RIDING IN THE WIND
A Prison "Shot Caller's" Ride to Freedom

Chaplain Roger Burdge

Strategic Book Publishing and Rights Co.

Strategic Book Publishing and Rights Co.
12620 FM 1960, Suite A4-507
Houston, TX 77065
www.sbpra.com

ISBN 978-1-62516-014-0

DEDICATION

To Cindy Johnston,
Chester's beautiful lady and all those who loved him.

TABLE OF CONTENTS

ACKNOWLEDGEMENTS

T his project began at The Spiritual Life Center on Parchman grounds. Once Chester came to know and trust me, he began to share his story. My office provided the solitude necessary to hear and record it. My thanks to Chaplain Ron Padgett for allowing me to work as a volunteer chaplain; his memory and mementos of days past provided much background information. To Chaplains Bays, Chason, Williams, and Scallions, and others who formed a brotherhood necessary for the prison environment. To Director and Pastor Andrew Hawkins, I owe a debt of gratitude for choosing me to be his camp spiritual director at Unit Twenty-Six. Also to Pastor James Wilkerson, who so many times provided a listening ear, also necessary at Parchman.

Thanks to Marilyn Corbin, who served as secretary for six superintendents, for facilitating my tasks and assisting me in reducing red tape, of which there is much in MDOC. To retired Warden Jacklyn Parker, whose time and understanding brought comfort and acceptance at Parchman early on. I thank all the area wardens who permitted my access to their facilities. To the officers of all the units I served, especially Tony Champion, who acted as a leader at Unit Twenty-Six when much of the security staff did not understand the changes being enacted. To the men and women in blue who had my back and those who didn't.

To the special officers who grasped my purpose and made me a part of prison life for a minute by locking me down at count time, and told me to "grab my rack."

Then there are the inmates who told their stories and made me feel welcome in their "houses," zones, or on their tiers. Special thanks to inmates Walter Lott, Billy Wallace, and the others whose name are long since forgotten, but whose faces and stories remain forever.

Now on to the most special persons who made this story come to print. Of course, Cindy Johnston, Chester's "beautiful lady," who has and always will believe in him. She made all the documents regarding the murder of Mr. Edwards available and offered additional personal contributions to this story. My book is Chester's story, but gives honor to her for being the great wife and lady she is.

To Jerry Mitchell of the *Jackson Clarion Ledger*, who has become my friend since the Sunday after the Pearl High School shooting. Knowing you support the underdog and have no fear in finding those who bring harm to the undeserving, I give my appreciation and thanks.

Then, to my lady, Gracie, who has read and reread this manuscript so many times with highlighter in hand, tuning out my gripes about my mistakes while correcting punctuation and spelling, of which there were many errors. I thank her for committing to our ministry at Parchman, working as the Internal Affairs Investigative Assistant. She at times was at risk there. She loved knowing all that was happening at Parchman and was loved by all. To all the Internal Affairs chiefs and investigators I owe a debt of gratitude for watching her back. A special thanks to Investigator Tara James, who became Gracie's confidant and friend while at IA.

Last and most important, I want to thank my God, who always had my back, whether teaching on the zone, walking the cells on death row, or holding church in stinking dining halls late at night.

To the guys who cleaned up faster so we could have church.

God is truly good. My prayer is that many will be thrilled by the life of a desperado turned devout disciple of Jesus. I know Chester's prayer, and mine, is that God will receive the glory for all.

Finally, to all the people at SBPRA who have added the "spit and polish" to this book.

I know I probably have omitted the names of some who contributed to telling this story, so, whoever and wherever you are, thanks.

INTRODUCTION

A merica is at war on the streets of our cities. The war is against crime and violence, and sadly, we are losing badly. The purpose of the enemy is to disband Christian values. Drug lords, crime families, and street gangs lead the assault on family unity and morality. Their commander-in-chief, Satan, has patiently waited while crime and Supreme Court decisions destroy our lifestyle.

Trillions of dollars spent by the government during the last thirty years have had little effect, and the bad guys are winning. Urban renewal spending to relocate gangs and slumlords in federal housing has failed, for the most part. Millions spent on education to change young gang members' minds only encourages truancy. Yet with all the sure-fire social programs, well intended public workers and teachers, and well funded programs, more ground is being lost daily.

Sociology, psychology, and criminology have not prepared a successful strategy.

Police and human resource personnel lose their lives, while others simply lose hope. Local police departments as well as the Federal Justice Department's case files are too large to manage. Jail and prison systems are overflowing, so early release of dangerous criminals has become a solution. New arrests are added daily. The enemy grows and our nation's defenders dwindle.

Drive-by and drug killings, teen pregnancies, "gangbanging" in schools, murders, rapes, and muggings become the daily lead-in stories on the six o'clock news.

The problem of crime and violence in America has risen to one of the top priorities in the minds of American citizens, more frightening than the soaring national debt. Where do we go to look for answers before the streets are completely captured by society's enemy? Government has proven it can't find a solution. Billions of dollars have been just a Band-Aid. More cops are not the answer. More prisons, housing projects, or money for schools has not worked. We throw money at the problem without success. Law enforcement forces have been enlarged, more and improved prison facilities constructed, but the problems grow.

The crime question stares all of us squarely in the eye.

Perhaps the answer to the nation's dilemma can be learned from the lead character in this book. His name is Chester Johnston. He has fought since childhood. He battled in school, was assaulted by his father, and after finishing high school, was shipped out to Nam. He came home when his tour ended, to be rejected by society for his service.

Marriage battles returned him to the biker life, a new war zone. Chopped Harleys, black leather uniforms, and chrome chains distinguished the soldiers. Thick beards and hair tied in ponytails designated their allegiance. Tattoos were their defenses.

Then came prison!

This veteran's life shows that Chester Johnston knew the soldiers and their battle plans. He is intimate with the combatants on both sides.

Chester's prison life reveals incarceration is not the solution. What occurs at times in prisons is ugly. Men and women who are "locked up" behave as animals. This book is not intended as an expose, or to point a finger in any direction, at the field of Corrections, or at those who could have changed. It is what I know, heard about, and saw during the six years I was a chaplain at Mississippi State Penitentiary. Yet it will also show men and women are capable of changing their lives; it's possible!

Chester's story will present the powerful testimony of a converted bad ass and dedicated criminal, describe the mind of the biker culture, and take you inside one the most dangerous prisons in the United States to show how Chester once ruled it. He was called the "shot caller" because he ran the lives of the men inside the fences. The power of Jesus to change the life of a social "throw away," into a powerful witness to change hearts will also be seen. The same power that transformed Chester Johnston's life can change our discarded young people or "throw aways" into strong soldiers in the Lord's army.

While this is the story of Chester Johnston, it is also about thousands of men or women who are transformed in prison, and the formula for those who are not changed.

This is the message of a prison "shot caller."

***

P.S. I acquired Chester's story only after I gained his trust and acceptance. Others had come to him before with requests, but were turned down. This man's story is so unique that many saw an account that would make a great read and contribute to our understanding of out of control teens. Thankfully, Chester chose me for this labor of love, the telling of his story.

One last word: the names of those who were Chester's antagonists and who contributed to his life sentence have been changed. This editing is for my protection and the publishers, not theirs. They know who they are and of their dreadful lies that kept Chester in prison for life. I only pray they have asked for forgiveness, as the one accused did.

The Author

CHAPTER ONE

THE HOSPITAL

Parchman inmate Chester Johnston, #44464, lay on starched, white infirmary sheets, staring at the yellowed ceiling of the prison infirmary. Every time he took a breath, aches and pains reminded him of his lost battle the night before, with Parchman "police." Penitentiary guards and officials considered Chester a troublemaker from his arrival. The day he arrived at Parchman, he was housed in the "hole," or lockdown Camp 24. That day at "the Farm" featured a battle with an inmate, who he beat to the floor. He later fought his way to the leadership of the Aryan Brotherhood. Chester became a fierce fighting machine with extremely fast hands and soon received recognition by the incarcerated population as the top man, or the "shot caller."

An old MDOC sergeant recalled Chester's earlier years. "Yes, Chester use to get out of line once in a while," he alleged with a sly smile on his face. A captain who knew Chester before his conversion remembered him as a real tough customer who made a tremendous change later in his stay.

He fought several guards to maintain his role as "prison boss." Officers came to move him from his "house" shortly after he had been moved once, and his pride forced him to fight. Swarms of

5

officers overwhelmed him and sent him to the hospital. Years later, he received seven thousand dollars from the state, along with scars and infirmities that would never go away.

He lay on his cot in the prison sickbay and thought about last night's battle with the officers. He believed they required him to fight. If he had moved peacefully, his reputation might have been blemished and other prisoners would suspect Chester was becoming weak. Yet, the soreness from his mouth, his ribs, and his groin raised the question: "Was it possible he had been better off to pack his stuff and move to another cell?"

The medication made him drowsy. He struggled against the desire to sleep. His mind wandered back, remembering all the battles he had fought. He had always won in the past, but broken bones and lacerations proved he had finally been defeated. Chester smiled to himself as he dreamily remembered all the officers it had taken to restrain him.

The sound of a guard walking through the ward brought him to reality. Quickly, he remembered past battles with the biker, Gunslingers, in Vietnam, and on the streets of Jackson ran through his mind like fast-forward pictures on a VCR. He had fought since he was a kid, when his dad had put the gloves on him and his brother.

He began to think how pointless each fight was, those with his brother and the others, especially, in Nam. Really, thinking about them, he thought about how futile, senseless it had been. They always created troubles.

In his youth, he fought to gain an image. Later, he was drawn into additional battles to prove Chester Johnston, the Desperado, was a man to be feared. Throwing his closed fists with lightning speed and enormous impact, biting, kicking, gouging, and stomping a fallen foe with his boots made him somebody. Fighting became the only avenue to recognition in his world.

As the pain medication played dream games with his brain, he slipped back to his grandmother's house. Living with her was good. He got defensive when it was time to leave her and go home. If he had lived with her, maybe things would have turned out better. The patient envisioned the little frame country house he loved so much.

Quickly, the pleasant dreams of the country life faded and an ugly scene replaced them, one of lush green vegetation everywhere. Screams of pain above the whine and explosions of incoming rockets captured his senses. Bodies of comrades lying in rain-filled foxholes; burned -out villages dotted with incinerated corpses brought a cry of anguish from his soul.

Finally, the medication took control, removing the pain and hopelessness he had lived with since a child. He slept.

Hours later, Chester awoke; time for chow. Inmates serving meals clattered metal trays and utensils as they moved through the ward. Chester motioned them away with his hand and turned on his side.

His pain was easier now. The last thing he remembered from last night was being loaded, strapped on a gurney, and placed in an ambulance. He had been injured before; a gunshot wound, several stabbings, and he had scars from other battles. But he had never been wounded like that.

A question formed in his mind. *Was the battle worth the pain*? Was maintaining the position of top dog, prison "shot caller," worth the pain accompanying the position?

Chester thought back to his grandmother. He pictured her teaching him to pray. "Now I lay me down to sleep." Her words, and Chester repeated them. The next line followed. "I pray the Lord my soul to keep." Chester contemplated the word *Lord*. What did Grandma mean, "Lord?" Did she indicate someone, some power, somewhere who would heal his wounds? He wondered if the "Lord" his grandma described and taught him to pray to would bring healing and change his life.

Chester fought against his last shot of painkiller and its power to put him to sleep. Before he dozed off again, he remembered Chaplain Lankford. He was the chaplain who had often tried to talk to him about God, but Chester never had time. Maybe he knew the answer. The last thing Chester remembered was saying, "Lord, Lo-rd, Looo-rr-d," as he dropped off to sleep again.

Little did he realize there would come a time when God would be the only solution.

CHAPTER TWO

JUST A "THROW-AWAY" CHILD

Some camps at Parchman are called "throw always." Camps are where prison officials place unmanageable, undesirable, and uncooperative men. Much time will pass before these men return to regular prison life; worse, they may die. "Doing time" is most difficult here. These men are no longer considered redeemable.

These "throw aways" will waste away in solitary confinement; some will lose any hope of freedom, and die from the inside out. Others will be killed under the cover of night from a prison-made shank shaped from a piece of scrap metal or old screwdriver. Life has little value here.

An argument over a "punk" (girlfriend), unpaid debt, or disrespect to another inmate will result in a stabbing, causing severe wounding or death. Officials care little about these deaths, as the men have already been classified as non-recyclable into normal prison society; thus, they are "throw aways."

Once an inmate is killed, if the family does not claim his body, they are placed in a plywood coffin; after a brief chaplain's service, they are buried in the desolate State prison cemetery. Later, a stone marker showing the inmates name and MDOC number is placed by the grave, soon hidden among the weeds. Even in death, the prisoner belongs to the State of Mississippi. The thought brings new meaning to the old prison saying, "Your heart may belong to Jesus, but your ass belongs to me."

Our society contains many "throw away" children. They are from homes where career or status or poverty leaves little time for raising children. Physical needs are generally met, but there is little love. In the mind of the child, they have become discarded, lost.

Chester Johnston believed he had been a sixties' discarded child. His parents didn't intend to disregard his needs; it just happened. Sara Ann was eighteen when she married; and Chester Senior was twenty. They exchanged wedding vows but they were not ready to have children and raise a family. Squabbles, for whatever reason, always got in the way of being a family.

Two children were born soon after the marriage. Ann, the first-born, came first, and a son, Chester Junior, a year later.

Chester describes the early days of his childhood. "I don't remember any love in my family, ever. My dad drank regularly." Chester Senior worked as a service station attendant or co-owned a station with Chester's uncle Bill. Arguments seemed to occur nightly when Chester Senior came home from work.

The arguments began with harsh accusations and ended in loud shouting matches. It appeared to the son there was always a quarrel going on in the house. Chester Junior believed he had been born in domestic "War Zone." The battles always followed the same process; arguing, followed by attempting to shout the other down, and, lastly, drinking.

For older sister Ann and Chester, the aftermath of the disagreements was always the same. "We would be loaded in our car with what few clothes we had and taken somewhere else to live.

"I was like a fifth wheel, always living from bedpost to bedpost, living out of a suitcase on the road. The bottom line was, I didn't feel wanted or needed, just there, just existing."

I once asked Chester, "Was there always fighting?"

"To me there was!"

Sometimes the kids were moved to Spanish Fort, Mississippi, where Chester Senior's parents lived.

"Mom would take us to Grandmother's. But in a week or so, Dad would come to get us. We would go back home for a while . . . then the fights would start again."

Mom and Dad made a few attempts to soothe away the hurt of the family fights and the children's relocations that always followed.

"Sometimes Mom would stop the Snow Cone truck and try to make everything hunky dory, you know, like everything was fixed with a snow cone. But another battle and drunken words would have Mom loading us up again and we would be delivered to Grandma's, or somewhere else, once again. But we knew in couple of days, Mom or Dad would show up to take us home and we would try to be a family again."

Chester and his sister knew only the uncertainties of shouting, heartless, curse words, and being loaded into a car. They suffered when separated from their dad and a house they called home. Leaving home hurt, even though it was a battle zone. There would be hurt again when they returned in a few short days and the domestic conflicts began again.

Accurate or not, strife is what Chester remembered about growing up in conflict no one remembered when or how it started. The result was a feeling of being thrown away.

Summer was the only time Chester actually felt like he was a real person. When summer came, he went to stay in the small white country house with his Grandmother and Grandfather outside Spanish Fort, Mississippi. Then frame house was still equipped with a hand water pump in the kitchen and a privy out back.

Chester loved working with his granddad.

The country store was a large wood frame building with a sunken porch and sloped roof showing its age. Everybody who lived in the area came a least once a week. Some came to buy or sell, others to sit around the black, rusty stove or on the porch and catch up on the local news. The old store was the local gathering place.

"We would get some ice and put it under the canvas on the wagon and then go to the fields and pick watermelons. That was a neat thing to do for me 'cause someone took time with me. Granddad would show me how to roll the watermelons over and put hay under them, to keep them from rotting."

Chester didn't mind gathering melons in the hot sun. Granddad's care and attention was what the young boy needed. It was the balm for his wounded self-esteem he never received at home.

Another "neat thing" to Chester was a reward from the rolling store. "I remember the rolling store . . . the old candy man would come by. He drove an old model car or dented truck filled with candy, chewing gum, little packaged cakes, and all the other sweets kids love."

To country kids, the rolling store was like the Good Humor ice cream man to city kids.

Chester's grandma and grandpa believed in giving rewards for completing chores. A candy bar for bringing in the cow or helping to churn, or the chance to lick the spoon when Grandma made a cake were some of their rewards from Grandma.

"When I got a reward I felt good, worthy. I had done something they were happy with me about. It made me feel deserving. I never got any praise at home, never a prize. There was never no fighting or fussing going on there."

During the restoration of genuine life in the summertime, Chester caught some glimpses of God. "Grandma had a Bible she read to us. She taught us to say our prayers. But I don't remember going to church regular. Once in a while, we went to a black country church and sat outside and listened to their beautiful gospel songs and hymns."

Black gospel singing was an institution in the South. Blues stars like B.B. King, Muddy Waters, Robert Johnson (who supposedly sold his soul), and many others had their roots in a country church. It was here they learned the notes and how to express their emotions in song. Summertime homecoming gatherings featured choirs singing and swaying in praise.

"I liked my Uncle Elliott because he shot marbles with me. He'd win my marbles and store them in a trunk. He said he had a right to keep my marbles 'cause he won them shootin' fair and square. I'd tell my grandma and she'd help me get my marbles back."

"Grandma taught me to say 'yes ma'am' and 'no ma'am' to adults . . . and thank you; things like that. She taught me God is always up in heaven."

Chester still replies, "Yes, sir," or "No, ma'am." Grandma's God always stayed in the back of his mind.

Grandma also tried to repair the family problems. "Grandma would say, 'Your mom and dad don't know how to love you when they're drinking. That's why you should never drink.' She told me they didn't mean what they said or did when they were drunk."

Chester knew grandma loved him, but all her words could not fill his empty space, and when vacation was over, he would return to the house that had no love.

Even when young, a bitter cup of division was brewed between Chester and his brother, Vernon, by his dad. The two brothers were made to fight when they didn't want to, weren't mad at each other. The bouts between Chester Junior and Vernon were supposed to be lessons in the manly art of self-defense.

"I remember my dad, when he used to come home, would make me fight my younger brother, Vernon. If I hit Vernon too hard, my dad would hit me. So, I would never hit him hard. I guess that's why I grew up angry like I was. Not really being able to fight back."

When Chester hit too hard, he received penalty blows from his dad. The one-sided lessons lit a fire of meanness. As a biker, the base of anger and bitterness caused Chester to fight fiercely.

"I always pictured my dad when I fought, and I wanted to get revenge on him or something like that."

The anger fueled by his bitterness would not be extinguished for many years to come.

Chester learned a system of survival at an early age. It enabled him to prevail in the killing fields of Nam, the California biker world, and the camps of Parchman State Penitentiary.

Chester Johnston felt like a "throw away" child. Born to a man and a woman who had married too young, too immature, what love there may have been before the wedding soon dissipated into distrust. They began to accuse each other of unfaithfulness and turned to the bottle for trust.

His anger continued to grow. Soon it would show in all his relationships.

CHAPTER THREE

THE END OF THE FAMILY FEUD

California promised to be a land of golden opportunity. Like the prospectors of 1894, Chester Junior, with his mom, would find nuggets of opportunity in the second chance of California hills.

Their first California home would be in Oceanside, with his Aunt Belle, Sara Ann's sister. She had lived on the West Coast for several years.

Soon after arriving in Oceanside, the curious country boy discovered strange brown people living in his aunt's garage. The big garage door in front and the small passage door in back were always locked from the outside, but Chester sneaked a look inside through a window. The rear door of the house also had a security lock on the inside. Chester didn't understand all the security locks.

Chester sneaked a look inside the garage; he saw several rows of bunk beds. No kitchen or bathing facilities, only beds. Chester wondered why Aunt Belle would have bunk beds in the garage. The youngster soon learned that Aunt Belle was transporting and hiding illegal immigrants.

Truckloads of illegal Mexicans were transported to Oceanside from just across the Mexican border. After they arrived, they were locked in the garage until their passage to LA or further north became clear. During their wait for safe passage, the immigrants were fed and given water. Belle would not take a chance on any of them getting loose.

Just up Interstate 605 was a customs station. All vehicles were checked for imported vegetables or fruit. They also checked the documents of truck drivers or any passengers. Chester's aunt's boarders were secluded in the garage until the custom booth closed. Sara Ann would sit in her car on a hill above the customs checkpoint as a lookout. The service station just off the interstate provided the safe passage sign using their large sign out front. Once Sara Ann signaled, her sister would cram the Mexicans into a van and transport them to their waiting employers. Upon delivery, Belle got paid $125 per person. A nice return for a week's work moonlighting, California style.

When the immigration checkpoint became too risky for Sara Ann, she and Chester moved to the north side of LA.

After the move, the blonde kid from Mississippi found a freedom he had never known. With Sara Ann working, the house was vacant when he returned after school. He became free to go wherever, do whatever, he wanted. His freedom soon led him to an old repair shop used by a local biker gang to hang out and work on their machines. Here, Chester met the riders of the West Coast Gunslingers.

School in West Covina had different rules from Mississippi. Most of the children had military parents or were children of migrant Mexican workers with little in common with Chester, so he made few new friends at the clubhouse.

His shirts made from cotton sacks and his faded blue jeans made him stand out from military kids, who wore store-bought clothing. He didn't understand the Hispanic children speaking Spanish, so after school, he went to the privacy of Sara Ann's apartment.

Chester quickly learned that California school attendance wasn't mandatory. Since his mom left for work before school opened, he had nobody to pack his lunch box and hand him his school books and make sure he attended school. The school did not check on him when Chester began to play hooky. He would fill his days with any pastime he choose.

"They didn't force you to go to school back then. School officials never did check up on you. Most of the kids left to pick cabbage or fruit some time during the school year, so absences were normal."

So Chester used the school's lack of interest to find new adventures.

Chester wanted more than anything to visit the clubhouse close to his apartment with the bright, shiny motorcycles and the bearded riders who cruised by. For a time, the old haunting fears of the unknown made him keep a distance from the clubhouse, but with each day, his curiosity grew and drew him closer to the white stucco repair shop. The magnetism of outlaw men dressed in black and their loud, chromed machines finally drew the truant to their open garage door.

"Hey, scooter rat; grab that wrench and give it to me." A gruff voice of one of the giants was speaking to him; it was his invitation to come in.

Chester stumbled over to the rack, retrieved the tool, and handed it to the greasy Harley mechanic. Working with his grandfather on the farm had given him a basic tool education. His knowledge of what to give the greasy mechanics provided his passage.

From the first day, the shy Mississippi kid became a part of the West Coast Gunslingers, one of LA's many feared biker clubs. As the days passed, Chester would find acceptance in the dirty garage of the stucco clubhouse. The allegiance would last for many years.

CHAPTER FOUR

BIKER CLUBHOUSE

T he gruff but inviting voice belonged to a biker nicknamed Bear. Bear was the Gunslinger "Enforcer." He was part-time mechanic, and full time club Sergeant at Arms, enforcing the code of the motorcycle clan.

The meeting place reeked of gasoline and oil mixed with sweat and beer. Not like any odor Chester had experienced before. The garage was always busy. Men in sleeveless denim shirts, with bulging muscles, bearded, with shoulder-length hair either worked on their machines or just drank beer. Other days they just partied.

Chester remembers. "The people seemed happy and I wanted to have a part of their joy."

His words contain a hollow empty ring when he speaks of his search for completion.

The clubhouse of the West Coast Gunslingers provided the kid acceptance and affection he never found in the Johnston house. Chester longed to be a part of it. The Harley household was a mixture of "patch holders", as members were called, and others who lived at the Harley residence. Some had kids; others simply lived together and disdained the thought of children.

A small stucco house was attached to the garage that housed

the unit. Some slept on cots or sleeping bags on the floor; there was no fancy furniture or carpet to cover the floor. Theirs was a Spartan life, easy to live by.

To the eleven-year-old boy from Mississippi, the bikers were real family. Perhaps a far cry from the Brady bunch or the Cleavers, but they were still kin. Soon, Bear and the others planned to make Chester a junior member of the Gunslinger family.

"Where do you live kid?" questioned Loser, another Gunslinger.

"Around the corner and up the street."

"With your mama and dad?" he continued.

"With my mom . . . they're divorced."

"Hey, rat; if you hang out with us, we have to check you out. Show me your house. I want to talk with your mom."

As he walked toward the apartment complex, young Chester was wide-eyed. The bikers were going to make him a member. They would like his mom.

Loser and Bear accompanied the prospect to the place where he lived, about two blocks from their garage.

Sara Ann became somewhat alarmed when two burley bikers with tattoos on their arms appeared at her door with her young, blonde son. The son appeared small and out of place beside the two giants.

Bear and Loser would quickly become the father figures Chester had never known. He trusted them. They accepted him as he was. Really, the bikers' visit would assure Sara Ann that her boy was in good hands down at the Gunslinger garage. They wanted her to know they were keeping an eye on him after school since no one was at his home.

Sara Ann was pleased Chester had a place to go after school. She could see pride in his eyes because the bikers liked her son. She found the two macho Harley riders slightly attractive. Chester passed the background test and was now part of the gang. Chester lived a new life accompanying his junior membership in the outlaw organization.

Chester thought, "I'm a part of them; things are going good in California."

The son figured, "Mom didn't get beat up any more, never cried, they had their own place."

This place had permanence; he wasn't moved in and out. The best part was belonging to biker family. Oh, he wished Mom was home more, so they could talk. Sometimes he came home and she would be in her back bedroom with a friend. He understood never to disturb her when she had company in the bedroom.

The Golden Gate state opened a brand new world for Sara Ann, and her Scooter Rat found another home. The enormous motorcycle riders kept their promise to Chester's mother.

"Don't get me wrong. I couldn't do anything I wanted to. They said, 'Get your butt home and go to school in the morning.' They kept me in line, but they never put their hands on me. Bear and Loser made me do the right things about school and all. They kept me in fresh clothes, wrinkled but clean."

The kid from Mississippi with blonde hair discovered new friends and was part of a new family. Who cared that his family was outside the mainstream of society; it made no difference to Chester. He was accepted in the greasy garage and clubhouse.

In his new home, Chester found another set of rules to live by. The code was more than a bunch of dos and don'ts. The riders made an oath which must not be broken. This allegiance would become a part of him for the rest of his life, burned into his soul.

The motorcycle patch is a cloth insignia worn by bikers on the back of their denim or leather vests. Chester has one tattooed on his shoulder. Each club's patch was known throughout all California and most of the nation. The cloth emblem was shaped like a military insignia and modeled after an army sergeant's shoulder patch. However, theirs were much larger.

Written across the top rocker (curved edge) was WEST COAST, and under the bottom rocker was GUNSLINGERS. Embroidered between the rockers was a robed skeleton with a hood over his head, which represented the Grim Reaper. The word "Death" was stitched above the grisly figure; underneath him were the words, "Death without Dishonor," the motto of the Gunslingers.

For that matter "death without dishonor," is the mantra of all bikers. The Hells Angels California organization was the prototype membership and had originated the code. They believed in dying before bringing shame to the brotherhood. Any member who "gave up," or ratted, on another member committed the most serious degree of dishonor. The code became universally accepted by all outlaw cycle clubs in the nation. Each member lived ready to die before aiding himself by turning in a brother to the law.

Snitches were speedily disciplined. No dishonor was allowed among the riders. Strict authority reigned within the West Coast Gunslingers. The top positions of the club's chain of command were president, vice president, sergeant at arms, and treasurer.

The prez, the nickname for the president, was head of the group; however, this was not an elected position. Top position was accomplished on the field of battle. No Ozzie Nelson figure for their family head. Their leader resembled a Conan the Barbarian figure. The president ruled by the power in his fists.

When a patch holder decided he wanted to lead, he issued a challenge to the top man to combat. Once the verbal gauntlet was thrown down, the club knew a bloody fight, perhaps to death, came next. The biker code demanded all challenges be accepted and settled immediately.

The sergeant at arms, as the "Enforcer," resolves troubles in the family as necessary. He collects outstanding debts and polices the clan in all matters as the leader dictates. Many motorcycle clubs terrorized the LA area. The Nomads lived in the desert; another group is the Pagans, with hundreds of brother gangs holding gatherings, called "blowouts," in the desert.

Today, nine hundred biker gangs exist in the United States. The most famous of all is the Hell's Angels. Sonny Barger, the prez of this group, was Chester's idol then. Chester would listen to the talk around the cycle shop. Outlaw riders mostly discussed Sonny and his clan. The club's junior member began to document a history of biker clubs in his mind as he listened to their stories.

Each day after school, the scooter rat would go to the clubhouse. Bear began to teach him about membership in the biker organization, the Gunslingers. Slowly, Chester learned the code and was molded into the group.

The gang motto was, "Satisfaction money back guarantee." The motto means that the code of honor will be respected without exception.

The group had taken the young Mississippi rooster under their wing. He closely watched and remembered everything he saw, and imitated every move of the warriors. Chester learned the language and the ways of the biker family. Chester's heart swelled with pride when Loser or Bear would place him on the back on one of the powerful Harleys. He felt the power of belonging for the first time while riding behind the bearded men, roaring up the interstate on the powerful, cut down bikes

**

Chester's grandmother taught him a reward system for services rendered. She believed work performed well should receive compensation. Some of the club's training methods were similar to those of Chester's grandmother. They, too, believed a diligent worker should be recompensed.

Chester gained his acceptance around the garage by retrieving tools for the motorcycle mechanics. He also cleaned up the garage when the day was over and performed other odd jobs. His first reward came as a result of his hard work and fierce desire to be totally admitted into the family. He loved feeling a part of them and wanted to become more involved in their activities. Little did he realize money was the basic drive behind all the bikers' schemes.

One morning, the novice biker arrived at the garage, and a moped motorbike had been parked outside the shop. This small scooter looks like a Western Flyer bicycle with peddles. Mounted on the bottom of the frame was a small gasoline engine. The motorbike's engine was started by peddling until the engine started up. Once it was started, the miniature motorcycle propelled itself.

Since the moped was Chester's first bike, to him, the bike was as big and bad as any of the full-sized Harley machines parked under the carport at the club, genuine because Bear or someone had painted a small Harley-Davidson emblem on the side. Later on, his new mentors would give him a Honda 150, and after that, a dirt bike.

The outlaws rode holy Harleys, and in the mind of the newest member, his ride was a Harley, also. The name Harley meant "top of the line;" it carried prestige. Harley was the Cadillac of motorcycles.

"I didn't know no better. The bike came from the outlaws; they said the bike was a Harley. If they would 'hold up' [back up the statement], I knew I was all right. The gift was a cool thing for them to do for me."

When the new scooter rat received his prize, his chest swelled up. The poor kid from Mississippi had worn homemade clothes and never enjoyed a birthday party or Christmas tree. The scooter made him beam with pride.

"Mother wouldn't let me take my bike to school. I would brag to the guys on the playground I was going home to ride my motorcycle, my scooter. They didn't believe I owned one."

Chester's outlaw machine helped develop an outlaw's heart.

"They had taken me in and practically raised me."

His years with the Gunslingers became the most formative years in Chester's life. Years later, he would return to the security of the clubhouse many times.

The same afternoon Chester received his gift, Bear explained that since he had a scooter, he had to deliver papers on a paper route. Now he had a job of his own. The novice could make a real contribution to the family's treasury, more than just helping by retrieving tools in the garage.

Somebody in the gang had draped a gray newspaper sack over the back fender of the scooter. The carrier was dirty from the ink of thousands of papers stuffed into the canvas paper sack. Hollow white plastic tubes lay inside the paper sack. The tubes protected the newspapers. The bikers provided him with all the equipment for a fully outfitted paperboy. Young Chester was ready to be a fully accredited member of the club; however, the route was a disguise for another business venture for the clan.

Drug distribution was the main source of income for the outlaws. The newspaper sack had a few rolled newspapers inside, which was a front for gang drug deliveries. The program was that one of the members would give Chester an address or tell him a place to deliver a paper. Chester was instructed on each delivery to put the paper in the hands of the one to be delivered to.

Papers were rolled up, secured with a rubber band around them, and stuffed into the plastic tubes by one of the gang members. All the young carrier had to do was deliver them. The gang's secret what was rolled up inside the paper.

The delivery list wasn't long, as paper routes go, but Bear would remind Chester each time he left the premises to be sure he had the correct address before he "gave up" the paper. Bear explained the reason. "People get mad when they don't get their paper," a simple, but false explanation.

Now the country boy from Mississippi had a job in LA. He delivered the papers daily. Some days, no papers had to be delivered. He went about his business with painstaking care, always confirming the address and recipient before handing over the paper. The list of deliveries changed daily. Some days, the list had new names; sometimes the names were removed. But the kid biker never made a mistake and delivered his papers with pride and devotion.

His final instructions were, "Don't stop until you arrive, ask for the person at the specific destination, like a Texaco service station down from Denny's Restaurant, and if he ain't there, wait for him."

Chester recalls brief conversations at the delivery point. "I'd say, 'Loser sent you a paper,' and hand the newspaper to them. Then I'd leave and go on about my business."

Who was going to suspect a kid delivering papers of doing anything illegal?" Paper routes were as American as hot dogs and mustard.

"I thought I was a cool dude 'cause I'd rev my engine up like the big bikers and go on down the road taking care of business. After I finished my deliveries, the bikers would tell me, 'You did a good job; go get you somethin'.' Then they gave me some money. I'd go home and tell mom we were going to the Jack in the Box and get a hamburger and fries, my treat."

The paper route provided the youngster a feeling of accomplishment, helping his mother. There would be no more gloomy days of packing and unpacking, no more searching for a place of security and serenity.

When Chester showed the scooter to his mom, she cried. Sara Ann knew this was a gift she couldn't give him.

"Boy that's something," she exclaimed. She was proud for him.

The bogus paperboy just grinned, the same boyish grin I have seen many time since I have known him.

"I guess that's when she began giving the bikers some love she didn't know she still had. They took care of her "youngun'.""

Today, Chester has accepted his mom's wild lifestyle. He understands why. Later in his life, he learned he must be forgiven; he also learned to forgive. He has long since forgiven Sara Ann her sins of the flesh.

"Bear and Loser started hanging around the house pretty regular. I mean, to be honest with you, all the time. I didn't get into Mom's business, but I wasn't stupid. I would rather her hang around with my friends than them old things [service men] she had dated in the past. They'd always take her off and I'd have to come back home to an empty house."

Chester's paper deliveries began to build a foundation upon which he would organize illegal club operations in the future. Sara Ann's dating practices soon ended her life.

Chester's new family showed their loyalty after he got into a fight on the school playground. A group of older Mexicans jumped him at school one day and beat him up.

I had been "flashing" my paper route money around, I guess. Three or four of the Mexicans jumped me when I was buying a soda and grabbed my money. They tore my shirt plumb off and robbed my cash. I knew them old bikers would hold up for me. I couldn't get home fast enough to tell them. I went and told Loser what had happened. I didn't mind fighting them one on one, but one of the Mexican guys was a grade or two above me and I knew I couldn't whup them alone. I tried to fight the older guy and the others at the same time, but I got beat. When my mom saw my black eye, she got upset and cried. Bear or Loser one had taken me home and said to Sara Ann, 'That ain't his first whuppin, and it ain't going to be his last. He's all right.'"

When the bikers left their place, Chester told his mom that Loser and Bear were going to make things right for him at school. Chester left and spent the night at the Gunslinger clubhouse.

"The following morning, Loser sat me behind him on his motorcycle. We rode together to the school playground. The same dudes who beat me up were there again. I pointed them out to Loser and he slowly got off the big Harley and walked over to where they were. The biker's huge appearance made them draw back. Loser really scared them when he warned those playground thieves not to jump on me again. I thought I was something big when Loser rode away on his big Harley. Now the dudes knew my big brothers would back me up if anything happened again. From then on I was the cock of the walk at my school."

Biker clubs had their greatest fun on their weekend party trips. They call the parties, "blowouts."

Chester narrated the agenda for the weekend get-aways. "Sometimes we rode to the Big Bear Mountain area on Interstate 5 or to Mexico down the Santa Anna Freeway to I-605 through San Diego, like a family outing to us."

The Harley's were cleaned and their chrome polished by their riders. Engines were finely tuned and the chrome tanks filled with gas in preparation for the trip. Food, drinks, and other camping supplies were stored in saddlebags on the back of the motorcycles. Once the bikes were loaded, the clan was ready to party.

Chester's motorcycle family helped dress the junior member in proper clan attire. They donated clothing to dress the prospect appropriately. Somebody tossed Chester an old grease rag and he tied the do rag around his growing curls for a biker bandanna. Someone else gave him a pair of black boots, scarred from wear and with a few holes in the bottom; but they were real. Chester cut the sleeves out of an old shirt to cover his hand-me-down tee shirt with the sleeves rolled up. Next he tucked his pants inside his motorcycle boots. He was a miniature version of the warriors as he prepared to ride down the interstate.

Once they formed the dual lines of motorcycle and began to cruise down the road, they resembled a military escort more than a family outing. Each male and female Gunslinger was dressed to match, in blue jeans and tee-shirts with head bands or bandannas tied around their flowing hair.

The West Coast Gunslinger proudly displayed their insignia on the backs of their leather jackets.

Chester arrogantly rode on the black leather seat of the Harley behind Bear or Loser. The riders slowly formed their ranks as they pulled out from under the metal covering outside the cycle shop. Next, they eased in pairs down the avenue with engines sputtering. When they rode onto the main thoroughfare, their cycles roared forward; black smoke streamed from chromed exhaust pipes.

Anybody riding on the street shuddered in fear as they heard the roar of the scooters and saw the frightening bikers approach. The riders had a mindset of warriors from old times riding their powerful, metal, two-wheeled steeds. They smiled as they sensed the fright of the citizens when they passed.

Chester though this was really living as he rode on the back of the scooter, dressed like the older riders. The bikers displayed fierce pride in who, and what they were, and they rode outside society's borders. Their power demanded respect.

Once on Interstate 5 East, the Gunslingers urged their mighty machines to full speed with a twist of their wrist. The finely tuned engines jerked the bikers forward as they rode, two by two, eastward down the concrete highway.

They were a small, arrogant company of soldiers racing toward a desert R&R. Once among the sand and cactus, they would bivouac with many other California biker groups. Together, the separate biker parties appeared as a giant army when all the clubs arrived. Tents were raised and fires started as the party seekers roamed or rested on the sand or rocks. Hundreds of polished Harleys parked in rows in the sand just off the dirt road that lead into the camping area.

Party time had arrived.

Chester quietly accepted his role in the lifestyle of his new friends. He remembered the loud arguments of the Johnston family, so he had no problem becoming accustomed to the riotous party ways of the bikers.

The West Coast biker society began their two-day fiesta ritual with eating and drinking. The partygoers popped tabs from ice cold beers and laughed when the spray spewed on them. They guzzled beer, and some of the men used hunting knives to cut slender limbs from the desert brush on which roast hot dogs. Others made grills using large rocks for the fire pit and wood spits to cook meat on.

When the sun began to set, dried wood was gathered and piled upon the campfires to build a crackling, blazing fire. The warriors sat and watched as the desert wind whipped the blaze higher and higher. The blaze was the grand opening of the party weekend.

The refugees from the city had one goal: to indulge in all physical pleasures possible in their desert hideaway. Desert parties were an event the Mississippi kid could never have imagined back home in the Magnolia State. He was intrigued as he watched the bikers as they began to party.

Once the flames of the fires reached toward the darkened skies, the party began to appear like a Hollywood Viking celebration. Portable radios were turned up louder and their music blasted across the sand floor of their party arena. The sounds traveled to the low hills in the dark and echoed back toward the party makers. They all continued to drink beer; others began to smoke marijuana.

The alcohol and drugs made their exchanging of "war stories" about parties and combats louder and louder. Soon, some of the women began to feel excluded from the party. They entered the circle around the fire of storytellers and lounged beside the men. Next the women would pull and drag their reluctant drunken partners from the storytelling and away from the fire.

Once the warriors were away from the fire and in the shadows, they mellowed to the advances of their female partners. Drugs and booze dulled their senses. They stopped fighting the kisses and sensual rubbing from their ladies. Next, biker women stood and began to move slowly to the playing music. Their sensual, swaying shadows were cast across the sand as they slowly moved away from the fire. As more beer was consumed and weed inhaled, the party's intensity continued to rise to an even higher level. As the bikers smoked weed and drank beer, their sexual desires caught fire.

All discussions of battles past and motorcycles were forgotten. The heat of the blazing campfire, accompanied by the loud, driving beat of the music, intertwined the warriors and their women into pairs making love. Some of the weaving female dancers removed their clothes as they moved toward the men. The burley, stumbling biker soldiers chased the dancers into the desert darkness. Cries of sexual pleasure mingled with the blasting music to float across the desert.

Later, the endurance of the drunken and weary soldiers would run out and they would stumble back to their tent or bedroll to sleep the remainder of the night. The morning silence would not be broken until the sun had fully risen. As the sun climbed, it would chase the family members out of the sleeping bags to shake themselves awake, and then it was time to party again.

Understand the scenario from which Chester learned a false definition of good times. His was a biker definition, not real morals and virtues, as his social training was learned from an outlaw gang.

CHAPTER FIVE

FROM SCOOTER TO RIVER RAT

The West Coast lifestyle of living in Biker Land came to a sudden end. Chester, now fourteen, was unprepared for the death of Sara Ann.

Emotion spread across the face of the hard ex-biker when he goes back in time to thoughts of his mother. Even though she had her shortcomings, Chester loved her. She had always been available for him, especially when martial battles raged and she had protected her son.

Chester returned home from the clubhouse and opened the apartment door. He saw his Aunt Belle sitting in the living room, crying. She never came to West Covina; her job and her second income kept her too busy.

The apprentice biker glanced around the room. He couldn't have been prepared for his aunt's tearful announcement that his mom had been killed. Belle broke her bad news abruptly. "Chester, your mother has been killed in a car accident."

There was no preparation, and no soothing words to soften the blow; just the hard facts of her demise.

It was his last day in their California apartment. The aunt told her nephew to pack some clothes; he must stay with her until they left for the funeral in Mississippi.

Chester would not view his mom's body until he and Belle returned to Mississippi. He would be in pain through the trip back to Mississippi. Chester was shaken and confused, and found his life quickly falling apart. Left behind in California were mother's love and the biker family attention.

His dad and sister, Ann, came to Chester's grandparent's house in Kosciusko to see him the day after he returned. Later, Belle told the details of Sara Ann's death. She and a date were driving back to her apartment, and her companion lost control of his car. Both occupants of the vehicle were killed in the crash.

Chester felt his mother's dates stole her attention from him. Now one of them had stolen her forever. Twenty-five years later, her death still stirred the tough convict as he turned in his mind to his mother's death. Now his words seemed thwarted by the extreme emotion buried from then. Chester's sighed painfully when he thought about her passing, revealing his lingering wounds. Sara Ann's shortcomings, her absences and drinking, are blocked out by her death.

Sara Ann Johnston was buried in a cemetery just outside Kosciusko, Mississippi. Chester desired to return to visit her grave for the rest of his life after incarceration.

The day after the funeral, Chester received instructions that he would go to live with his father and stepmother in Arcola, Mississippi, south of Greenwood on state highway 61. But Chester's heart longed to return to California, to live with Aunt Belle and be close to his Gunslinger family. His aunt clearly sent a message of rejection, so he would not return to the friends he left behind in California.

The death of his mother had separated him from all the people Chester loved and wanted to be with. His aunt could provide an alternative to living with his father; however, she didn't want him.

If he could get in touch with the Gunslinger family, he might live with them. But there wasn't a way to contact Loser, Bear, or the other outlaws. He had left without saying goodbye or obtaining a phone number where he could call them.

It would be several years before the bikers would learn where the scooter rat went. Chester's separation from everyone who brought completeness to him impacted him greatly. After the funeral, the blonde haired youngster felt empty. The "throw away" kid from a dysfunctional home was discarded once again.

Chester returned to a familiar house with some unfamiliar people. There, he found a new stepmom, just slightly older than him. He discovered, at least in his thinking, Brother Vernon and Sister Ann changed. Much of his future grief in the Arcola house could be attributed to his new stepmom's pregnancy.

Even life with his dad seemed different to Chester. But with the changes in the old unit's members of the Johnston household, the atmosphere remained the same. Chester's lifestyle was a drastic change compared to that in California. New rules came in Mississippi. The house rules were posted on the refrigerator and verbally explained to the new arrival. Moreover, more were just kind of made up as the days went by. At least that was the way it appeared to the new kid in the Johnston home.

Chester could no longer freely come and go as he wanted. All he ever heard from his stepmom was, "Chester, go help Ann with the dishes," or "Chester, mop the kitchen floor," or "Do you have some chore to be done?"

Chester's personality had changed since he left Mississippi with his mother after the divorce. He had enjoyed his mother's liberation of her "free spirit." Chester had found a new strength of his own. His time with the uncontrolled bikers had brought freedom to do what he chose. Hanging out at the garage, running his paper route, and the weekend rallies in the desert filled him with the biker free will mind set.

Behind his stepmom's back, Chester would imitate her orders. "Mop the kitchen," echoed the aspiring outlaw, then under his breath, "That's a girl's job." He wondered why a junior member of the Gunslinger should have do household chores.

It seemed the housekeeping chores fell on the children. His stepmother's pregnancy became supposedly the reason for the kids doing the housework. True or not, the young ex-Gunslinger just saw her lying in bed all day while he did her tasks. Understandably, what he termed "woman's work "did not set well with his California lifestyle, nor did his reluctance to perform it enhance his relationship with the lady of the house.

Chester remembers. "My relationship with my stepmother turned very BAD!"

His stepmom would not replace his mother to him. He did not want her to be his new mom. She didn't birth and raise him. In addition, he transferred some of the blame for Sara Ann's death to his stepmother. The split in their association widened when she gave bad reports to his dad. The emotions originating during his childhood spilled over after his mother's death.

Chester's poor relationship with his stepmother began with his summer visits in West Covina. They argued over petty things. She would end the squabble by telling Chester to go back and stay with his whore mama. It seemed to him no one would allow him to forget his mother's transgressions. Each time the uprooted youngster made a mistake, the reason was because his mama was "no good."

Consequently, the atmosphere here turned far worse than before. His mother had been a refuge. He sat on her lap and she would tell him what a good boy he was and how much she loved him. All boys growing up need a mama's refuge, need to hear they are loved. Sara Ann guarded his hiding place.

Underneath the surface of fussing and arguments, a deeper and more serious predicament was developing. While on summer visits from California, Chester helped some of his friends cut yards and did other odd jobs around town. Sometimes his friends paid him with an ice cream cone or soda; other days, they would split the proceeds from the jobs. On his last summer visit, Vernon and Chester mowed yards together. However, Chester was never been allowed to keep what he earned.

"How much did you make today?" his stepmother would inquire. "You used our lawn mower, so it belongs to me." She would confiscate his earnings. After working all day in the hot sun, the boy received no compensation for his labor.

Chester articulated the problem to me. "I didn't mind working as long as you gave me my issue." *Issue* is prison jargon for pay. His grandma taught the young boy the Bible saying, "A laborer is worthy of his hire."

His emotions, then and now, are the same as when someone takes or withholds your issue, pay. The action is nothing short of robbery. His grandmother taught him one's labor is to be rewarded. The lesson also was part of his California street smarts taught him by the bikers. To him, it became a fact of life.

Chester, like all children, was programmed by the instruction he received and examples he saw. Lessons observed far outweigh lessons spoken. Chester worked hard and his work deserved pay in return. He became perplexed when his earnings were taken from him, and especially angry because his stepmother pilfered his earnings.

Dysfunctional families almost certainly produce mixed up children.

Chester believed that what he earned belonged to him. No one, family or not, had a right to take his wages. Theft by force or by kin was still theft. Thus, a new lesson replaced an old one. His stepmother's example taught him that taking from others was satisfactory when one has the power to do so. He would live by this erroneous thinking for many years.

Chester's living with his re-constructed family did not last very long. He found no positives to offset the negatives of his mental checklist. The time soon came for Chester to leave the divided household. He would no longer take orders to perform housework or have his money seized for work done for others, and no one in the future would take it without severely paying for it.

"I hired out on the river boat when I was fifteen."

He did this to escape the slapping around by his father and the disputes with his stepmother. Why stay? They even stole his earnings.

His opportunity to leave came when his uncle made arrangements for him to work on a barge on the Mighty Mississippi River.

During our discussions, I asked Chester how long he lived with the new Johnston family after his mother's death.

"Un, Unnh," he mumbled as he considered the query. "I didn't stay long."

The street-wise kid knew he could make it on his own.

Uncle Bill worked on the barge line as an oiler and maintained connections with the owners of the line.

"He got me on 'cause he knew about my problems at home and that I had proved I would work."

"Did you like working on the river?" I inquired.

"Anything was better than living with my dad and stepmom. We worked thirty days on the boat and then fifteen off. The tugboat pushed barges from Greenville, Mississippi, to St. Paul, Minnesota. Then we returned with another load to New Orleans and wound up back to Greenville. I liked it . . . yeah."

Chester could live in this world any time he was being treated fairly or at least thought he was.

The steel tugboat had small living quarters containing two bunk beds per room. Two crewmembers occupied each room. Chester's first work assignment was to clean the wheelhouse and captain's quarters. Looking back, the small living area would help prepare him for a six by nine cell later on in his life.

During his free time, he sat in the wheelhouse and listened to stories the captain and crew told. Stories about the river and how the Mississippi changed constantly. The "Big Muddy" was never the same from one trip to the next, creating a new bend, a new mud flat or sand bar, or some other thing. Each trip the tugboat made, "Old Man River" changed his face.

From time to time, their river tales had been interrupted by another tugboat about to pass. The captain called on the marine, ship to shore radio. "Motor vessel J. Page eight; this is River Belle at mile marker two twenty-five. Do you read me?" came a voice on the radio.

Chester's tug captain took the radio mike and replied, "Motor vessel River Belle, this is J. Page eight; we read you. Go ahead."

The reply came, "Motor vessel J. Page eight, we are going to pass you to the starboard at mile marker two thirty-four. Do you read?"

"We read you, River Belle, loud and clear; look out for a sand bar about fifty feet from the bank as you make the next turn. We nearly went aground there." Each captain kept the passing skipper apprised of the river's changes.

The new cabin boy especially enjoyed hearing the Cajun captains. They spoke with a strange brogue hard to understand. The sound of their language had a musical ring to it. The flowing softness of a Creole French accent sounded like a song as they spoke on the ship to shore transmitter. The Cajuns were delightful to listen to as they passed by.

Other times, when Chester was off duty and the water was "good" (deep and unobstructed), the captain turned the big chrome steering wheel over to him. That was the most fun of all. Chester loved looking over the huge brown barges the tug was pushing. The sound of the hull breaking the river water and the drone of the diesel engines drowned all thoughts of his previous home. All his problems seemed forgotten amid the sound of the barges and the river.

Non-functioning children will become co-dependent when they do not think they are acknowledged in their house, and will search for security elsewhere. It happened when Chester found the Gunslinger's clubhouse and it happened again with the tugboat crew.

Chester found a new family to believe in. They filled the same emptiness the Gunslingers had done in California. While working on the river and gaining the trust of the crew, Chester worked on his uncle's desire to complete his formal education. Chester's Uncle Bill made sure he took his school books each time the boat shoved off. Chester studied each day of the voyage so one day he might complete his GED.

The hands on the tugboat made Chester a part of the crew. While the stories were fun, life on the river had a definite negative side to it, a decided down side.

The last day of the river voyage was payday. Life on the river was nomadic. Spending part of a one's payday in a river honky tonk temporarily removed the loneliness of the river. The captain and crew would charge into a bar and begin to order up drinks. Chester had become part of the crew and was permitted to join their party. Following close on the heels of the bars, beer, and whiskey came other pitfalls of river life; loose women and drugs. All the river passages became study halls in the cabin boy's informal education.

After several trips on the river, the young hand had another surprise waiting for him when he left the boat. A new life lesson was gained when he returned to his screwed up family.

Several months before, Chester priced a new Harley Sportster motorcycle. He shopped for a two-wheeler at the conclusion of one the river trips and found one priced for $8300. After four trips up and down the river, he considered his savings to be about half of the required price. His dad was to deposit his earnings each time he returned home to Crosby, Mississippi.

Now, when he returned to his dad's house, he believed half of the bike's price was in the bank. With steady employment, he could make the other payments, so he could purchase the Harley.

Chester is still shocked when he recalls the incident. "You know, when I got ready to get my money, it had disappeared. What happened was I went to my dad and asked him if he would co-sign a note for the balance of the price of the motorbike. I reminded him more than half the cost was deposited in the bank. Then I asked him if he would sign for the remainder."

That's when Chester Senior's wife said to him, "We need to talk to him, don't we?"

"My stepmother did the talking. She explained they took the money and paid the fees for the other kids, Vernon and Pat, in Deerfield Academy. They blew it off like it ain't no big deal. I got pretty angry; a lot of what was said by them was to justify what they did. But I didn't want to hear it. I told them I was going to have them put in jail, and they threw me out of the house. Since I was so young, a kid, I had no way to prove the charges. I left town."

From that day forward, when the cabin boy got off the tugboat, he went to his grandma's or uncle's house. Chester had spent his last night under his father's roof. His alienated stepmother, who partnered with his father, had betrayed him. They took his money without asking. He would have given it to them had they asked, but they never asked; they just took it. After years of so many family disappointments, now came family theft.

His grandfather attempted to soften the fact that his dream for his first real scooter had been shattered because of the stolen money. He dragged a 1945 Army tricycle out of his barn. The old man had bought it from the government years before. Now he gave it to his grandson to subdue his anger and attempt to soothe the hurt.

Chester accepted the motorcycle, but nothing ever mended the damage done by his deceitful parents. In February of 1970, Chester would turn eighteen. He decided to join the military right away, even though he had not reached the legal age. Chester asked his dad to give his approval and Chester Senior signed his son's admission papers. The son had grown to become a man working on the riverboat, and now he had become ready for new challenges. He had become also ready to leave Mississippi.

"The Viet Nam thing was going on and I thought it had become the macho thing to join up."

Chester had a cousin, Sammy, who agreed to join with him on the buddy system. So, off both of them went, to the Army Recruiting Center in Greenville, Mississippi, and joined up.

Shortly after, the ex-biker, ex-river rat and his cousin took off to Leesville, Louisiana, for basic training.

CHAPTER SIX

BASIC TRAINING

C hester, former biker novice and tugboat hand, left home to join the Army. He and his cousin, Sammy Johnston, responded to the trumpet call of their country. A battle was raging in a distant country, Viet Nam, and soon they would go to represent the Red, White, and Blue there. The action of being a soldier and war seemed exciting.

The Greyhound bus from Greenville was sweltering on the ride to Fort Polk in Leesville, Louisiana. Our young recruits crossed the invisible boundary at the fort's sentry post and stepped into a new world. It was a world of order and Army drab, things they had never known before.

For the next six weeks, their DI would be their mama, papa, and instructor. It was a life of six weeks' of reveille before the sun rose and into bed early at night. The recruits fell onto their cots each night too tired to party or write home. Daily, they marched, jogged, exercised, and drilled on the sandy soil of Louisiana in hundred-degree heat for hours without end. Sleep was their only relief.

"The two things I hated most were peeling potatoes on KP and typhoid shots."

The combatant-in-training relished the impending battle, but still disdained women's work. The soreness in his arms from the shots soon worked out and was lost in manifold aches from drills raising and lowering his rifle thousands of times each day.

The United States had never before fought in a territory like Viet Nam. Regardless, the new recruits prepared for battle. They crawled on their bellies on the coastal sandy soil, slithering under barbed wire and across the fields and bogs of Louisiana. Live rounds of .50 caliber machine gun fire whistled over their heads. The terrain and combat strategy would change in Nam, but the young soldiers learned the basics of soldiering. First lesson: keep your head down. Staying low is necessary training for any battle terrain, jungle or open.

Chester always loved to drive. He started driving with the scooter the Gunslingers gave him. Later, he drove a bright yellow Plymouth Duster he bought while working on the river. The U.S. Army chose to use his talents by assigning him to drive a deuce and a half supply truck.

The recruits were taught how to drive under combat conditions. They were issued a metal helmet and a shield for their face and groin. To reproduce battle fire, other troops with high-powered air rifles shot BBs at them.

"One of them air rifles wouldn't kill you but the BBs would sure sting and raise a welt," Chester recalled.

After six weeks of sweating and saluting, graduation day came. Just like in the movies, the now experienced troops marched across the camp parade ground in long, straight lines, their rifles carried smartly on their shoulders. The young heroes were led proudly by their drill sergeant. Six weeks before, they were a raggedy bunch of country boys. The drill sergeant drilled, exercised, and screamed them into a fighting machine. The young soldiers held their heads high as they paraded in front of the dignitaries sitting in the reviewing stand.

On graduation day, they were proud, even arrogant, and ready for battle. Then, none of them dreamed glory and victory would be erased by an unseen enemy's bullet. Others would have their bodies shattered by a buried mine or a whining artillery shell. Those unscathed by enemy shells would return after combat in the rice fields only to have their bright dreams destroyed. Reading the rejections of an unsympathetic press, like being called baby killers, when they returned, they were robbed of their future. They all wanted to put this unwelcome war behind them.

Chester was given a thirty-day leave after graduation at Fort Polk, then to report to a base in New Jersey to embark for Nam. The young soldier packed his duffel bag, put on his dress uniform, and headed home to Mississippi and his family one more time. He just knew they would provide a grand reception for him as a U.S. Army soldier and now they would be proud of him. The young soldier left Fort Polk prepared for combat. He looked like a professional in his green uniform and brightly polished brass. His return trip across fertile Louisiana countryside followed the same Greyhound route he and Sammy had ridden to boot camp.

Underneath his spotless, green uniform, his muscles were toned for battle from basic training. After six weeks of training, his mind had been disciplined to kill. Every day at Fort Polk, the young soldiers were mentally prepared for battle. Now they were prepared to be the finest soldiers in the world. These recruits were better equipped, better prepared, and tougher mentally than any other soldier in the world.

But soon they would all learn they had not been prepared to fight the unseen enemy in the rice fields and jungles of Viet Nam. When they completed their overseas tours, they would be confronted by an unforgiving adversary back home they had not been prepared for.

"I was proud riding home to Mississippi in my Army green uniform, going home before leaving for Nam. I wanted my daddy to see now I was a soldier . . . a man. He would be proud of me for the first time."

After Chester's bus pulled into the station in Greenville, Chester found a pay phone and called home. His return from basic training would not be a storybook ending. None of the Johnston family seemed excited about driving to Greenville to pick up the young soldier going off to war. After a long, hot wait in the bus station, some of the family arrived to pick him up.

Chester had been brainwashed in training to believe his country was proud of him. He was a soldier, going overseas to defend the Red, White, and Blue . . . the land of the free and the home of the brave. However, if his country was proud of him, his family didn't have time to bother with him. He was rejected again.

The direction of a dysfunctional family is always toward more fragmentation, a family type without rules, devoid of a moral standard, and lacking focus upon the God or family. The movement is slowly, gradually, away from unity. Many times the separation is unseen. The Johnston family was becoming distant.

Life in the Chester Senior's household had not changed much. Ann had moved to Jackson to have a baby. She had not married yet. Brother Vernon used Chester's scooter deposit to enroll in private school, but his grades were poor and his training at home was even worse.

Although Chester was a member of his country's fighting corps, he simply became a wart on his family's nose. He answered the call to a war far away, prepared himself to wear the uniform, and was about to cross an ocean to defend American families. Yet, the struggle on his home front became so intense his family had taken little notice of him since returning from basic. The family was too troubled, too caught up in their problems, to welcome their soldier boy home. They had less time to wish him well when he left.

After one more clash with his stepmother, he responded to the roar of the California Harleys. He knew now was time to see Loser and Bear and the rest of the Gunslingers before going to war.

The seventeen-year-old soldier had enough sense to know this might be the last time he would see them. His last chance to hear the gruff laughter and the beer can tabs pop, and smell the oil and the grease of the cycle shop.

He caught a ride to Greenville and headed west on the Greyhound once again.

***

If Chester had ever trusted his dad, that trust dissolved the day the young deck hand discovered his savings for his scooter were gone. His father's lack of good emerged from the family's dysfunctional closets once again.

Abuse and favoritism drove Chester to choose his alcoholic mother after the family divorce. Now, his father's manipulation dispatched the young soldier to California once again. Personal bitterness cannot be measured. Even anger or anguish does not expose or measure an individual's internal fire. Chester, now equipped for battle, had returned home to seek his father's approval. Deep inside, he longed to forgive his dad's financial indiscretion. But again he found the same aloof, distant vibes in his father that he had known growing up. He had trained in the Louisiana heat and rigid boot camp discipline just to find favor in his family's eyes. All he found at homecoming was their empty stare of uneasiness.

Nothing had changed. The importance of his uniform he wore made no difference. He had been betrayed again. All the old memories returned. They fanned the coals deep inside. Coals from being slapped around when he wouldn't fight Vernon, constant yelling and screaming between his mother and dad, accusations his mother was "whoring around." The hottest coals were those of his scooter fund being used as an education fund for Pat and Vernon.

He still had most of his Army pay in his pocket. There were three weeks left before he reported to Fort Dix, New Jersey, to ship out to Nam. So he bought a bus ticket and headed for the one place on earth where he was loved and accepted.

It had been three years since he had seen Bear and the bikers. He had left the club members before without saying good-bye. Now, the once-biker novice could not leave for the killing fields of Viet Nam without seeing the West Coast Gunslingers one more time.

Again he endured a hot three-day bus ride across the country. He watched the countryside slip by. The rolling hills of North Mississippi and Arkansas flattened out into the plains of Texas and Arizona. Memories of his first trip with his mother invaded his solitude. Finally, after many rest stops and greasy meals, LA was the next stop.

A freed spirit and a yearning to belong stirred within Chester as he got off the bus in West Covina. He planned to see his aunt, but her visit could come later. Right now he wanted to fill his soul with the sound and aromas of the old clubhouse and the garage on the side. He looked forward to filling his heart with the laughter of the crazy bikers. Most of all, he wanted to bask in the warmth of being home.

His heart beat faster as he stepped from the taxi that brought him from the bus depot. He threw his duffel bag over his shoulder and started up the front steps. No longer a boy, he carried himself with strength and grace.

Old Loser was sitting out front of the clubhouse. He was the watchdog. Loser's job was to stop any suspicious person who wanted to enter, especially if they appeared to be cops.

"Loser took a long look at me. He just saw a man in uniform and wondered why a soldier had come to the biker club. I didn't even recognize Loser at first. Age had got on up on him."

The former paperboy drug mule identified himself. "I'm

Chester don't you remember me?"

Loser found it hard to believe the this scooter rat, once covered with grease, was now standing in front of him as a man in an Army uniform. The old biker rose from his sentry seat and examined the soldier in front of him more closely. His memory had dimmed in the three years since Chester left LA. Those years of working on the tugboat and the six weeks of boot camp had changed a boy into a man. The ex-scooter rat had become a battle ready soldier. His uniform and erect carriage caused Loser not to recognize him at first.

When Chester identified himself, Loser rose from his seat. "We wondered what had happened to you." His arms extended to the soldier and gave him a crushing bear hug.

A lost boy was found. The bikers' wandering novice had returned. It was time for the club to celebrate. The guard dog led Chester into the house and he threw his duffel bag in a corner. Loser went to call the rest of the family into the kitchen. While Loser was summoning the rest of the club, Chester opened the refrigerator and pulled a beer from inside, pulled the tab, and listened to the familiar whoosh of escaping CO_2 gas. He took a long swallow of the ice cold beverage and got ready to party.

The family members began to enter the kitchen from the garage and upstairs bedrooms, and someone handed Chester another beer. Tops were being popped all over the room as welcomes were expressed. Everyone hugged Chester. He finished his beer and accepted a third, cold and foam running down the side.

This was his home. These were his people. They were family. They did not care how long he had been away. This family did not accept or reject him on his achievements. He belonged and he was home.

Later in the night, the welcome home party began to die down. Trashcans were full and the floor was littered with empty beer cans. The women went to bed and the men stayed up to talk.

Chester related why he had to leave suddenly without saying good-bye. He described the day his mother was killed, how his aunt had rushed him to her house in Oceanside, then how they had quickly left for Mississippi.

Bear, Travis, Loser, and the rest of the club members listened as he described those heartbreaking days. Talking about that day revived his emotions over the death of his mother. Feeling is a part of family.

The bikers explained how they had become alarmed when Chester had not come around for several days. Bear and Loser went looking for him, but all they found was an empty apartment. Nobody knew where he had gone, not unusual for LA. Many people came, stayed for a short time, and then just disappeared.

During the next week, life was just like old times. Chester helped work on the scooters. He handed the tattooed mechanics tools or whatever they needed. Like always, he retrieved a beer when the mechanics got thirsty. The smells of the garage brought back old memories, memories of a time when Sara Ann would be home when Chester returned; when there were no rules. A time he felt at peace at being a junior member of the outlaws.

When his days began to run short, he rode the bus to Oceanside to see his aunt. As he rode, he thought about the unanswered questions with Belle still remaining. Questions about calls never returned to him at his dad's. Why couldn't he live with her after his mama died, and other questions. But for now, his questions could wait. It seemed fitting just to tell his aunt good-bye.

Chester rode the bus from West Covina to Oceanside. It was a beautiful trip down the coast of California. He walked from the bus depot through the beautiful village to where Belle lived. Nothing there had changed; it was the same white house with the garage in the back. Chester wondered if there were any illegal emigrants hiding there.

When his aunt came to the door, she looked at him, this time with suspicion. The nephew quickly told her he had not come to live, simply to visit before going overseas.

The afternoon with her was filled with him telling tales about boot camp and his thoughts about going to Nam. Neither Chester nor his aunt wanted to relive the events of his mother's death or his living in Mississippi after Sara Ann died. Both believed this time would be better for both of them if they left the past buried with his mother.

When the sun began to set over the Pacific, Chester knew his bus to LA would be leaving soon. He hugged his aunt good-bye and walked back to the bus station. It would be a beautiful evening ride along the coast to West Covina. He wanted to spend his last night in California saying goodbye to the Gunslingers.

The next morning, Chester rose early. He had to catch a bus back home. Loser and Bear gave him a ride to the bus station. It was tough to leave the burly bikers and their "old ladies." They had always treated him as an equal, and had become his only family now. But, this time was time to say "adios," knowing he must go to war.

As his Greyhound bus headed east, Chester began to think about another country far from LA, thousands of miles from his biker home. He had already learned Nam was a place where soldiers and civilians were daily shot and blown apart. The job he had been prepared to do loomed ahead. There was no more time for any more conflicts at home. A much greater and more deadly struggle loomed over the horizon.

Once back in Mississippi, he went to see his grandparents. He just had a couple of hours for one last good-bye to the only blood kin who seemed to care about him. Just enough time to say good-bye and get back to Greenville to catch the bus to New Jersey.

Chester may have looked like a man in his uniform, but he was still a boy in his heart. He found leaving his summer home and the love and care of his grandparents painful. Both of them had taught him so many values of life. The young soldier held his emotions in check long enough to kiss the old couple and leave. Tears ran down their cheeks as they embraced the grandson. They knew the hurt he still carried inside. They held hands for a minute, then Chester turned down the sidewalk and left.

In that moment, his grandparents' affection was Chester's crowd and blaring band sending him off to war. It was enough for him. He had a bus to catch at the Greyhound station. The bus ride would begin his long journey to the other side of the world, to a place named Viet Nam.

His forehead wrinkled as the Greyhound droned toward New Jersey. He thought about his job before him. The thoughts weren't as exhilarating as they had been right after boot camp. Then, he had been full of vigor and not excitement. The thought of going to a country with no personal incentive to go, except that Uncle Sam had ordered him there, stirred an unrest in him. He pondered the thought of going to represent a country he had little knowledge of.

Most of what he had seen of the United States was from the window of a Greyhound bus, a country not wanting their soldiers at war in Viet Nam. Regardless, he was going to fight for the freedom of Vietnamese people he had never met. Soon he would learn that the Vietnamese did not want him or his comrades in their country.

Life can become difficult to understand for a "throw away" kid of eighteen, wearing his country's uniform. Well, he thought, he had ducked and dodged the BBs fired in boot camp. He had crawled under the fire of live automatic weapons, and this time, it would be for real. He believed he knew enough to survive in the rice fields of Viet Nam.

Seeing his foster biker family for a week had quelled the bitterness inside for a minute. The beers and the camaraderie of the club members had cooled his anger. While his bus sped toward his final destination, he began to look forward to the conflict lying ahead. He could not know then, but his hidden resentment inside would find many opportunities to breed and materialize in the coming months. It would also play a major role in his capability to fight and stay alive in the battles now just in front of him.

The look of the military base at Fort Dix, New Jersey, was much like Fort Polk where Chester suffered through basic training. Soldiers in Army green uniforms or camouflage denim work suits assured him that this was an army base. The wooden barracks were laid out in rows like basic training. To Chester, most bases looked pretty much the same.

For Chester and the other Nam replacement troops, Fort Dix, in GI jargon, was a jumping off place. Their training was complete. Now they waited in the barracks, lying on bunk beds or pacing the wood floors. Their status was an illustration of the Army maxim, "Hurry up and wait." They had all rushed to get to the base; now they just wanted their orders to come through.

Chester met some of his friends who were also Army buddies. Their destination was set. The only secret was the time of their departure.

Rigorous basic training was like playing war. As the soldiers trained in Louisiana, the real fighting was getting closer. The promise of conflict and when they would leave for the dreaded country referred to simply as Nam occupied the thoughts of all the young soldiers while they waited.

While at Fort Dix, the troops did not maintain a regular schedule. There was no daily regimen of marching or classroom training. They got up, went to chow, and returned to their bunks. Some played cards for a while or just lay on their double deck racks. However, in a few days, their life in the USA, enjoyable or not, would disappear behind them. Stories of an unseen enemy and the terrors of Nam warfare flooded their minds. The enemy and his well-aimed bullets would soon be real. A concealed adversary would be shooting at them to drive the American invaders from their land.

Chester wished his orders would come. He wanted to get on with the potentially deadly encounters just ahead. Not because of a love for combat; he really despised it. He simply wanted to get all the possibility of death and horror behind him.

All the Nam vets I interviewed related the same wish prior engaging in combat, to go there, fulfill their time, and get back home. They all prayed it for real once in the combat zone. There, the entreaty was to come out without loss of life or some vital body part.

Once the soldiers engaged in the battle against the Viet Cong, blood-sucking insects, and chemical sprays, the only remainder of the original hope would be to get home. The young soldiers lay in their barracks and pondered the future. How many days of life did they have left?

Finally, the orders arrived announcing the day and time of departure. Their weapons glistened and operated smoothly from all the nervous cleanings of the past few boring days. Duffel bags were packed and the Nam replacements were loaded on C-47s for the long, tiring flight to Cambodia.

The boredom of the long flight returned the reality of the impending battle. Then the young GIs began to relish the thought of fighting. They reasoned that anything was more desirable than being cramped inside their flying cattle car. Their apprehension of the unknown combined with the discomfort of the cramped aircraft intensified their desire to "get this time on" to kill the VC.

After an eighteen-hour flight on the cramped C-47, Chester and follow soldiers landed in Cambodia. The replacements were temporarily quartered in base tents there. Next they would be transported to the beaches of Vietnam by Navy ships. The Navy transports would sail around the tip of Cambodia, then through the South China Sea to Da Nang. There, they would be discharged on the bloody soil of Viet Nam; then they would be at war.

CHAPTER SEVEN

VIETNAM

C hester recalled his first thoughts about Vietnam from the day he arrived. "In August of 1971, my outfit, the Five Hundred Seventy-Second Heavy Equipment Unit, landed in Da Nang. We sailed on the giant aircraft carrier U.S.S. *Kitty Hawk* from Cambodia, across the China Sea to Vietnam. Diminutive gray landing crafts took us close to the beach. When the bow of our vessel was lowered, it became a ramp into the surf and onto the sand. All new recruits stepped into the water of the South China Sea and nervously waded toward the sandy earth. We realized this place wasn't a beach club. Its beauty brought a false sense of security. Each of us realized we had to be alert. The sun on the white sand reminded me of a postcard greeting from an idyllic country. Really, it was an entrance to a bloody war zone.

"We swaggered across the beach like tough, conquering heroes. I guess we believed when the enemy became aware of us they would evacuate. Then we marched down a muddy road toward a strange village called Da Nang.

"Poverty in Nam is unlike anything I had ever seen. I grew up in Mississippi where small, frame, unpainted sharecroppers houses dotted the Delta farmland. I knew about Hispanic poverty in LA, yet Vietnam was primeval compared to the poverty seen in America. I was soldering in an unfamiliar country, buying products with a unaccustomed currency, fighting a bizarre war I really couldn't comprehend."

To Chester, natives dressed in black with straw hats appeared as a cast of mimes. "Short in stature, from a distance, each one resembled the next one. It reminded me of the old Charlie Chaplin movie where all the characters in the picture were dressed the same and walked swaying sideways, as did the silent film star. But they tended to their business. They were polite, as all oriental people, but they never spoke to us.

"The first section of Da Nang contained rows of gray, wood or tin shacks serving as nightclubs. Far different from the glamorous neon-lit river joints I visited working on the Mississippi."

"Roads in front of the dilapidated bars were slick, muddy tracks bordering the rice fields. Each run down club boasted crowds of soldiers and Vietnamese females. Local girls sold their bodies for whatever a GI had to trade, a can of tuna, soda crackers, a small package of cigarettes, or a few pieces of chewing gum. Love and life had little value in Nam.

"In Da Nang, the bars never closed to GIs. Slim Vietnamese bar girls were dressed in bright printed dresses slit up the side to expose their thighs and legs. They survived by prostituting."

No city health department controlled the women. Many of the GIs contracted venereal diseases after sleeping with them. Other GIs woke up to discover they had been robbed after they fell asleep in a rented room.

In Nam, bar girls and foreign soldiers lived life in constant danger.

"Even while on patrol, village girls, some pregnant, approached and undressed before our squad. They showed no shame in displaying their bodies to the GIs for gain. The prostitutes would giggle and smile and invite the GIs off the trail for quick sex where a bomb trap was set to kill us.

"The constant pressure of hidden explosives, fighting an unseen enemy, and disease would soon affect all of us. We imaged the veterans who had been in Nam for months. Words for the Nam natives labeling them all alike became part of our vocabulary – dinks, slopes, slants, or gooks – crept into our conversations. Then we also began to repeat the slogan of the vets who fought here ahead of us: One million of them ain't worth one of us.

"Slowly we were swayed to think all these poor farmers were ungrateful, unappreciative of our protection from the northern enemy, the VC. They didn't care if we lived or died and we gradually become persuaded the majority of them would like nothing better than to see us all dead or gone.

"Once the blood of our buddies spread in pools on the ground in our first fire fights, we begin to believe this country is fighting against us. The villagers' lack of gratitude breeds loathing in us. Loathing turns into a desire to kill randomly, to eradicate all of them. Young U.S. soldiers didn't know which of the natives dressed in black could be trusted.

"We all begin to wonder why we were sent to protect a country with people who never owned more than the clothes on their back and a bowl full of rice. How come our comrades, dying to preserve a life style poorer than any in the States, were giving their lives for a populace who didn't care anything about us?

"We came to believe the Vietnamese natives were crazy to think the struggle to defend them was because of colonialism. Why did Washington order us to Viet Nam? Our thinking was that every-body must be demented. We were dying for politicians seven thousand miles away. Someone must be crazy!"

"After resting, we began our march from Da Nang, ten clicks inland. Our equipment unit would join the 18th Infantry Brigade.

They already had camped at a village named Ah Khe. Our march there saw the soil quickly change from sandy into green, marshy rice fields."

Rice is the staple food of the Vietnamese people. Peasants grow enough to feed their family and sell the excess at market.

"Peasant families worked in the rice paddies without looking up at us as we passed by, remained stooped over the rice plants. All the farmers were dressed in traditional grower attire. Black trousers neatly gathered and bound at their ankles, and dark shirts that matched their pants. Narrow faces with slanted eyes were hidden behind pale, cone shaped hats. Some were the enemy.

"Our troops approached the village, a little cluster of mud and straw huts containing some vendor shops. These huts and marketplaces were the town of Ah Khe. The GIs had nicknamed it Firebase Winnie."

Ah Khe became a staging area for Chester and his fellow troops. They arrived and unpacked at the village and learned the town had become a commercial center on the now famous Highway 1.

Camouflaged Army trucks rumbled up and down the highway all day. Some transported soldiers going to or returning from battle. Others contained food, supplies, and ammo from Da Nang, or they returned empty. Lines of trucks filled the road in a steady, endless rumbling caravan. Soldiering at Firebase Winnie always simply repeated the previous day's events. The soldiers rested and waited for their battle call.

The marketplace sat in the center of the village. Two-story, makeshift buildings served as the backdrop of the primitive market jumbled along side each other in a wacky assortment of shapes and sizes. The exterior paint, chipped and faded, barely hide the wood underneath. The stores' ground floors opened onto an earth sidewalk. When the rains came, the walkways became a giant bog of mud.

"And the rains would come," Chester assured.

The Ah Khe market sidewalks stood in front of poorly constructed booths with tables displaying domestic and imported goods. Native-sewn pants and shirts hung on racks and straw hats were piled upon each other on temporary tables. Canned foods, rice, and fish are also available. The grocery stalls were easily identified by swarms of flies and insects hanging over the food in the hot, breezeless air.

Imported items were also offered. Air Vietnam flight bags, identified with the airline initials and insignias, were hung from poles. Stacked beside the flight bags were B.F. Goodrich sandals and cartons of black market cigarettes. The more enterprising vendors offered radios, wristwatches, Zippo lighters, and even Army fatigues.

To Chester's mind, it seemed to be a miniature mud mall. "Outside the shopping center, intersections were restricted by coiled strands of shiny concertina wire. Each exit displayed a military checkpoint. Soldiers lounged against burlap sandbags. Inside the sand fortresses, other soldiers leaned over steel grey machine guns ready to fire.

"When the soldiers got drowsy. they simply dozed off. The rest stayed alert, but nervous. The nights in the joints before going on duty made them seek sleep; those awake stayed in their tents. Regardless of the previous night's entertainment, they guarded all the approaches to the market," Chester explained.

The roadblocks were necessary because the VC loved to sneak into town and fire upon unsuspecting soldiers or unfriendly natives.

Chester continued. "Firebase Winnie sat just four or five miles from the heavy jungle fighting. Even at that distance, the camp filled with hollow sounds of artillery fire. If the wind blew hard, the boom, boom, boom of the big guns seemed to be right next door."

Yet, life is almost bearable for the young GIs based at Firebase Winnie.

The former soldier tells about the humid, sometimes bloody days as a grunt in Nam. "Orders from command for us to move out into the countryside come too often. Our outfit is always aware of the war even at the supply base. The staccato beat of chopper blades beating the air is continuous. At times, small arms fire could be heard from the distant countryside. Finally, orders come and it is time for us raw recruits to seek out the enemy, to kill and destroy him.

On his first day out, Intelligence reported the adversary had been spotted and gave Chester's platoon leader a map coordinates.

"Order are given to move out, you load your weapon with ammo and put your pack over your shoulders. Sweat begins to stream profusely down chest and back. The humidity mingles with fear of a firefight and opens every pore. One can smell the fear.

"We move slowly out of the camp, our shirts clinging to our backs. The sticky camouflaged uniforms become wet and uncomfortable. The straps of our M-16 rifles and backpacks begin to cut into the flesh of our backs. We notice how the Vietnam scenery changes as we move closer to the real war.

"The road we are on narrows into a twisting, rutted dual path, barely wide enough for a Jeep to pass. Civilians ride past us on Honda motorbikes or bicycles. The dirt roads are boundary lines dividing the owner's rice patches. It is the ancient landowner system.

"Green hedgerows, impenetrable to one's vision, rise eight to ten feet high, fencing and towering over the small rice fields. Engineers riding their bulldozers follow in behind the foot soldiers. The operators of the huge earthmovers push the green brush covering into gigantic piles to be destroyed. The hiding places of the enemy are uncovered so they cannot fire into the passing columns of U.S. troops later."

After the hedgerows are burned, the soldiers can see more small rice gardens separated by earth mounds serving as dikes or dams. The helicopter pilots see a beautiful picture of the framed marshy sections of land. The paddies appear as painted mosaics in a myriad of pastel colors, blue, purple, and green, tile-like pictures that momentarily hide the ugliness of war to the observers above.

"We silently walk in a line past the muddy fields of rice. The peasants scarcely glance at us, stooped over tending the plants. During a firefight, it will become difficult to distinguish males from females, adults from children. All are dressed alike. The peasant farmers maintain a stoic trance as me and my buddies pass by them.

"Unexpectedly, the hush across the area is broken as artillery shells begin to rain down on us. Everybody scrambles for cover in a rice paddy or hedgerow. Recruits quickly learn to survive in this dangerous place; you either learn, or die quickly, face down in the soggy mire of Nam.

"I crouch down in the obscure water and pray the peasants we passed are friendly. We were trained only to fire when the enemy is engaged. I wait with finger on the trigger of an M-16 at my shoulder, aimed in the direction of the Vietnamese. I nervously await a sign of hostility from them. The workers just rise and watch as the road explodes in enormous clumps of mud and foliage from the shells. Good news, the men are friendly."

After the incoming artillery fire ceases, the villagers return to work and the American troops continue their search.

This had been a good day for Chester and his friends. The young GIs marched for hours and did not encounter any VC. The road back to Firebase Winnie begins to widen. Peasants appear, carrying goods in green, plaited baskets tied to bamboo poles between them. The natives are either going to market or returning home, and the soldiers are either going to the fields or returning to camp. Everyone always seems to be constantly moving in Viet Nam.

"We move back inside the tent camp and gaze upward as the sun begins to dip below the rim of the trees. High above us are fading white vapor trails. The evening sky is crisscrossed with white trails of friendly F-15 exhausts. They are our air defense. Smaller, narrower tracks lazily float high above the earth, leaving evidence of our protectors as a warning to our enemy. The smaller vapor trails are SAM missiles, a nightmare for our courageous jet jockeys.

The SAMs, Mother Russia's contribution to the North Vietnamese forces, have slowed down our air attacks on the enemy Vietnamese Regulars. The decrease of U.S. fighter's attacks turns the pressure up on American grunts on the ground.

"There is comfort knowing the guys in the sky are there for us; in this awful jungle hole, we need someone.

No one had died on Chester's first day in the field. A day without body bags and friends with tags on their toes was a good day in the rice bogs of Viet Nam.

***

"Barely eighteen years old when arriving, I didn't know what to expect in this place simply called Nam. But the land we had come to liberate from oppression was not like the place I had imagined."

Chester learned Firebase Winnie was suitably named. The base was the supply depot for all the U.S. platoons poised to move inland.

"I soon learned the basic battle plan for Nam. To the North Vietnamese, we played the role of an invader. We came armed with artillery, shells, and rocket launchers, protected by jets and choppers in the sky, ready when called to destroy the VC's jungle hideouts. VC soldiers had the option to run and hide when the barrage got too hot from rockets and napalm.

"We moved our supplies in heavy green and black camouflage, one and a half ton trucks. The VC army moved what supplies they had on their backs. Our soldiers dressed in black and brown camouflage uniforms. We were heavily armed with the latest model rifles, grenades, and torches. The VC are armed with weapons supplied by friendly Communist governments or taken from dead U.S. servicemen.

"I learned the battle plan was really quite simple. Surround a village where the VC had been reported hiding, crank up our artillery until the village was knocked down, then us grunts moved in. When the enemy stayed to fight, we killed as many as we could and chased the survivors into the dense jungle."

The goal of battle was to destroy. Obliterate crops, animals, houses, and whole villages of people where necessary. Those failing to leave the settlement of thatched hootches would be destroyed. Staring death in its ugly face, the soldiers had no time to decide whether the remaining people were friendly or not. Most times, the troops had no information from U.S. interrogation if the villagers provided crops or animals or support to the devious VC. With the might of their American firepower, they were just devastated.

"Once we chased the enemy out, we began phase two. All huts or hootches still standing were burned to the ground. What remained of buildings torn apart by the artillery was also burned, and animals and crops were destroyed. Nothing was left the VC could survive on.

"When the artillery bombardment stopped and the firefight ended, the bulldozers came and pushed all the debris and ashes into the jungle. After the area was cleaned up, we set up tents for the villagers to return and live in. In the new tent village, the natives could be closely supervised and segregated from the hidden enemy."

Chester learned General Command had a dual purpose in the battle plan. One, kill the adversary and destroy supplies and arms concealed in the village. Two, move the peasants into an area where they would be protected and watched. The friendly Army of the Republic of Vietnam assisted with the guard duty.

"Sometimes the adversary, the VC, hid deep in the lush jungle foliage or outside a small village. When we found them, the procedure was for the U.S. foot soldiers to move back into safe position on the perimeter; then the big guns went to work.

"Kinda like bird hunting in the Mississippi farm fields. The grunts, played by the hunters, moved into position, where the birds, playing the role of the enemy, hid. The artillery, like bird dogs, were released to flush out the coveys of birds, the foe, hidden under the growth of grass and bushes. Once the dogs flushed the hunted into flight, the hunters then shot scores of escaping birds. In Nam, the artillery flushed the enemy VC infantry and killed them as they fled."

The battle plan never varied. Sometimes the VC returned with larger forces. Then, they drove the U.S. invaders from the village, again and again, and so went the war.

***

Chester had not been prepared for the struggle in Nam. He was depressed in a demoralizing country. From the minute he arrived, a depression came over him that he would never shake.

"My thoughts were mixed about being a U.S. soldier in the Viet Nam conflict. I was proud of the uniform I wore and the country I represented, yet at times I also felt myself as a bloodthirsty killer. I swore loyalty to my fellow soldiers, men I went through boot camp with. On the other hand, when I came to learn the Washington politics of the war, I began to wonder if the government I came to rescue was worth the effort.

"Our brainwashed thinking believed our fight was aimed to save the peasants from a corrupt and evil enemy. However, the poor people of Nam had no interest in our variety of help. The peasant farmers and the enemy looked alike. We could not discern between them, as those who looked like peasants were the enemy and at other times they were simply peasants."

This conflict was confusing for a young soldier boy from Mississippi.

Even so, the U.S. grunts had been trained and sent into this county to eliminate the enemy. Our commanders appeared interested only in body count, the final tally of how many of ours and theirs were buried. Numbers seemed to be the only important issue; the reporting was totally impersonal.

***

Another day in Vietnam came again began for the young soldier. The morning mix of the night air and the day's ground heat creates thick fog of humidity.

"On humid days, my biggest enemy was the hungry insects attacking me. During breakfast of K-rations, our platoon leader says today we will search for VC military further inland. The opponent rarely moves in daytime, so the battle plan is to seek them out and demolish them."

Experience taught our soldiers that the VC forces are battle-hardened and expert in concealment. They blend in with village peasants or hide underground in elaborate, covered trenches running for miles. The grunts job is to dig them out, to put the uniformed soldier in black in a burial ditch before he puts you in a body bag.

"Prior to falling in and moving out, we check our M-16s to insure they are operating properly. The four grenades issued are clipped to the ammo belt around our waist and diagonally across our chest. Insect repellent is double-checked. We saddle up and move out.

"There is silence among the men of the platoon. Our lieutenant briefed us about the mission. Large numbers of VC had been reported by village informants. We know we will engage in a firefight before we go back to Firebase Winnie. The unspoken question is, how will I return."

A platoon of GIs with black-streaked faces stealthily walk past the ever-present farm ponds off a narrow muddy path. Silence is broken only by a passing chopper or jet high in the azure blue sky.

"We become edgy and chills race down the back of our necks at any unusual sounds. Panicky fingers pressure the metal trigger of our weapons. The solid green foliage raises a curtain impossible to see through. We all have heard about complete platoons being 'wasted' by an unseen enemy hiding behind theses massive curtains.

"We walk several miles, passing countless farms being tended by their bowed and silent farmers. Dual tracks beaten out by rubber tires and shoe leather merge into one and become just a faint trail. Our group moves forward into territory new to us; the veterans call it 'Indian Country.' The Indians are the VC irregulars. They walk the same endless mud paths as the American GIs, called the Cowboys.

"Once in occupied territory our eyes constantly move up and down searching the heavy foliage. We stare down, probing for a tin can or scrap of paper that could be deadly. The VC hide land mines with any item that might attract the foot or hand of an unsuspecting soldier. A slightest dislodging of the camouflaged device will detonate a bomb, called a booby trap, resulting in death or dismemberment.

"Our minds play a game of search with the eyes, but the mind sends alarms faster than the eyes can focus because we all know a firefight could erupt at any minute. Our column enters a large clearing where a village stood only months before. It takes a moment for me to adjust to the change in the lay of the land. A savage firestorm of small arms, artillery, and flamethrowers had leveled the large cluster of thatched hootches. Once the battle ended, the ground was scorched by the heat. The only remnants were withered brown grass and blackened soil.

"In Nam, the ground has amazing resiliency. Small tree seedlings will quickly push their way through the soft green earth. A few palm trees felled by shell explosions lie dead on their ugly thatched sides. Several charred jagged palms remain standing erect, blackened on their top by an exploding artillery shell.

"This area is strangely silent. Only the sounds of nature, oblivious to warfare, are audible. We sense an uneasy peacefulness on the leveled village site. The jungle foliage reaches out to the charred ground to install a new carpet. The few remaining trees stand as stark monuments to those who died here."

The word picture Chester describes is of cultivated rice paddies, now filled with weeds. Peasant farm families have been relocated to a tent village.

"Fear is always resident. It rises in intensity until your skin feels as if it can crawl away from your bones."

The soldier's fear is activated by the always-present hidden enemy. When the silence is not right, your "brain races to try and focus on the situation. When will the enemy attack, in the light, or the dark? We can feel they are close. Our questions: where are their hidden holes, how far are their disguised tunnels, have we walked right over some?

"There is movement in a neighboring rice field. Instantly the silence is alive with the tat-tat-tat-tat-tat of automatic weapons firing and the hollow bomp-bomp-bomp of heavy rifles. Someone is screaming, 'Stop firing, stop firing,' as a loud ka-plash is heard and a spray of brownish water dances above a pond. Our first firefight has been won by the good guys. Score: U.S., one; water buffalos, zero.

"Indian Country is a free fire zone; here, we shoot at anything moving."

The downed water buffalo lies in an expanding pool of red. It has almost been blown to pieces by the massive firepower unleashed by the nervous grunts. We thanked God the enemy could not return our fire.

***

Another morning comes for the GIs in the scenic country of Viet Nam. Chester explains the rainy season is when rain falls all day every day. His platoon's mission today is to check out a little village where native spies have reported the VC hiding and growing small patches of vegetables and rice. Intelligence has no information about the non-military natives in this cluster of huts.

Each day, the young troops repeat the occurrences of the previous one. Walk through muddy trails past scrubby bushes, on trails marked with string. One stray step off the marshy walkway could result in death. When a GI dies in the rain, his corpse lays in the mud of this merciless country.

"By dark, we are only a couple of hundred meters away from the small group of hootches. We are given orders to make camp in a narrow clearing. Our force consists of three squads of soldiers and four civilian Vietnamese, in all about forty men.

"We all dig in and form a perimeter circling around the camp. Sentries change every four hours. The rest of company use trenching tools to remove the surface muck on top, then dig short trenches further into the fertile soil underneath for protection through the night. By now, the adversary knows where we are and are discussing whether or not to attack.

"We slump down in our trenches. Water begins seeping into the shallow cover. Ponchos disguised with green and black foliage are drawn tightly around us as we settle in until first light.

"The only word to describe our situation is miserable. The rain is miserable, our foxhole is uncomfortable, and the war is wretched. I wonder if our adversary will attack tonight. I hope not. My mind turns to home and a frantic feeling of despair creeps into my mind. I am wet and helpless; I hate everything about this God-forsaken country. Only one thing will conquer my fear and ominous feelings: THC. I reach into my shirt pocket and light a joint, not the best grass in the world, but sufficient me for now.

"I lean back on the muddy side of my foxhole and inhale the drug that hides the pain and fear for a short time. The soft pop of a flare igniting snaps me out of my haze. A reddish glare semi-illuminates our clearing; instantly the night is alive with the sound of war. Agonizing screams rise above the firefight din. A soldier on the boundary of the camp has been hit, steel ripping flesh apart, and quickly shock captures him. I wonder who he is.

"Flashes of red flame appear quickly and vanish in the shadowy curtain of vegetation. I spot a VC and fire a burst in his direction. I empty my ammo clip randomly into the rain and darkness. More cries and screams are heard as men close by are hit, as well as those on the outskirts of our camp. Explosions shake the ground and spray us with wet encampment. I raise my head after an explosion and there is a shadow moving toward us. I empty another clip in his direction. If I live until dawn, I may know if I can add one more to the enemy body count.

"As suddenly as the flashes of flame appeared, they vanish. Has it been long since the clash began, a minute, an hour? How does one measure fear in time?"

The enemy is gone, on the run, dragging their wounded with them. Their blood trail will have washed away by daybreak in he rain. Medics attend to the wounded GIs. They apply temporary medical aid until daylight arrives. Firebase Winnie is contacted by phone and choppers will arrive at first light to evacuate the injured and dead.

"I reach for a second joint, light it up and hope I live until tomorrow.

"Daybreak is announced by the arrival of two helicopter gun ships. Our company cautiously emerges from our burrows in the ground; another new day has begun. After the choppers depart with the load of stretchers and body bags, another fire mission is called in to command center. Almost immediately after the coordinate is confirmed, the shrill pitch of artillery shells breaks the gloom. We watch as the small native village begins to be lifted from the earth in a succession of explosions. The ammo fired from miles away crisscrosses the hootches and dirt road running through the farm community.

"Like magic, the artillery shells stop falling and the whine of jet engines join the chorale of the jungle. The sound of whoosh-whoosh-whoosh in the sky indicates a rocket has been fired at the helpless cluster of huts. The ground erupts in fire as the rocket burns through the huts. A smell of gas and cinders floats toward the clearing we're in. Where a settlement of natives existed now is a glowing firebox of cinders.

"There is no movement as we approach the charred remains of a tiny village. Even the forest animals have fled the fire and explosions. Only a few patches of flames remain and they flicker and die. The earth is black and scorched for several hundred yards on all sides.

"Our first squad crosses the seared sod looking for charred bodies of VC, there are several. The scattered remains of a truck garden is found on the backside of the village. The informants were correct. We capture several Communist soldiers and find the bloody and torn bodies of others. Most of the guerrillas jumped into tunnels when the firefight began and are out of the country by now. Some may still be a couple of feet away in a shallow hole hidden by the vines and leaves of the jungle."

After the dead are buried and the fires extinguished, it's time for the cleanup to begin. Another day of warfare ends in a country far from home. Very soon, death would visit Chester in a close and personal manner

CHAPTER EIGHT

AL

One of Chester's war experiences always eluded our discussion, as he became evasive during my many interviews with him. I had known for some time that his closest friend was killed in Nam. He died a few feet away from Chester. Chester refused to discuss event. He had never even discussed Al's death with Cindy, his wife.

Most of my early interviews with Chester took place at the Parchman Spiritual Life Center. Chester worked with the chaplains and I served as a volunteer chaplain. One day we got together for another interview because not much was happening at the building. Chester mentioned we had finished the Nam section, but he had not related his friend death.

The warfare in Viet Nam continues in the minds of every Nam vet. The conflict provided many experiences that shape and molded who Chester had become. He went to fight at age eighteen, still a teen.

The blend of know-how and temperament sought their proper fit. Today, the experiences of Nam continued to haunt and challenge his emotions. Twenty years after his best friend's demise, there is still a deep festering wound in his soul.

Discussing Al's passing activated the brutal war experiences of bombing women and children, buddies maimed and covered with blood, and all the horrors of the Vietnam as if they continue in the present.

Al's untimely demise has been like a piece of shrapnel imbedded so deeply it cannot be surgically removed. Each time Chester thought about his death, the memory aroused the always-resident pain.

The day I wrote this chapter, I understood that, for his story to be complete and for the cleansing of Chester's soul, we must together put Al to rest forever.

***

In Nam, Chester learned that losing friends during battle is painful. The Apocalyptic Horseman riding a pale horse is indiscriminate as to who he rides over. In the lush green killing fields, with an ever-present, unseen enemy, death often came without warning.

Al arrived in Nam two months behind Chester.

"What attracted my attention first was his curly red hair."

Al was one of the replacements who came into the area where Chester's platoon was bivouacked. He was a burly, stocky kid from Connecticut, of Italian descent.

"I don't know what drew us, but we became partners."

For Chester and Al, the bond of friendship tightened quickly. Soon, they dug their foxholes and got high together, shared ever-immediate, inevitable danger with each other. Both smoked weed in an attempt to remove the constant fear of dying. Their partnership was based on trust. Al would catch his back and visa-versa. The element that drew the cord of friendship tight was promise of a future.

I asked what they discussed in the narrow confines of a foxhole.

"You know, Brother Roger, you talk about the desire of going home, what we talked about mostly, what we exchanged. We spoke mostly about expectations."

What the two soldiers discussed was a return to the USA alive. They looked forward to meeting each other's family. Foxhole faith concerns the "here and now," not the hereafter.

"Al shared what he hoped to do when he went home to Connecticut. Al was a laid back guy, not like me. He talked about his loud, Italian family, where he lived, how everyone, family and neighbors, acted when they had a deep snow. He taught me about skiing and skating and shoveling snow; things I had never done."

Al's desire was simply to return there and resume life. Chester's hope was woven around a fine lady sitting behind him on a "righteous" scooter and being "in the wind." His was a reverie of biker freedom.

They shared the prospect of riding free together . . . once they returned safely to the States. Their vision would be complete as they rode across the country on Harleys. Go fast and feel the wind in their face by day and get high at night. While slumped in a muddy hole in the ground, Al and Chester defined their true freedom.

Chester dreamed Al could meet his California biker family and then they would "settled it in" (go to work and raise a family). They passed the hours sharing dreams and smoking weed in their foxhole long after darkness hooded the jungle of death around them.

"We picked one another up."

Everything concerning life was negative in Nam. Chester's fighting spirit died the night Al was killed.

"Some time about dusk, our outfit had been cutting down hedge rows while taking incoming artillery from rocket grenades off and on. Our job was to protect the rice paddies so the people would have food. Cutting walls of shrubs was an everyday job to eliminate enemy hiding places, a necessary task to stay alive. Our duties changed daily. We cleaned mud out of our bulldozer's roller tracks and kept them oiled. You might be an oiler one day and on 'point' the next. The lead man stayed out in front of the clearing work and watched for VC. Enemy attacks came suddenly with little time to find cover."

Chester and Al had been on point the day Al was killed. Fear was part of being the point man, and both Al and Chester had been stiff with dread since morning.

"Out front, the greatest danger was land mines, which were buried everywhere. Some planted by 'Charlie' and others by our guys. Any time anyone stepped on one or a bulldozer ran over one, you never knew whose bomb it was, ours or theirs"

The grunts referred to the native marijuana as Thai stick.

"Many of the natives made rope by drying out the fiber of this leafy plant; they didn't understand its mind altering properties. Most of the GIs did. I saw some bushes growing twelve to sixteen feet high. The Vietnamese had been aware of THC's medicinal quality for centuries. They chewed the THC, or sap, out of the plant to kill their pain when injured."

The leaves can be dried and crumbled and rolled in cigarette paper for smoking. The chemical agent THC locked inside brings precious relief from fear and death and depression.

"The marijuana was growing in abundance around where we had trenches. A warning was given not to collect the plant once we received the command to "Dig in." Al and I dug our hole and circled the camp perimeter with sharp concertina wire. We thought our supply of Thai stick would last for the night and we settled in."

Chester and Al hunkered down in their recess below ground level and waited; it was like a death vigil. A firefight could begin with rocket grenades or a bullet fired from a tree within the circle. Smoking weed made the waiting for action more bearable.

"Al began to crawl out to where he had seen stick growing, just beyond our perimeter. Artillery shelling and some light weapons fire had begun from outside the camp about the same time. Our training had been to stay down and look for the enemy. Even with light rifle fire, Al thought he could crawl out, get some smoke, and return to safety. He slid out of our hole and started sliding along the ground. He had crawled four or five feet and I heard a muffled sound like a soft 'womp.' Al stopped crawling and just lay in the mud.

"A flying piece of metal had struck Al beside his eye, close to the temple. The object may have been a sniper bullet or shrapnel. I never found out. He didn't make a sound; no scream or holler. I looked over and whispered to the guys in the next foxhole, 'Hey, Des; Al's been hit.' I called his name softly through the darkness and rain, but I heard no reply.

"My partner laid belly down, still clutching the soggy ground outside our foxhole. He was dead. I've seen a lot of 'em blowed up or shot, and you just become hard. You see the hospital trucks with large red crosses painted on the top going back to Nang or the base, full of GIs with their heads all busted and bandaged up and blood everywhere. Some missing arms or legs; most of them you don't know, so it doesn't bother you as much.

When you've been together with someone every day, been kicking it, gettin' high, I guess death affects you more than the ones you never met."

One small piece of enemy steel had dissolved Chester and Al's partnership and plans for the future. More grief would soon come down the road.

All through modern-day military conflicts, the metal dog tag has been the method of identifying a GI. The soft metal tag is stamped with the soldier's name and serial number. When new recruits report to basic training, they receive uniforms, shoes, and a bright metal tag on a chain. The recruit hangs two dog tags around his neck. The tags will remain around his neck until the soldier leaves military service.

Identifying a dead soldier is a gristly process. Each man is issued a tag with one purpose only, to identify a person when he is killed.

Most Vietnam veterans I have talked to expressed one common fear beyond death, a fear of being killed and their body not being identified. Their remains could not be returned to a hometown and family and they would be buried and lost in an unmarked military cemetery plot somewhere. No one wanted to be killed in Nam. Yet what they feared most of all was being buried in this remote jungle country and forgotten.

After WW II, a new procedure of assuring identification of the dead began, a chilling process, but foolproof. The dog tags are removed from around the neck and one inserted in the mouth, behind the teeth of the dead GI. The process must be done almost immediately after death, while the jaw can be opened wide. After the tag was inserted, the jawbone is driven upward, lodging the tag in the upper roof of the mouth. The blow that drives the tag upward is delivered by the boot of a comrade. While cold and chilling, the process assured the soldier he will go home. Perhaps in an effort to put the thought in the back of their mind, they made a joke out of it.

"I mean, it wasn't really a joke. They would say, 'Hey, man; if I don't get through this one tonight, make sure I'm tagged right."

Chester and Al had made a bond with each other. Whoever might be killed first, his survivor would insure identification. The oath would keep their hope of going home certain, even in death.

"You know, Roger; when it came down to it, I didn't have the guts."

Chester paused as a living picture of his partner's death flashed by for the millionth time since the day he died.

To Chester, a warrior's loyalty is proven by his keeping an oath . . . or dying for it. Chester had been unable to keep his, for lots of reasons. Since Al's death and during our interview, Chester struggled with the fact he had not being able to carry out the pact. To lose a friend one moment, then kick a metal plate into his friend's mouth overwhelmed him. Perhaps he could have done it later . . . the next day. But he could not do it right then.

But he did do the next best thing; he made sure it was done.

"It's not like I let him down. I saw it done right. But it was my job, my oath. He said he would do it for me. He wanted me to do it for him. But when it came down to it, I couldn't do it. From that day on, even after I got home, I just wanted to get high and stay out of it." [Not be involved in any new relationships.]

Chester continued slowly working toward self-forgiveness. Talking about that day helped. For the mud-covered grunt, it was a war to just go home alive, and to hope your buddies made it, too.

***

The Viet Nam memorial, or "Wall," just off the downtown mall in DC is a high, black structure of glistening stone tablets anchored in the soil of the nation's capital. Hundreds of thousands of Nam vets, many riding Harleys, and scores of other visitors file silently past the Wall throughout the year. On the base of the monument are tokens left to fallen comrades: a letter, picture, even a pint of a comrade's favorite Tennessee sipping whiskey. Visitors came to see the awesome spectacle, others to rub the impression of a name recalling a soldier who died in Nam. The bearded vets appear to find peace at the Wall.

Their peace comes from knowing their fallen comrade is remembered here on a silent stone wall. The remembrance is enough to provide comfort to the outcast men and women who fought in Vietnam. Chester will never visit this healing place, but today he has found peace.

CHAPTER NINE

GOING HOME

C hester finally received new orders in March 1972. After living in the mud and blood of Nam for eight unforgettable months, his thoughts had become, "Praise God, my tour is over in this war zone."

Then, Chester knew little about God but had enough sense to recognize that a higher power had helped him escape Nam with life and limb. The soldiers who arrived in Nam with Chester nearly a year before, those still there, not killed or wounded, had orders to ship out to Finland. They would stay in Finland thirty days on R&R. Finally it had come time to leave the bloody battlefield.

Sleeping occupied the initial time in Finland. Rest had been a luxury none of the soldiers on the front in Nam enjoyed. When get-up-and-go had been restored, next on their schedule was to check out the Finnish lounges and clubs.

Finland boasted a reputation for having many bars with single women and a vast supply of drugs. The guys checked out the scenic and historical landmarks of the country, then found little else to do except visit the nightspots.

"I would sit in the bars and watch the girls hustle drinks from our soldiers," Chester remembered. "It mirrored the life in the clubs in Da Nang."

American money attracts men and women. Some came to rob or steal, others to sell whatever from Fort Dix to Vietnam, Germany to Finland. The game is the same. (My comment, not his.)

"The sting operation happened while our guys tossed down strong drinks, their companions feigned drinking along with them. The bar girls drank cherry colored orange juice without alcohol. They got paid for every drink they hustled. When the bars closed and the couples went outside, boyfriends would show up and the girls disappeared. The fake offers vanished with the GIs dreams. The less fortunate soldiers were robbed, beaten, and left in the gutter for the police to take to jail."

The end of R&R always came too soon. But Chester's new orders put him on board a military transport plane to Heilbronn, Germany. Here, he would finish his obligation to Uncle Sam.

***

The one travelogue concept the soldiers knew about Germany was cold weather, strong beer, and blonde women, Oh, yeah, and drugs; weed, acid, speed, and any other drug desired. Germany also boasted numerous "all night clubs," where companionship could be purchased. In Germany, Chester permitted his foxhole habit to resume, using marijuana to make the nights easier to bear. Yet the shorter the THC made the night, the greater the craving increased. In Nam, smoking had been approached as medicinal; now he began the use for pleasure.

Chester's new duty in Germany was as a stock clerk in the motor pool. His assignments included inventorying and issuing parts for Jeeps, deuce-and-a quarter trucks, and bulldozers, everything from bearings to brake shoes. They inventoried any part needed to repair the vehicles and return them back action.

His new position took Chester back to his first love, fixing scooters at the Gunslingers' garage. It returned him to the loud sounds and harsh smells of the California shop.

Now, far from the shells and the bombs of Nam, life became easy. Work filled his days, but nights and weekends remained unscheduled, empty. To pass the time, the GIs chose to drink, get drunk or high, and chase women.

Even with the laid-back lifestyle in Germany, some would pass time before erasing the horrors of the bloody rice fields of Vietnam. Chester would wake up screaming at the backfiring of a passing truck or car, and the memories would rush back.

"You sat up in bed and thanked God you had moved away, far from the firefights and rocket grenades of the jungles. We felt safe from the enemy in Germany, like a horror movie which played every night in my dreams."

A guy could lay back in Germany and enjoy friendly people, beer flowing freely, and drugs on every corner. German girls loved American GIs and Chester enjoyed working in the military garage.

Soon, another adversary showed up to be faced, unknown because their only news was from *Stars and Stripes*, the army publication. There were no accounts being reported of the depressing postures building at home against the war by a anti-war press promoting ill will and hard feelings directed toward the young soldiers, some of whom lost limbs or lives for democracy.

In Germany, news from the U.S. became far more available. Here, unconstructive comments by the U.S. media existed all over. Local and armed forces networks aired the latest protests in the States daily.

Chester had done all his country had asked him to do. He had ducked enemy bullets, located and disarmed VC land mines, and given two years of his life and lost his best friend, but that was not nearly enough to satisfy his countrymen back home.

Weeks turned into months that quickly passed in the motor vehicle maintenance shop. Weekends, some he remembered, some not, all faded from memory. Work and pleasure faded into a kaleidoscope confused by chemical substances. Finally the day to go back to America, not to return, finally arrived, and the sound never sounded so good.

CHAPTER TEN

LIKE FATHER, LIKE SON

Once back in Mississippi, Chester seemed to have put Vietnam's bloody rice fields and charred hootches in his past. He put his Army green pants and coat away in mothballs. Chester moved in with his sister Ann in Jackson, Mississippi; there was no "Welcome Home" banner or sign at his dad's house. Still, from time to time, he would visit some of his kinfolks in Arcola, Mississippi, not far from Jackson. The missing scooter money and past conflicts seemed buried for the time being, but not deeply enough.

Chester soon met his uncle's stepson, an Army warrant officer and a helicopter pilot. They shared two common interests: Vietnam and girls. He and his cousin, in Chester's words, quickly "hooked up," became good friends.

Chester told about meeting his future wife. "One night, we went to Shoney's Drive-in, a sit-down, fast food restaurant chain in Jackson. We noticed two pretty girls sitting alone. I thought I looked pretty cool in my new clothes, with my hair parted in the middle and tied back, so I started 'picking' [making cute, "pick-up line remarks] at both of them.

"Later that night, one of the girls and I went out to a park in Jackson. We talked about a lot of different things. She talked about her high school activities, and I talked some about my Nam experiences. Time came to leave, so I got her name, Rita, and address. I really wanted to see her again. Rita worked after school, so she gave me her work phone number."

Soon Chester would learn why Rita didn't give him her home number. She was dating a soldier and she didn't want him to know she was seeing Chester.

In Nam, the grunts sang a little soldier ditty about their girlfriends' faithfulness back in the States. They chanted: "Hey GI, don't look down, Cause Jody's got your girl an gone."

The courtship of Chester and Rita lasted from April until September of the year they met. They married in October, and Jason, Chester's son, was born the following May.

Their wedding was in Pearl, Mississippi, a small suburb five miles east of the capital, Jackson. The anticipated nuptial joy of the wedding ceremony was dashed by more family problems, bringing additional anguish. Chester had looked forward to both families gathering for the wedding. He hoped that by starting his own family and settling down, he finally would find his father's acceptance he had longed for from his youth. His hopes vanished when the ceremony began and nobody from his family showed. The wedding ceremony became another family rejection added to a history of disappointments. His pain burned more brightly.

I asked Chester how he felt about his families "no show."

"I've wanted to talk to my daddy about it several times, but I never have."

Beat an animal repeatedly, and, in time, it will reach its pain threshold. From then on, it becomes numb to additional pain and will slink away and lie down.

Soldiers learn to accept pain, both physical and emotional. Warriors can only endure pain until they reach their limit then they, too, become numb to more suffering. Chester's history of rejection brought his pain threshold to a new breaking point on his wedding day,

Chester had become insensitive to his dad's family after enduring the pain for years growing up in an abusive and alcoholic home. More emotional blows rained down on him when he got no praise for joining the Army. His rejection on returning from the horror of Vietnam only continued his angry aggression. The family nonattendance at his wedding finally numbed him to any more pain, just like the beat-down dog.

The pressure inside him challenged him to confront his father, to openly thrash out his embarrassment when his family snubbed his wedding day. Their other plans served as an excuse to Chester, reopened the festering wounds. He chose to temporarily dismiss the pain from the wedding rejection. He would reopen the case another day.

Even without his family present, wedding vows were exchanged between Chester and Rita. The church bells proclaimed a melody of matrimony. Another couple united before God and company.

Chester sums up his family's absence: "Just another letdown in my life."

Chester Johnston Junior, ex-biker apprentice, riverboat hand, and Viet-Nam veteran had officially become a husband. Chester and Rita began their life together in a small, rented apartment across from Millsaps College.

The new bride, a senior in high school, and the groom, barely twenty, would both discover twenty was too young an age to begin married life together. Like Chester's parents before him, they really didn't know each another. Subtle, silent forces were working against them even though they didn't know it. More importantly, Chester's living in Jackson would result in a crucial turning point in the ex-GI's career.

Soon after wedding bells stopped ringing, a son would be born. With the joy of having a wife and a family, Chester would not dream he had embarked on a long, disastrous, downward slide in his life. The bottom of the slide would be living a life sentence in the state prison of Mississippi.

The wedding candles were blown out, cake and punch served, then the newlyweds settled in their new home in Jackson. Chester began a new career in addition to his role of husband. His uncle arranged for him to join the Carpenters Union located off Logan Street in Jackson. Chester applied for and received his union card. He went to work as a laborer on a nuclear power plant being erected in Vicksburg, Mississippi.

The new groom joined an economical car pool to the work site. He loved the ride through the beautiful country of the Magnolia State. The hard, outside labor presented the change needed from Nam. It provided a safe environment and fair pay, all in a free country with no bullets zooming past him.

Many bikers like Chester who had lived in California held construction jobs during warm, summer months. Jobs seemed easy to find and they needed the money to support themselves. Members of Mississippi biker gangs worked among Chester's work crew on the power plant. During lunch breaks, their discussions turned to bikes and "riding in the wind"; the bliss of knowing complete freedom.

An old restless itch stirred inside him. His mind kept being drawn back to the California clubhouse where he had always been accepted, offered the hand of brotherhood. Each time Chester had problems, his call to them always seemed to be heard.

Two nights a week, Chester's car pool returned to Jackson. He attended night classes on these nights, learning to read construction blueprints. He hoped this training would assist him to advance his career in the future, but he couldn't deny an itch for freedom deep inside.

His old yearning for a bike, a scooter, came alive. Rita drove a blue Mustang her mother had bought when she was a senior in high school. Chester wrecked it, then gave in to the temptation to purchase a motorcycle with the insurance money.

"I used the insurance money to buy a used 750 Honda motorcycle with loud drag pipes."

Chester would ride the bike to pick up Rita at school. He wanted to send a message to all the young high school heroes; Rita chose to be his woman and no high school punk could stand up to him. The scooter's loud pipes and Chester's long ponytail and denim biker image accented his message

In October, the newlyweds learned Rita was pregnant. As Rita approached graduation, her son grew inside. She became so large she no longer could climb stairs to their bedroom at night in their apartment. They solved the problem by moving Rita back to her mother's one-level house. She could live there until her baby arrived.

Satan can always find a way to create difficulty in our lives. He can bring turbulence into all tranquil environments. He is an expert at trouble and found an opportunity to invade the lives of Chester and Rita.

Chester confessed to having an affair. Rita ordered Chester out and Chester rode away on his noisy 750 Honda to join his biker comrades. They brought no accusations of any type. Their rules of conduct welcomed sexual pleasure. The bikers once again simply took Chester as they found him.

Rita was pregnant and becoming lonely. She called her husband and asked to come home; she could forgive him. Chester agreed, and shortly after his return, their son, Jason, arrived.

Chester held his new son, Jason, for the first time on the day he was born. The new dad wanted to be a better father than his dad, but, biker freedom called to stand in his way.

Since Rita had separated from Chester, he had been riding with the Banditos, a Jackson biker club. As a man, not a novice, Chester immersed himself in a patch holder's life of drugs and parties. He knew that, for his marriage to be successful, he must shove the biker life aside. Leaving the bikers would also mean eliminating heavy drugs, but Chester continued to "use" on a regular basis. Drugs and freedom had become part of his life. They heightened the freedom call.

Chester began to drink beer and smoke marijuana in Nam to drive away fear. He had not been able to lose the habit when he left the battlefield. In Germany, he "used" to combat the boredom. Back in Jackson, the drugs became part of his recreation. Now his addictions controlled his life. They would continue to control him, even confined in prison, until a man from Galilee set him free.

Chester knew the problems in his marriage must be resolved if they wanted to provide a happy home for their new son. He tried. He found a small brick house in Hermansville, outside Port Gibson, Mississippi, and bought it. It would be close to his work and away from his seductive mother-in-law and compulsive Banditos. He knew he must put distance between him and his Jackson sexual compulsions. If not, they would destroy his marriage.

For a few months, the marriage seemed to be successful. A new son and a new house combined with returning to construction work made Chester and Rita appear as a normal, happy family, but serious arguments continued.

During an argument, Rita would crush Chester's ego by saying Jason wasn't his son. She said it in return for his adultery, and it was a solid punch to Chester's pride. The statement would floor him momentarily; later, it stirred up the wanderlust sensation inside of him.

He had learned from childhood to run from internal problems. Now, as an adult, he developed a desire to get away, putting the experience behind as he closed the back door and left.

"Hey, back then, I was not going to go for that kind of talk. I'd climb on my scooter and put some air between us."

Like his dad had done.

Once again, his marriage dangled on the ropes. He pictured himself as a rejected fighter in a new conflict; this one with his wife. When their arguments started, Chester rode off and Rita stayed home to sulk.

The marriage ended one day after a dispute. Chester returned home from work and found a note Rita had left. The message Rita left stated she had gone back to her mother's house. She had done this several times before. Chester describes her as a "mama's baby." Her leaving did not alarm him.

Chester really believed he had tried to make their marriage work. "I tried to be a husband and a father. I would come home from work and spend time with Jason. But it takes two people to make a marriage work."

Thinking back about their relationship, it is evident it never could have worked out. They had met at Shoney's and got engaged in a sexual relationship from the beginning. Once Rita learned of her pregnancy, Chester had done what he believed to be the right thing . . . he married her. Just like the case of Chester's mom and dad, he and Rita had never really known each other. Alcohol killed his parents' trust; infidelity would end his.

Chester and Rita suffered through lessons they never learned, which ended their marriage. They never learned about the real other person, and never shared dreams, just a bed. They stopped talking about the important issues of their lives. Both responded to their physical desires, their relationship was purely sexual. Because of their immaturity, it became procreative, neither believed to be at fault . . . both had been.

When they learned Rita was pregnant, they did what they believed would bring cohesion to their relationship; they got married. That only compounded the problem. They thought they could produce a solid relationship with a baby. Marriages don't work like that.

How often the way of a father is followed by a son.

Chester's infidelity with Rita's mother provided a weapon for Rita to use in their arguments. She often threw it up at her husband. Later, she would tell him she had forgiven him; however, in the next marital firefight, she would mentally bludgeon him with his affair again.

Now Chester wonders if he should have pursued the marriage further; tried harder. Perhaps things might have changed and their marriage would have been different.

After he read the note, Chester began to wonder. Had her old GI boyfriend returned from the Army? Could this be another Jody from the soldiers' song, "Jody's got your girl and gone"?

"Back then, I handled a problem by leaving it alone and getting some yonder.' Ride into the wind and put distance between me and the problem. I'd put my clothes and carpenter tools in a duffel bag and just go."

And go is exactly what Chester did. Go back to the bikers' lifestyle of heavy-duty drugs to burn out his bad memories. So Chester left the honeymoon cottage in Hermanville and returned to the Banditos in Jackson.

***

Each time Chester had money, he would ride to Rita's house and leave it for Jason's support. The final round of their marriage bout came after one of these visits.

"I had come back to Jackson to leave some money with Rita. When I got to her house, she had gone. Her daddy told me she had gone to the store with her mama."

Chester decided to wait for her. "I laid back on my scooter and began to shoot the breeze with her brother and some neighborhood kids."

Deep inside, the estranged husband needed to confirm his

suspicions about his wife and her former soldier boyfriend. He suspected Rita's last return to Mama's had been for another reason other than their latest domestic dispute, to see her old boyfriend.

Chester waited in the driveway. When Rita and her mother returned from the store, Chester stayed sitting on his motorcycle. When Rita and her mom drove into the driveway, Chester saw them and some dude sitting in the front seat, little Jason was in the back.

Mary Ann, Rita's mama, knew her ex-son in law well enough to realize there would be trouble if they got out.

"I saw them coming. They pulled into the drive and almost ran over me. When Mary Ruth saw me, she put the car into reverse and hurriedly backed out of the driveway. She wanted to avoid trouble. I started my bike and followed them down the street. I couldn't stop them. They got to the intersection with the main road. They saw a lot of traffic, and were blocked from going on. I pulled my Honda alongside them at the stop sign, and I laid my scooter down [put the kick stand down]."

"As soon as Jason saw his daddy, he called out 'Daddy, daddy.' I opened the back door and Jason jumped into my arms. I took Jason and hugged him. Immediately, Rita jumped out of the car and began to make a scene.

I'll never forget. When Rita jumped out, that dude jumped out too, shouting, 'Put him down, put him down' and came toward me."

Chester refused the order from the boyfriend. He was about to learn Rita's ex would be more than a match, at least physically for him.

"I told him, 'get out of my face, punk.'"

He came toward me telling me to put my son down. I handed Jason back to his mother and went up side his head."

Chester won the battle but lost the war. The boyfriend charged him with aggravated assault. The result was that, from then on, every time he wanted to see his son he had to call and receive permission.

The deepest wound of his breakup with Rita was being separated from Jason. Unlike his boyhood experience, Jason had been too young to choose to live with his daddy when the marriage broke up.

Chester's marriage scorecard showed nothing but zeros. Zero from the wedding ceremony when his natural family showed their lack of respect by staying home, zero from their relationship primarily about sex. Zero because the son from the marriage was taken away.

The ill-fated end of his marriage reflected his losing the battle to live in society. Then, he did not realize it. But Chester declared war with a world of structure and balance. A war with life as society prescribed it, also a war with himself. A conflict to find his place in society and the family he had been estranged from almost all his life.

Once again, it came time to "put some air" between his problems and himself. This time, he rode his bike back to the river, to work there once again. He could communicate with "Old Man River;" the river kept silent. It was like the river soaked up all his questions, but never responded with pat answers. He sought comfort in the arms of the river, but the river became an unwilling lover.

CHAPTER ELEVEN

THE GUNSLINGERS

After the fight in Pearl with Rita's boyfriend, Chester knew nothing could repair his marriage. His beating up Rita's boyfriend showed total disrespect for her family, and now the time had come for him to leave Jackson.

Even though he was home from Nam, a battle raged inside Chester. His fear of rejection had exploded into a rage, causing him to beat on Rita's new live-in. Chester knew he had go somewhere else for acceptance. It would not come from his dad, Chester Senior. The relationship with Rita was destroyed, and he was barred from her house; now it was time to move on.

For real, he had only one choice, one place he would be acknowledged for who he was. He believed he only had one real family. The only family he fit into was at the California clubhouse with the bikers.

His working on the river ended quickly. The small tugboat made him feel a captive. He couldn't find the freedom on the river he sought.

The aroma of the California clubhouse filled his nostrils; the perfume of oil and beer mingled together. He needed to hear familiar voices call him "scooter rat" with an affection he never found anywhere else.

He decided to be California bound, and walked down the tugboat gangway for the last time. He tied his duffel bag, filled with tools, blanket, and clothes, behind his rebuilt, electric blue, three-wheeler motorcycle, and headed for California.

He shot up some speed before beginning his journey. The two thousand-mile trip to California could be made in three days. Chester could ride straight through if he stayed high; no need for sleep when he had enough drugs to stimulate his energy. So across the U.S. he rode, free as the wind. Each mile put his broken marriage and family rejection a little further behind him. Each hit of speed blotted out some of the past and brought on the promise of a new future of belonging.

Chester carried a traveling Carpenter's Union card in his billfold. It would enable him to practice his trade anywhere in the States. He had divided the house sale proceeds with Rita and Jason, and in his mind he had severed all unwanted ties with his past.

Down the long highway lay freedom, and a belief he was a part of something. He was putting several thousand miles of "air" between him and all his bitter rejections of his Mississippi Delta family, and Vietnam's rejections. Freedom lay at the end of the highway.

***

Chester spent his first few weeks in California settling in. He found a place to live, and signed n with a local carpenter's union. Bectol, a huge construction corporation, was building warehouses in the area, so Chester signed on with them.

Once he started to work, he was ready to find his biker family. Many patch holders, club members, also worked for Bectol on several construction jobs. Each day on the job, he heard of local biker activities. He learned some of the Gunslingers had moved to the Riverside area. His old mentors, in biker lifestyle, Loser, and Bear, had retired or "laid down," in their jargon. However, California is the cradle of biker clubs, and many existed when he arrived there.

Chester located the West Coast Gunslinger clubhouse, and drove to it one weekend. The welcome was joyful, but with many questions. The leaders of the club remembered him from his days as a scooter rat. He would soon become a member, but he was not regarded as one at first; he had to be initiated. Becoming a member patch holder for an outsider was different. It was difficult and time consuming for the "wannabe" to gain the trust of the club. Some initiates never received a patch of membership.

For all initiates who desired a patch, an intense background investigation was conducted. The family's privacy and the secrecy of its business was too precious to allow just anyone into the organization. Police and federal law officers often attempted to infiltrate the clubs. They had little success because of the club's close background checks.

Chester commented, "If you think the FBI can conduct a through investigation of someone, just let those scooter tramps get ahold of you."

During the first phase, the club asks the prospect where he is from. Then the club directs several members to accompany the prospect to meet his family. The initiate had better have a family where he says he has. Here, the members can find out what he is all about.

After the family check, the biker investigators move to the local police station, where there is always an officer who can be slipped a couple hundred dollars to run a police background check. Even after these intensive checks, a prospect is not allowed to "come bobbing in," as Chester put it.

Next, the prospect is taken on a weekend run. Someone will throw a piece (pistol) at him, and tell him, "Take ten pounds of marijuana] to Houston, Texas." He knows what he is to do. One of the other members may accompany him. If he is sent alone, after he "lights out" (takes off), he is followed by a member traveling at a safe distance behind him. A record is maintained of all the stops he makes. Every phone call is recorded by the member shadowing him.

"You got to be cautious," Chester explained.

After he has proven trustworthy, he is taken by a proven associate and educated in the ways of the club. When the prospect is ready to undergo initiation, he must have three members who vouch for him, say he can "hold up" under pressure situations.

"Initiation is not too hard after you have proven trustworthy. Mine came one day when we pulled into a service station. One of the members unscrewed the cap from a quart of oil, turned it up, and drank a considerable amount of its contents. About the time I thought, 'Man, what's happening here?' he handed the plastic bottle to me. No questions asked, I knew I was supposed drink the oil like he had."

The club member will not ask the prospect to do anything he himself will not do. But the prospect is expected to do whatever his mentor does without question. It is a trial of trust between the gang and the prospect.

Chester continued. At the time, I thought drinking oil was stupid, but I was just a prospect."

His initiator wanted to see if Chester would get angry or repeat his demonstration of toughness. It was simply a test of loyalty.

The oil initiation also cleaned old Chester out. Both he and his mentor had to make several pit stops on the remainder of the trip. Chester laughed loudly as he remembered the purifying results as he made his entrance into the club.

Some of the initiation ceremonies were more difficult.

"I have seen prospects put in the back of a vehicle with a roll bar and kicked off, traveling sixty miles an hour down the interstate, to test their mettle. If the prospect lived through it, they received their patch of membership."

The Gunslingers, and all the motorcycle clubs, realized unity could not exist without loyalty. "Death without dishonor" declared their motto, and members must strictly adhere to it. Nobody could be permitted to hold a patch without a background check and a check of their loyalty. The success of the club depended upon it.

With his initiation, Chester became a full patch holder in the Gunslingers. He had wanted membership since he got named scooter rat and his mother still lived. He felt alive again, as he had when he as a novice in the club.

***

Once Chester found the chapter of the Gunslingers, he quickly found them and began to ride with them on weekends. They had scheduled a Three-Day Run in Yuma, Arizona, a fundraiser for the Godfather of all bikers, Sonny Barger.

The Godfather had made parole and was ready to exit prison, and sibling clubs had established a fee of twenty-five dollars for the run to provide money for him to live when he got released.

Barger began the club known as Hell's Angels. That club struck dread throughout the State of California; Hollywood had made movies about them. The Hollywood version of their lifestyle portrayed them riding into a small town and totally taking it over. They struck fear into the hearts of local citizens on the West Coast. True or not, it gave the bikers a fearful reputation.

After the formation of Hell's Angels, many other clubs had been gradually formed. The biker spirit spawned as disenchanted veterans of Nam or displaced wanderers joined the motorcycle club ranks. Biker clubs appeared all over California and on up the West Coast to Washington State.

Then the Godfather, Barger, found himself convicted on nine

counts of murder. Some of the deaths had resulted from gang killings within the club, and others were contract killings against rival clubs. Sonny had not personally committed any of the murders; his fellow members had. But the law held him responsible as the prez of the club. Since he ordered them, he had to serve time for his role in ordering the killings to be being carried out.

Even with their Godfather in prison, the clubs continued to grow. The biker movement swept across the U.S. and into neighboring Canada.

Now, after his release from prison, the fledgling clubs planned to show their respect for the Godfather by a fundraiser, a welcome home party in the desert.

Chester could feel strength and power filling his veins as he rode his Trike, a three-wheel motorcycle, into the gathering area for the run. This turned out to be a respect event. More than nine hundred clubs' colors would be flying on display in respect to the old man who had given them their birth.

"Hells Angels, Banditos, Gunslingers, Nomads, Outlaws," and hundreds of other club members gathered on the sand floor of the desert, a biker "gathering of the clans." Their Harleys' roar voiced the riders' contempt of the conventional world. Black leather or denim uniforms established which side they belonged to, society or outlaw. They had grown into an army. Many had not just felt indifferent to society; they grew into invaders of society. They feared no one who got in their path. They had fought valiantly for their country, and been refused entrance back into society. This gathering of club flags became more than a desert fundraiser; it served as a demonstration against names like "baby killers," and worse. The happening showed a unified stance against all society stood for, and their rejection of it.

They gathered, burly men with flowing hair tied back and untrimmed beards with do rags for a helmet. Women and children dressed in leather and denim to match. The men welcomed each other as they moved around the desert site, roughly shaking hands and pounding each other explosively on the back in greeting.

Women and children set up tents and unpack pots and pans for the evening meal. Kids ran and played in the nomadic setting. Located away from highway, thousands of parked bikes in endless rows of bright colors and shining chrome gave new color to the painted desert.

Many patch holders are Nam veterans. They have no fear of small town citizens or police after Nam. They fear nothing.

The biker assembly serves the same purpose as their desert predecessors who wore war paint a century before. The rally is to display their rejection of modern society. The bonfires, encouraged by the alcohol, raise their rage higher. The bearded giants dance around the fire with greater courage. Tattooed warriors drink and dance in the desert like their red skinned predecessors.

Once the party begins in earnest, the kids are taken by their nannies to a remote camp area. Even these bikers realized their primitive pleasures are not to be witnessed by their children. Once the kids are taken aside, the party becomes more intense.

"Once the Barger merrymaking kicked off, the beer flowed freely. Drugs are everywhere. The evening's first entertainment event is a wet tee-shirt contest. The feminine contestants are doused with beer until their clothing sticks revealingly close to their skin.

"The contestants begin dancing sensuously to the music. Both male and female biker desires are aroused. The booze, and speed create a catalyst for a drunken orgy. Soon after, the aroma of marijuana and shouts of pleasure fill the desert."

The panorama Chester describes is that of all the patch holders evolving into a sensual frenzy. It defies society's acceptable virtues, and cuts against the grain of its acceptable mores.

Chester and his fellow bikers grew up within established social boundaries. Now they chose to live outside those boundaries. Most of the bikers had been siblings of the "free lifestyle" sixties, and the "give me" seventies. Some came from the nation's Sunday churchgoers, who then fight and abuse each other through the week. Some are the offspring of parents who boozed and fought until divorce finally split families.

The sad truth is that the young West Coast Gunslinger learned from his primer of adult behavior by those who raised them. Parental dos and don'ts left confusion about acceptance, family, and love.

But a code of conduct covered biker family relationships. Nobody would sexually abuse a child; sex is always between male and female. No one would ever "come out of the closet." Biker communes have no closets.

So Chester watched his first desert orgy, with drunken women in beer-drenched tee-shirts dancing around the leaping flames of the fire as men staggered to catch them. Once together, they sought darkness and cover of the desert.

The desert orgy was a fundraiser and homecoming for the biker Godfather.

In this family gathering, Chester would start over. His warrior spirit would allow him to climb to the top of the club ladder. Once on top, he would use his physical prowess, motivated by buried emotions, in his climb to power. This became the world he chose.

CHAPTER TWELVE

IN THE CLUBHOUSE

N ow living in California, Chester's daylight hours were taken up with erecting warehouses for Bectol Corporation and the nights and weekends were devoted to biker activities. Now an adult, he felt he really belonged in the Gunslingers and he was a vital part of the club. It was his first real sense of belonging.

Some of his spare moments were spent rebuilding a Mach I Mustang he had bought. When the car had its engine rebuilt and a new paint job, it was ready for the championship of drag racing at Irwindale, California, the home of the famous Winter Nationals for dragsters.

The Mustang was beautiful. Both the interior and exterior were a deep, rich black. Mounted under its hood was a rebuilt 351 power plant. Chester had repainted the block Ford blue and added chrome accessories. Atop the block was a chromed four-barrel carburetor. A Cleveland shifter guaranteed a rapid takeoff from the start line.

He continued to save his money and began to put a new look on his War World II scooter. Only an expert could see through the 90 percent chrome job and new paint to the discarded military bike it once had been. Now he had a motorcycle for sport and Mach I for his racing business.

Life was going well for the recent addition to the West Coast Gunslingers. He had already discovered how the club was run when a teen in the West Covina clubhouse. Chester knew how the club paid its debts. He learned the cash sources to keep the vehicles in top condition and for funds for the desert parties.

"We used several methods to make money. Some of the younger biker ladies were hired out. They worked as a waitress in the local bars and lounges where an attractive lady earned a hundred to a hundred and fifty dollars a night from tips. Or if they looked good, they worked as an exotic dancer in the strip joints thriving on the West Coast. Their tips bought groceries and paid the rent."

But the ladies' income was a small portion of the club's total earnings.

"We set up crystal meth labs, which produced what we called speed. Meth shipments were made south to San Diego and Mexico. When we returned from Mexico, we smuggled kilos of weed, marijuana, across the border. The drug sales provided a lot of cash for our operation. More capital was taken in by transporting ten-pound packages of cocaine into LA. Our kickback was four pounds of the haul. Runs were made by mules, female members who, hopefully, would not arouse police suspicion.

"The weed was imported from Mexico and the Big Bear Mountains of California. Our club grew marijuana there, as did many other clubs. Only members involved growing smoke or farming operations were located high in these mountain areas. These farms were protected by men carrying automatic weapons and by buried booby traps. Anyone snooping around could end up getting killed."

Chester explained. "One had to find out who had turf rights to a specific area and receive the club's blessing. All plans had to be done by the organization's rules."

The top run of the membership power structure was the presidency. Chester completed his climb to the club's top position during a weekend party. He suspected the president's weakness would present an opportunity to take over the leadership. While serving as sergeant at arms, he learned the Prez had become soft. Now, Chester was a fierce rival of many other club members and those of rival clubs. Fear was beginning to creep into the existing president's mind.

Chester chose a drunken weekend party to take the coveted President's Patch.

"I called him out once he was drunk. I told him he was a weak so-and-so and didn't have any God-damn! business running the club. He was sitting on a couch with his old lady by his side. As he rose to his feet, I saw fear in his eyes and I knew he was through. He couldn't grab a weapon before I placed my sawed off shotgun between his legs. The other members also saw his fear.

"I knew I could take him. I squeezed the trigger of the shotgun and blew some meat from his legs. He yelled in pain and the others knew to fear me a little more quickly."

Whether the other club members considered him crazy or courageous mattered little to Chester. The bravado of the challenge and results of the shotgun blast elevated Chester to the head of the club and eliminated all challengers. His plan had been risky but he had waited for the right moment and seized it. Now he was commander in chief of the West Coast Gunslingers.

Other patch holders either bowed out or fell into line. Other riders had come to him earlier about the president. They were concerned with the waning leadership abilities of the former Prez. Whatever reason the biker family had for following him, whether from a sense of fear or admiration, made no difference. The house had a new president, and because they had seen his ferocious takeover, the other associates would stay in line.

We discussed his ascent to power, so I asked Chester how other bikers felt about weakness. "Do other members disrespect weakness?"

"Absolutely," came his rely. "You can't be weak and stay around long. Even though I beat the president, he wasn't ousted. He had our blessing to stay on as a part of our group or to leave. It was just like a government take-over. You know; you either accepted it or moved on. You just can't show you don't have the courage to stand up."

Lack of strength and fear were two emotions Chester had left in the farmlands of Mississippi and the rice paddies of Vietnam. Controlled by emotion and filled with rage, Chester blasted his way to the top of the Gunslingers.

***

Life in the gang, riding under the insignia of the Gunslingers, was very ordered but simple. They were ruled entirely by the male members. The ascension to power was always achieved by deadly combat. The club lived by strict rules.

Chester's life in the biker world was more multifaceted than Hollywood's stereotyped profile. Their existence is more complex than behaving like a herd of wild animals. Their philosophy is "kind of" patterned after an Indian tribal structure. The warrior fights to protect the lives and ways of the family. He rides proudly on his Harley like a soldier on a fine horse. His job is to hunt and fight. The women raise children, prepare meals, and keep their old man happy in the wigwam. Those are the biker roles.

The president is like the chief of the club. He and his counsel of vice-president and sergeant at arms plan all the activities of the club. The code, "death without dishonor," is maintained by all members.

The bikers presume to play a viable role in society, its alter ego. They claim to have overcome the materialistic constraints of the world in which they were raised. Their confrontation is against the injustices of corrupt police, judges, and politicians, as they see them. The people in leather claim they have withdrawn from a corrupt civilization to a just one.

Each member must perform his role for the club to function successfully. Male members have specific duties. They are responsible for seeking out new drug sources. Prior to a drug run being made, they scout the route to determine if they will encounter police or DEA agents along the way. As necessary, law enforcement is paid off to insure a "clean" (safe) route. Patch holders operate within an elaborate web of many clubs who provide information about bad cops. When a run is planned, they will inquire of informants the names of police officers who will assure success. There are always pay offs assuring there will be no interference by law enforcement.

Chester advised, "You can't make a delivery without someone being paid off down the line."

Any goods going through an area where honest police might be waiting, or where no pay offs have been made are sent in an alternative direction, with a law enforcement escort. The dope transporters know there is always someone somewhere in proper society who can be bought. The corrupt are sought out and paid off so business can be carried on safely.

The president and his enforcers don't take a hands-on role in narcotics trading. They plan the work, make the contacts, but never touch the product. Like their Italian gang counterparts, the leaders are several spaces removed from the violence and illegal operations of the club.

Biker "old ladies," or females, are the "mules" that actually carry the contraband between maker and market. As mentioned earlier, their vehicles are vans or family type cars with a "Sunday outing" appearance to avoid suspicion.

The ladies also take care of their offspring. They make sure they go to school. The club's leaders don't want a nosy truant officer paying a visit to the club's residence. Their lifestyle is too expensive and their illegal gains are too valuable to permit unwanted visitors.

The female's role is one of submission in the biker family. Women are to do whatever they are told. They know their position in the club structure and will be expelled if they fail to fulfill it, and normally, they have no other place to go.

Chester's comment was, "If your old lady doesn't mind her old man, they get abused, and I have seen some bad abuse."

Abuse is the course of action to create submission.

When a woman is abused by her old man, she can appeal to another member to accept her as his old lady. Drunken abuse is simply not allowed. Any affiliate drunkenly abusing his woman is taken before the club and severely disciplined with a beating. The bikers know and respect their women as their bread and butter; she is the moneymaker. Abuse cannot interfere with the club making money.

I inquired of Chester what created the underpinning of club family living.

"Unity and respect for one another. You had to have rules to have respect. Before you bed my old lady, come to me and ask me. If you want her and I don't mind sharing her, ask me; it's respect."

Respect is also required in all business dealings.

"Don't go out there and get involved in a deal putting us in the limelight," the ex-biker instructed. "Freelance operations are not permitted. If you want to make a deal, you get the blessing of the membership. The expression *blessing* is what we call getting the club's approval. All issues are on the table or out in the open."

Every phase of the family is done in the open. Total agreement; "Everything has to line up," is Chester's way of defining respect in the family. "If not, you will be dealt with accordingly."

The older riders are also vital to the organization. They are held in high esteem by the younger ones. This brand of respect was demonstrated by Chester in his relationship with Bear and Loser, his mentors, when they retired. I asked Chester to talk about this.

"Most definitely they are respected. They still live in the house or nearby, just not in the limelight anymore. The older guys are like grandpas to younger ones."

While "acceptable" society places their seniors in nursing homes, bikers make them the most respected part of the family. Retired members still have their old bikes and ways, and maintain complete respect. They may participate in a party or desert outing, but are inactive in the club's business dealings. The retirees spend their evenings in a local bar or strip club, reflecting on the past.

"They just want to be left alone."

The club rules are as standardized as the traveling design when they ride down the highway in pairs, side by side in a perfect line from front to back. An affiliate performs his or her duties under the rules. Any associate who gets out of line receives swift and harsh discipline.

More than twenty years have passed in Chester's life since living with the biker members. Now he sees much of their lifestyle was wrong, going against God's law; the desert parties and the unmarried partnerships are violations of His commands. One element of the past society of the patch holder is he still "holds up for," is loyal to, the honor code.

In his past, he might have called on associates to help him; there were times when testimony against others would have reduced or eliminated his jail time. Biker band riders in Mississippi could have produced an alibi for him when he was arrested for murder, but he did not ask for their help because he would have put them in legal jeopardy. He still lives by the code of death before dishonor.

Chester still wears the patch of the West Coast Gunslingers

etched in ink on his back. Years later, he no longer rode under that emblem, but the code from his outlaw days would be taken to his grave.

***

Runaways, mainly female, are still an overwhelming problem in our society. Even Christian teenage girls think about leaving their home. Running away is a subject Chester always confronted with visiting high schoolers when they visited on Parchman tours. He described their conduct by bikers and pimps who rescue them, "like a piece of meat."

I asked Chester to speak about how kids who abandon home and family are located, picked up, and enslaved to the streets.

"In every town, clubs know that, when a girl leaves her home, she will ride the bus. Those who prey on these depressed girls hunt for them at a bus station or truck stops. They can be recognized by a knapsack on their back or the suitcase sitting beside them. If they have any money, they will rent a room in a fleabag hotel. Those who are broke will go to local bars. That's were they will hang out, the locations where they are discovered by the predators.

"Once they arrive in a new town, they get afraid. Usually they have spent all their savings getting to town and have no money to buy food. So they are found, shaking with fear and hunger, and promised that we will take care of them."

The courage and dreams of the runaway soon disappears when they become lost in a new town, dismissed by a city's cold shoulder. Once there, money is spent quickly and they are unable to find legitimate jobs because they are minors without work experience. The promise of freedom turns into a nightmare; they don't know anybody and the new location offers no help. The metropolis is unresponsive.

Any time any predator finds a scared and lonely teen in a second-class bar, they are noted. Leeches buy drinks or offer some weed, and later, when high or drunk, an invitation is extended to them to join their exciting biker life. Alone, broke, and homeless, the runaways need protection and food, and they accept the biker invitation.

A few young women will quickly crawl back to their family because they can't make it in the club. A very few will be sent home by compassionate club members. Those who stay will be pumped full of drugs and used or abused like, in Chester's words, "a piece of meat."

The hometown truants who remain with the club never become part of the family. They are never given inside information about the club's drug deals. The bike riders won't trust the young girls enough to enter the inner circle. Generally, the older family women reject them as a challenge because they fear the pretty young girls will steal their men.

Every runaway's story winds up the same once she is picked up by the bikers. She is passed around until the men tire of her; then, next, she will be turned into a prostitute, waitress, or dancer.

"Prostitutes are what they are used for, Roger," was the ex-outlaw's forthright comment. "Young girls bring money into the club. The money earned by selling themselves is turned over the club treasurer; that's why they are picked up."

Prostitution is the fate of most runaways who seek shelter with the biker club. They ran away because they believed they had no freedom at with Mom and Dad.

Runaways are turned into slaves when found helpless. The bondage is partly accomplished by addicting them to drugs.

"We gave them drugs so they would do what we wanted them to do. They were supplied speed to keep them going and marijuana to make life bearable."

Chester's graphic lesson to teens is always the same: don't run away. Young men suffer identical bondage as the women.

The immature runaways want to find a new life without rules, and to "find themselves" when they sneak away, but no money and no job leaves them defenseless. They try to find help from whatever source they can. The glamour of biker living fades into ugliness. Later, their bodies age as they are abused sexually and physically, and their minds are wasted by drug use. Runaways are turned into possessions dictated by the warrior mentality and quickly bend to the rules of the club lifestyle.

***

Few biker soldiers have knowledge of or trust in God. They don't see a need for a higher power. Like a soldier, they trust their strength and that of their comrades. The president leads the band of renegades. They are desperados, far from God and society, and depend only on their strength.

Their gun and knife are the sword and bow in the lyrics of the ancient songs. A biker's vicious appearance and loud motorcycles strike fear in most people they encounter. The outlaw knows he has an advantage over a terrified opponent. With his gun and knife, he will defeat any foe that does not run away.

The biker's war is against the "establishment;" their battle cry is freedom. He respects "old glory" as his flag, not society. He believes it has abandoned beliefs that once brought independence to America. His enemies are the police, the politicians, or the public when they invade his domain.

Every biker warrior carries a knife or gun. However, the most vital part of a biker's battle gear is his armor. This is his defense. A biker's defense is his pictorial tattoos. Their symbolic plating is etched into the skin, designed to strike fear into enemy hearts.

Their plan of intimidation works. When a member of the middle class is driving along a highway and sees several motorcyclists approaching from behind, riding sleek, new bikes with radios and other fancy gear, there is no concern. The cyclists in his rear view mirror are just Mom and Pop out for a ride in the country.

But when a he hears a loud exhaust engine blasting and sees

men with bandannas or helmets, denim vests, thick beards and flowing hair, sitting low in their saddles, the driver thinks Hells Angels are behind him and about to go around. As they come around, he doesn't want to look, right? But his curiosity prevails. He glances out and perceives a line of outlaws and their old ladies, and they all stare as they pass him. Fear overtakes the civilian as he sees brawny, intimidating arms covered with tattoos, vests with outlaw insignias, and a intent look on faces inviting conflict. The everyday person prays they will just pass them by.

Mostly, their drawings brand them as the enemy. They display White Supremacy, power of some origin. The biker goal is to break down society's defenses, to make sweat pop out on its skin, and to generate a sick feeling in the depths of politically correct stomachs.

The inked graphics are part of the outlaw persona. The graphic designs function like a home defense system, warning a possible intruder to stay away to avoid great cost. It is a mental caution to society to move on or suffer the consequences, to breed fear. That fright provides an invisible safeguard for each rider, from the first to the last, in their military-like formation. Their persona becomes their protection.

Unseen and unknown to society are the etchings created with ink hiding the rider's worry, not fear of combat, for they welcome warfare. Many learned in the jungles of Nam. Conflict is a part of their life that they relish. Their only concern is a loss of their freedom, losing the right to ride anywhere with the wind in their face and their old lady behind them. The trepidation of independence lost would expose their true feelings about society's rejection hidden deep behind the drawings all over their bodies. Their apprehension is one of festering emptiness from so many past rejections. They, like Chester, have been rejected by society for whatever reason. The emotions of being locked out must not be seen, so they keep it out of sight, hidden like family skeletons in a closet. To reveal the wounds from rejections long past would erode their defense.

Moreover, the images embossed on a biker's flesh tell the story of who and what they are. The images are a mural of the organization's ideals. Etched everywhere on their bodies are the outlaw's writ of everything they hold sacred. Each drawing represents a value they will give their life for.

***

I never had opportunity to closely examine a biker's tats until meeting Chester. I asked him to explain the meaning of his multiple etchings. I suggested his descriptions would provide a clearer understanding of the outlaw protective covering and the values they stood for. Chester's colored images run over his body like a fascinating color slide presentation, a production of the biker constitution.

Chester began his description with those on his right arm. His tattoos progress from the shoulder down to his wrist; both arms are covered completely. Almost no flesh is uncovered by blue and red ink.

The first picture on his bicep is an American bald eagle. The same image stands proudly for America. "This symbol reminds us of our pride in our country." Chester reminded me, "Most of us fought for our country. The proud bird represents our loyalty to the code of honor of all the patch holders."

Under this emblem of honor is a portrait of a lady with a skull placed in her stomach. "She is the Queen of Diamonds, from the song 'Desperado.' Beautiful but deadly. It's her who deals you the cards in the game of life. When you get her, she will beat you every time. Once beaten, you lose your ante, the skull which is your life."

When Chester talks to visiting teens, he describes his previous time as a desperado. He refers to the message of the Eagles hit song. "Young people, I thought I was a desperado. But I found out I needed someone to love me. Listen to the song; find someone to love you before it is too late." The Queen is a warning not to love a women like her, as she brings death in the end.

Next comes a drawing of the Grim Reaper. Club members do not fear death. Strangely, the outlaws know his purpose and that he will visit them some time; the knowledge is a death wish. Without realizing it, perhaps they know, deep inside, that the only release from their pain inside is to die.

The robed reaper holds a sickle in his right hand; he is busy reaping his crop. In his left, he holds a heart. Injected into the red human heart is a hypodermic with a serpent wrapped around it. The portrayal is the Grim Reaper's killing instrument, a needle stuck into the vein, and the man in the robe and hood collects his harvest of souls.

The syringe illustrates the biker's "habit," his method of satisfying an empty heart. The hypo, if filled, is his remedy for being alone. The liquid injected is like a serpent's venom. The chemical cure makes the heart beat faster, raises excitement, but in the end, it wears out and the hooded skeleton reaps his reward.

Chester's drug of choice was speed. Speed is crystal meth in rock form, diluted and injected into a vein, generally in the arm. Preludes, a form of crank known in the eighties, became his energy to push on.

Continuing down his arm is a series of pictures. Next comes the insignia of the West Coast Gunslingers. The patch is a copy of an Army sergeant's symbol. In the center of the patch, the Grim Reaper is seen again. This time he is carrying weapons. In his bony right hand is a pistol and in his left is a knife. Underneath is the 101 percent shield, which testifies to the oath to remain silent under questioning until one dies.

Located under the Gunslinger patch is a White Supremacy, or Southern Pride, slogan. This is a bearded biker wearing dark glasses, sitting atop a Harley. He is looking back over his shoulder with his hands on the controls of his bike. Seated behind him is his old lady, flashing her breast. They are riding free in the wind. The biker and his old lady are not ashamed of being who they are. She is not afraid of displaying her body; in reality, she is flashing society.

On the outside of Chester's arm, just above his wrist, is featured the Old Gunslinger. He resembles Yosemite Sam of cartoon fame. He wears a wide-brimmed hat, and his long hair is flowing from underneath. A huge handlebar mustache and beard completely cover his face. In one hand, the Gunslinger holds a pistol, and a knife is on the opposite side. His portrait is a warning of the fierceness and tenacity of the patch holder.

The last imprint is a thin chain around his wrist. Attached to the chain are the letters SWP (Southern White Pride). The S is large and bold. The other letters are inked smaller. The bracelet refers again to the arrogant pride of white supremacy.

Now, to the protective covering of Chester's left arm. Like the other extremity, the line of tattoos goes from the shoulder to wrist.

Imprinted across his shoulder is a Gemini bird. This creature is part lion and part eagle, with the head and feet of an eagle. The creature's body, back feet, and tail are those of a lion. The eagle portion in the picture represents the biker's belief of superiority and the lion part symbolizes the club's omnipotence and strength. This ancient, fabled bird shouts dominance by the outlaw riders.

Next in the inked flesh mural is a nomad warrior exiting from a skull. This combatant is the Aryan Brotherhood Enforcer. No member must ever forget that the intimidator stands ready to require compliance with the brotherhood code.

On the right of Chester's bicep is a prison tower. The spire represents confinement. On top of it is a pointed turret with an unfurled flag. The slit windows are dark and foreboding. Jutting from the tower wall is a black iron fence with a gate with an antique keyhole. This picture represents the despised Mississippi correctional organization. The brotherhood calls it the Mississippi

Corruption System. Many Aryan Brotherhood members have been incarcerated behind this iron fence with no key for the lock. In the past, the system has been brutal.

A Klansman with a hood over his head is peering around the tower. He is the protector of the Aryan way of life proclaimed by outlaw biker clubs. The Klansman's message is that the system will not guarantee a white establishment, but the Klan will.

Old Man Time is shown running to jump on a Harley-Davidson scooter. The keeper of the clock has a wide grin on his face. His loose robe is flying and his sandals are flapping as he chases his fleeing motorcycle. The envoy of time is the conscience of a club member. Father Time reminds the outlaw that the drugs he uses are bringing him down and his time is running short. His life is illustrated as a race in time to catch the scooter, or to get off, before it is eternally too late.

A montage of pleasures decorate the lower part of Chester's arm. In the center of the mural is a female with her backside bare; she boasts that she is the member's ideal lady. The naked partner is "righteous" because she is loyal and true to her man. To the right of the "righteous" female is a table with several lines of crystal, or speed. Above the table are reproductions of 714s or Quaaludes. Underneath the woman's bare bottom are drawn two leaves of top quality marijuana. On the left of her is a picture of Tennessee's finest whiskey, a bottle of Jack Daniels, the biker's choice of sipping whiskey. Framing the bottom of the mosaic is a sawed off shotgun. The shortened weapon is the biker's choice against the enemy, the establishment. The short barrel of the gun can create a bloody, gaping hole at any enemy gathering.

All these items are the "finer things in life" to a club member. They will bring pleasure, either a high or a low. Add the "lovin' of a fine woman" and you have depicted a biker's dream, and a one-way ticket to Hell.

Finally, on the wrist is displayed the Motorcycle Clubs or M/C brotherhood patch, wings from heaven attached to a new chain mark, or fresh beginning. On the band, the initials FTW stand for "free the witness."

Between Chester's shoulder blades is a large West Coast Gunslingers M/C patch. The illustration reaches from his shoulders to his lower back. The representation is framed with top and bottom military-like rockers. Between his shoulders, the words "WEST COAST" are enclosed within the framework. Just under this is a hooded figure wearing dark glasses. The bottom rocker frame contains the word "GUNSLINGERS."

When all the representations are combined, they create a mural displaying all the desperado's ideals and lifestyle. The values and pleasures he lives are displayed on his arms. Having tattoos reminds him of his code and the club's pride in unity. The pleasurable things are illustrated by the Harley-Davidson bike, a fine woman, and the necessary chemicals to keep him "up," are the staples of life, the good times he looks forward to.

Mentally, all the illustrations serve to protect him. They serve as guardians, as garden gnomes outside a home, to ward off evil spirits, or candles ceremonially lighted to protect from the powers in the dark.

In the biker mentality, the tats are steel-like sleeves to protect his arms in battle. These safeguards bond the club members until the Grim Reaper comes for them; only death brings release.

***

Chester told me more about his club life: "Every time I had a problem in my life, I went back to the one place I felt confident, and had always been accepted. The biker lifestyle had been implanted in me by Bear and the others."

As he had done before, when he lost direction, Chester returned to the clubhouse. Once there, he moved quickly to assume power in the West Coast Gunslingers. The command of the presidency, the highest biker position, brings a heavy load of authority and responsibility. The president must direct the club's business operations.

"At the time I took leadership of the club, most of the older patch holders were behind me, so I took it."

As before, Chester seized the top spot by sheer strength and guts.

The smooth operation of the hundred-member organization required brains as well as brawn. Their profits from buying and selling drugs had to be continued. The women designated to provide cash had to have jobs in the local bars and strip joints. Discipline was a must in the organization. All work assignments were performed under the president's oversight.

To fully grasp daily life in the clubhouse, "being high and staying high" must be understood. In this environment, being high was a phenomenon that continued every waking hour for club members.

"It was nothing to swallow a downer or take some purple microdots and drink a beer to come down. I smoked pot at work on my breaks. I knew if I got sober I would have to face reality and I couldn't do it; the real world was my weakness."

The ex-club president exposed the totality of existence in the club. In spite of long flowing hair, beards, loud scooters, and a leather-tough image, chemicals enabled them to stay in a vacuum, in a world separated from real life. Drugs and alcohol were the ticket to their isolated community.

The club members daily lived in a drug-induced microcosm, separated from the outside culture. Their reason to live was different. The definitions of words they used in their conversations changed. They adapted life and their approach to it to fit their own desires.

Understand that one goal drew outcast bikers: simple acceptance. They feared it, but sought it at the same time. I asked Chester about the importance of being accepted.

"You put all feelings aside to be a part, right? Acceptance, love," he responded. "To me, they went together. Yeah, they were the same thing...in my mind."

Other patch holders, mostly rejected Viet Nam vets, converted with teenage runaways, would have answered the same way. So, in their secretive world, goaded by chemicals, they lived their secluded way of life. Theirs is a strange paradox in that they have removed themselves from the society they seek to be accepted by.

My inquiry continued, "Love can mean different things to diverse people, right?"

Chester responded, "I thought being mean and having people looking up to you was love. You had prestige and it was everything; being number one was it. If I was the leader, every-body respected me. I believed, once you feared me, you accepted me, cause I'm bad. And you loved me for my prestige or for my macho image."

So fear and love in the biker existence were synonymous. As strange and distorted as Chester's words may sound, counselors assisting spousal and child abuse cases hear them daily.

Chester continued to describe the emotion of being devoted to in the biker clubhouse. "The patch holders and prospects looked up to you for leadership. They knew you could hold up for the code, death before dishonor, and they respected me. That respect meant love to me. Our family survived because there is protection provided for and by the group. Females may be passed around, but never when it would put the club in danger. Each person, from the president to the newest associate, had been bonded by the creed of "death before dishonor."

The members accepted an innovative way to live with original community rules. Each one suffered through the biker code to live, isolated, in the private society they are a part of. They had not found what they sought where they came from. Many had suffered much more pain in the biological family and social settings they had escaped.

On weekend runs, members met hundreds of other club bikers who lived by the same creed. Here, they found new emotional bonds. It was a family reunion they were a part of. Their society was one in which status, wealth, or other social standards were not a criteria for approval. Many found approval there for the first time.

Our ex-biker described living in biker garb as a "security blanket." He quickly asked, "Does that make sense to you?"

I responded, "Yeah, oh yeah." With his Vietnam experience and the breakdown of the nation's family as the canvas, I understood the illustration there.

The club leader's greatest responsibility was its drug operations. It was the largest source of income. They had to continue successfully to survive. The financial transactions of the clubs were fashioned after larger crime syndicates or the smallest street gang. Hidden behind the organization's private image was drug sales. They were the plasma to continue the heart beat of all operations; drugs used, and sold, were the biker's lifeblood.

The president and other leaders made all decisions on deals, purchasing or selling narcotics. The choices made were by mutual agreement of the hierarchy; no one board member could make a decision, and the top man had veto powers.

The money they laid out in deals was seen as belonging to all members, a community treasury. The profits enabled their society to stay alive.

If a member was arrested, the leadership decided if bond would be provided or if the club should avoid the release process for the safety of the rest of the club. It was their way, and each member knew and accepted it. Medical treatment was provided for when needed. The common fund paid for school expenses for the kids and made money available for weekend runs to the desert.

The bikers have community rules and communal funds. It is their way.

There were few genuine romantic relationships among the male and female club members. Most of the males lived with their biker mama, but there was no romance, no bona fide emotional ties between the biker and his lady. A man could either share his partner or privatize her, his choice. Emotional displays, like affection toward his lady, were an indication of weakness to the other male members. No expressive ties between male and female were found in the clubhouse. To show deep affection was a sign of weakness.

The top man knew all the members desired the top position some day. He could not afford emotional attachments to fellow riders. There would come a day when one would call him out. No one would ever be regarded as a friend.

"You always know somebody has in the back of his mind to try you, to take your position. You are constantly tough as nails."

The position of president came with a moat, setting him apart. When a member dared to cross that mental or physical boundary, he came to take your throne. This was the only purpose for crossing line.

I ended our discussion, by stating the obvious. "So all show of emotion was weakness, a chink in the leader's armor."

"Thank you," was the warrior's response. You had a 'kick the door in, whup butt, take names and leave it alone' attitude toward the others. Once a challenger approached, you pulled out your piece, fired off a couple of rounds, and stuck its muzzle into the challenger's mouth and listened to the meat sizzle. That was the way it was."

Any patch holder who failed in his quest for conquest of the president or on an assignment, knew the results; failure always brought consequences. Remember, in the biker organization, fear and love ride together as partners. Prospects that get out of line in a meeting are made an example

"You may fire off a round in his face or bust his head, but you keep the others in line; it's what you got to do to hold your position of authority."

The leadership rules by fear. At times, it doesn't matter if no one is "out of line." You snatch somebody up by the hair of his head to maintain the terror.

The president polices from his throne; fright is his scepter. Terror is the boundary around his throne room and his shield of authority. No man ever rose to a top position without a campaign of it and no one remains on the top without it. Once Chester joined the ranks of the motorcycle gangs, he utilized his fierce manner and quick hands to establish a facade to make his enemies and fellow bikers fear him.

At least on the outside, he had no dread of man or God. One day, this would change.

***

Being president, or prez, permitted Chester to maintain his front as a construction worker. He was on the job from Monday through Friday. His outlaw survival decreed he keep a low profile. Policemen were constantly looking for informants from the biker clubs and maintained a complete list of patch holders. The holder of the highest post had to remain discrete.

Chester kept his union card current so his work could create a front to the police. In California, he was employed by the largest contracting firm in the world, Bectol Construction. Its vast employee file would present problems later when he was confronted with murder charges.

The leader did not live in the clubhouse. Once on top, the he found a residence away from the visibility of the clubhouse. The meeting place was watched constantly by the "heat." Cops were always hanging around looking for bits of information. The biker leaders despised the police with their nosy ways.

The president had to maintain distance between himself and gang activities.

"You may be just across the street when a deal goes down, or a long distance from it. There must be deniability between the leader and any illegal activity. The only time I was seen with other members was on weekend runs into the desert, far away from prying eyes."

The loss of deniability between the leader and illegal activities brought the famous Hell's Angels organizer, Sonny Barger, down. The founder of biker bands failed to write a disclaimer into the bylaws of the organization that would hold him harmless from gang activities; rather, it made him responsible for them.

When the police began to find corpses of rival members and pressured fellow patch holders, some of them "rolled over," or gave evidence. They testified the bodies were the result of gang-related incidents. The cops arrested Sonny Barger as leader and top authority of the club and made him answerable for all the murders as leader.

Leaders of sister gangs quickly learned a lesson from their honored founder and changed their bylaws. Other outlaw bands in neighboring states legislated that their top people were not responsible for the actions of the members who rode behind them. They created leadership indemnity.

The club leader lived by day as an accepted member of working society. He appeared to fellow workers and those who lived close to him as a hard worker who never interfered in anyone else's business. They couldn't know that on weekends and at night he led his fellow club members in all their activities. He planned the drug deals and rode at the head of the line into the wastelands to party and "blow out" with other clubs. His Jekyll and Hyde lifestyle protected him from law enforcement and provided the safety and acceptance he sought.

However, Chester learned he couldn't fool all the police forever.

Sometimes, Chester, even as the top man, preferred to get off by himself, maybe to see the world once again as it really was, without drugs and illegal activities.

"Sometimes I would go up on top of Big Bear Mountain on my bike. I wanted to be off by myself, just look down on the world. Looking back, I could see the values my grandmother planted in me. I knew she was in heaven and thought about how I wanted to join her some day. I clearly saw her love. I think everyone needs to get off to think once in a while."

Chester reflected on living in the Harley-Davidson world. "I got the feeling of loneliness or despair. I sought after home where I could say, 'Look what I've done with my life.' But you don't want your family to see the ugly part of you. My mind was 'Look and see; I'm big and got a bad motorcycle and a nice car and a little bank account. If you think *things* are valuable, then compare your possessions with mine'.

"Way down deep in my soul, I knew I had a son and family where I grew up, and I wanted to go back. At times when I came off a high, I wanted to call home, but I didn't."

No matter how many times he suffered rejection at their hands, Chester never lost the yearning to win support with his family. Family goodwill was lodged more deeply than his biker code in his subconscious mind. The hurts were covered by scar tissue and the desire to go back to Mississippi was still deep inside.

Chester was ready to return and see his relatives again after living the club lifestyle for a year. His time to return home came when he had thirty days' vacation from his construction job. When he did call home, he would talk to Jason, who would always ask him when he was coming home.

Now Chester believed the time to return home had come, so he could show off his beautiful bike and his 71 Ford Mustang, look successful, and his folks would be proud, accepting.

Chester decided to combine a drug run with his homecoming. He rode his bike, and his old lady drove a van at a safe distance behind, carrying drugs. They took a detour to Yuma, Arizona, to attend another fundraiser for the recently released Sonny Barger, godfather of bikers. It was an attempt to raise money for Sonny to purchase a Harley and get back on his feet.

The rally broke camp in three days, and Chester and his lady headed for Mississippi. He was the prodigal, but the wayward son had made good, and maybe now he would find acceptance from his father. Perhaps they could put all the problems of the past behind.

CHAPTER THIRTEEN

THE ROAD TO PARCHMAN

Oh listen men, I didn't mean no harm,
If you want to do good . . . stay off
The Parchman Farm.
Bukka White, "Parchman Farm Blues"

There was another reason the new biker leader desired to return in to Mississippi.

The California police had discovered that Chester was a member of the Gunslingers and had begun to look at their activities too closely. Life was becoming dangerous to Chester's health, and freedom was far too precious to lose. Drug distribution in the West Covina area was being linked to the local biker gangs and the police were keeping close surveillance on all the outlaw clubs.

Chester was aware that the Godfather, Sonny Barger, once believed himself to be beyond the law, but now was in jail. He had no wish to make the same mistake. He sure didn't want to serve time on the west coast.

Chester had met the leaders of the Mississippi Bandito gang when delivering drugs there. The code of the bikers would force them to harbor him when necessary. Besides, he might just show them some West Coast tricks to increase the club's profits.

So Chester rolled up his clothes in a blanket, put his carpenter tools in a duffel bag, and fired up his three-wheeled motorcycle. Quickly, LA was behind him and he was "riding into the wind" again.

Arriving in Jackson, Chester wasted no time in meeting with the leaders of the top Mississippi biker club, The Banditos. Once he made contact with the local members, he and his scooter mama, Della, checked into a neighboring motel.

Upon arrival, Chester and his lady got involved in illegal Mississippi capital city activities. The Banditos quickly accepted Chester's West Coast Gunslinger patch and he began to ride with them as a full member. The ex-prez learned how to generate income and went to work to increase Mississippi profits.

Chester started planning new operations as a participant in the club. The organization's first business venture was purchasing a nightclub in downtown Jackson. It was a run-down bar named the 404 Club, located in an older, less desirable section of the capital city. The bikers leased the West Capital lounge for $350 a month.

Many Jackson citizens avoided the area because alcoholics and winos hung out in the there. This kind of clientele provided the base for the club's profits.

The bars devised a revenue system from the welfare checks of those down and out. Each pay period, the owners were permitted to run a bar tab. On the first day of the following month, social security checks arrived at the post office. Most of the alcoholics received their checks then. One of the bikers would accompany the patrons when they picked up their monthly pay. The lounge owners cashed the patron's checks. The owners paid off the tickets, then gave the regulars fifteen or twenty dollars to live on for the remainder of the month. Most of the SSI recipients didn't pay rent, as they lived on the streets or in local flophouses. The owners served free cornbread and beans each day to their regular customers so they wouldn't starve to death.

The Banditos built up a tidy business revenue from the street people. Bikers and wannabes liked to hang out there, providing more income. Local Jackson politicians also stopped in, as the club was close to the capital and government offices, and several of the legislators saw a possibility for making money with the bikers. They provided a larger cash flow for the club and provided a new money-making scheme with the bikers.

The lounge provided a good front for the bikers to hide from prying police eyes. Many of the Banditos patch holders came by to drink beer and plan more illegal business ventures. Quickly, the saloon dives were filled every night.

Generating income was a common objective of motorcycle gangs as well as politicians. The bikers soon hooked up with some of the politicians in a money-making scheme. This type of scam has been around for years. The nightspots were an ideal gathering place for the Banditos and government officials to scheme.

The first hook up between them involved a fraudulent payroll program the political bosses had running. It was a neat setup for both parties. The politicians had false employee checks printed and the bikers cashed them, a perfect joint venture. The officials placed phony names on state or county employment payrolls. Each month when the payrolls were written, checks for the ghost recipients were among those written. The payroll vouchers to fictitious employees were forwarded to supervisors, but only checks for actual state employees given out.

However, the salaried employees and government big wigs who ordered the fake checks printed had a problem. They couldn't cash them in Jackson area for fear of being recognized. Sooner or later, a local bank or business would recognize those receiving funds and might want in on the scheme. For the plan to be successful, they needed someone to redeem the fraudulent chits in another geographic area. Enter the bikers.

Some of the local officials drank at the 404 Club and became friendly with the Bandito guys. One of them mentioned the dilemma with the checks. The bikers referred the problem to the leaders and they figured out a solution. The Jackson outlaws would open a check cashing service.

Their check scheme worked smoothly. Checks were delivered from the government operations to the bikers. Club members carried the phony checks in their saddlebags or bedroll. No police would suspect a motorcycle group on an outing to be transporting phony administration checks.

They rode seven hours through the night to New Orleans without stopping. They had contacts there. The checks were cashed in the Crescent City at a discount by a local businessman or banker with an eye for easy profits. Once processed in New Orleans, the documents moved through the federal bank system, finally arriving back in Jackson where the payroll deposit was waiting. All canceled checks had been accounted for and stored away in file boxes, away from anyone who might suspect the scheme.

The Bandito bankroll grew rapidly. Both the bikers and the politicians involved in the scam became increasingly greedy. They had a sweet, yet simple deal. More fake employees were added; checks were printed and cashed. No one was ever the wiser.

Even with the successful check scam and its cash return, drug sales remained the king of the club's financial ventures. The Banditos had drug deliveries all over the state. Prescription pills and marijuana came from the west coast. Crystal, or methamphetamine was exchanged from the Mississippi club. Meth labs opened in the farm country around Mississippi. The California gangs returned home with the drug, speed, they had exchanged. Speed or meth provided a complete drug bill of fare for their business.

The outlaw organization had acquired friends in Mississippi high places. Protection for drug deliveries was available to be purchased if one knew the right contacts. The biker club learned to become invisible to the police. They found a greedy politician in a position of authority and bought protection.

On all out of state drug runs, the mules and their escorts stopped at the state line. There, they placed a call and waited. Within minutes of their phone call, an official police escort arrived from their entry point to Jackson providing an official safe trip. Of course they paid the escorts.

One of these drug runs resulted in an event that probably led to Chester's later rape charge. Returning home after completing a drug run, he traveled down Interstate 20, and a highway patrolman flashed his headlights and turned on his blue lights. The same officer had provided his escort earlier that day. The motorcycle cop knew Chester was carrying the day's cash proceeds. Chester pulled his car over on the shoulder of the road while the patrolman parked behind him and got out of his car. He knew him well and that he held the rank of major in the patrol.

Chester got out of his car also, and the two met between their vehicles on the side of the road. The major bristled and said he didn't get paid his thousand-dollar escort fee. The desperado knew the fee was always paid in advance of the run. That way, the police had their money even if a runner didn't arrive. He recognized the shakedown at once. The drug running game had been established far too long not to know all the moves. Shakedowns had become a common practice by police. Sometimes the man carrying the funds would pay more to stay out of jail.

Chester replied that the payment had been made in Vicksburg, as usual. The escort fee had been paid in full.

When the uniformed patrolman saw his scam wouldn't work, he became scared Chester might turn him in. He quickly pulled out his revolver and pointed it at Chester. "Either give me another thousand or I'll kill you right here and take everything you got," he declared.

The two men stood very close to each other now.

Chester replied to threat, saying, "Look, I paid you, and if you don't put the gun up, I'll take it from you and stick it . . ." Well, Chester described inserting the pistol into a part of the majors anatomy, or at least words implying the same thought.

"Johnston, turn over the money and get out of here," the officer replied.

Chester had been in too many fights for a lot less to permit the major to rip him and the club off. So Chester made a lightening fast lunge and grabbed the officer's thirty-eight. As they wrestled, Chester wrenched the pistol away and threw it over the embankment. Chester was filled with fury at the policeman's attempted shake down. The outlaw drove the major into the ground with a bull rush, then punched and kicked him into submission. One last punch to the his jaw turned his lights out.

Chester left the crooked policeman lying on the roadside, bloody and unconscious. He had won the shakedown battle, but later would lose the war for freedom.

Racehorse, or Della, Chester's girlfriend, was also busy making money. She took a job as bartender at a local lounge where area other government reps and businessmen stopped for a round of drinks before going home. She quickly got to know some of the state officials who frequented the place after the legislature dismissed for the day. Many workers had apartments in Jackson, where they lived away from home during the session. Della agreed to clean their apartments for them.

Even though the check cashing arrangement and drug operations grew more profitable for Chester and his political allies, this bargain may have been another cause of Chester's problems with

Jackson police. Sooner or later, the best of scams are discovered and a penalty must be paid.

However, apart from their scam being uncovered, most likely another point led to Chester's first arrest. The money scams were lucrative, but the government officials began to fear Chester and the others, as they knew too much about them.

Another money-making operation for the club was the manufacture and sale of methamphetamines. Chester told me how they found and set up a lab site.

"We would drive around on the back roads and find a deserted house way out in the country at the end of a dirt road. Then we'd put up our lab. We began to manufacture crystal. Our operators cooked in one area for several months and nobody got suspicious. We took the meth to Mobile or to the Mississippi coast. At times, we made longer runs to Houston, Texas to deliver 'meth to biker clubs there."

The female members served as mules to transport the drugs. They kept the male riders from being arrested when shipments were intercepted by the police. The men drove behind the women at a safe distance. Once the dope was delivered, the men arrived on the scene and received the payoff. Then everybody returned home to Jackson.

The manufacture of methamphetamines was, and is, a very profitable business operation for all. The chemicals then used to manufacture dope were cheap. Income derived from meth production is high. In addition, crystal, another name for meth, can be produced almost anywhere, enabling bikers to set up or move a lab quickly. Law enforcement officials staked out meth labs for months, only to find all the equipment and drugs removed when they finally made a bust.

With the growth of membership, additional income was required to continue operations. The bikers' next venture was the purchase of the Zig Zag Club, located on Highway 80 off of Ellis avenue. The club purchase was part of the leader's master plan to take over many of the downtown nightspots. They already had control of most of the city's drug business.

My narrator described the outlaw club's business expansions as attempting to take over the scene. It was like a turf battle. Every major city has seen criminal and gang elements wanting to corner a market in drugs or nightclubs.

Associate Banditos networked narcotic traffic throughout Mississippi and across the southeast to Texas.

The prez was rapidly moving up in the outlaw ranks. He became involved in many club activities. He wanted to show the members how gung ho he was. With his blessing from the Banditos as a Gunslinger patch holder, he played a major role in all the Mississippi club's activities.

The "throw away" kid from Mississippi had risen to the top of the ladder in the biker gangs. He rode with the most powerful outlaw organization in the state. He was recognized and respected by brotherhood clubs across the United States. His strength and planning posed a threat for the police to reckon with. Most of the members feared him; "mean" was the label applied to him. Fear did not reside within him, of man or God.

From 1976 into 1978, Chester worked several jobs. His time off was spent running drugs to and from the west coast. His knowledge of California gangs provided a sales market for their Mississippi methamphetamine. His adrenalin surge from uppers in the day kept him moving, and downers put him to sleep at night. The drug habit learned in the jungles of Vietnam increased as he rode in the club ranks, and developed into full addiction. Now drugs began and ended every day of his life.

To demonstrate his boldness, Chester found a tattoo artist to imprint a hole in his upper arm where he injected a needle to give him life. The tattoo was still on his arm as we talked, but has the name of Jesus written there, as his new source of life.

Entertainment came in the form of drugs, alcohol, and sex. All three vices usually were indulged at once. The blow outs, or parties, that took place on the Mississippi Gulf Coast resembled those on the west coast. Member clubs from around the state would meet on the beach and party through the weekend.

Chester draws a blank about most of 1976 and 1977. Drug and alcohol use created a mental haze during those years, eroding much of that time from his memory. In 1989, when facing murder charges, his faded memory would become an obstacle in defending himself. His lack of alibi would contribute later to his guilty verdict.

Chester described years 1976 and 1977 as, "Just the same old same old," a rehash of the previous two years as a biker chieftain in LA. Like the Freddy Fender song title, Chester's life was one of "Wasted Days and Lonely Nights."

***

Again in July of 1978, Chester stopped to assess his world. He temporarily discarded his narcotics usage and permitted feelings of his biological family and home to creep in. Other than short visits, he had not been home in three years.

It was time to go home once again. Perhaps, now in the money, he would find respect from his dad and stepmom. Della packed their possessions in the trunk of his restored 1969 Chevelle for the trip home.

They began their journey with Chester riding his chromed tricycle and Della driving their car. The biker president and his scooter mama headed for home.

A return run from California required two days and nights of sleepless traveling to arrive at his dad's house in Crosby, Mississippi. Chester, with Della, pulled up in front of the house and got out. Both traveled high on weed.

Nobody seemed to be there, so Chester went to the back of the house to wash up. His yellow coveralls were covered by the dirt and grime of the long trip. He found the water faucet and stripped off his top to wash up. A full beard covered his face and a bandanna held his hair in place. A long ponytail extended from under his bandanna. He fully resembled a Hell's Angel.

As Chester bent down to wash from the faucet, someone approached from behind him. He heard a deep voice growl, "Stand up and put your hands in the air," as a shell was injected into the chamber of a weapon.

Chester knew when the odds were against him, so he followed orders. Chester turned and was looking into the face of his father, who was holding a shotgun firmly in both hands. The shotgun was pointed dead on Chester.

Chester said, "Hey, Dad. It's me." Knowing he had not identified himself, he added, "Chester."

His father had failed to recognize him in his biker attire and full beard.

Chester and Della spent the night with his dad and stepmother. The next day, they moved to Jackson, Mississippi. Chester remembers now how his dad begged him not to return to Jackson. Senior knew the police had been looking for his son there, but Chester was determined to go. Chester was determined to see Jason, his son, and Rita, his ex-wife, the reason he had felt called to return to Jackson. He wondered if his relationship with Rita and Jason might ever be mended.

Chester and Della found a inexpensive motel room and checked in. Once they had their belongings inside, Chester left Della there. He had not seen Jason or Rita in far too long.

Chester went straight to Rita's house. She told him he had custody of his son for the day. Chester put Jason in the chromed sidecar beside him and the two of them "got in the wind." Chester pointed his Harley toward the Ross Barnett reservoir. They left the interstate and rode off the pavement onto gravel back roads.

Jason was excited but nervous riding in the sidecar. The wind blowing in Jason's young face made the speed seem faster than anything he had ever experienced. He clung to the side of the bullet-shaped passenger compartment.

Chester showed Jason the beauty of manmade Lake Ross Barnett and the woods that surrounded it. The dad was being filled with his son's affection. It was a special father-son time like Chester never experienced as a boy.

Their second stop on their day of adventure was the Metro Mall in Jackson. They walked through the stores looking around and watching people. They bought clothes and a stuffed rabbit for Jason. They just had fun.

The two of them made a comical picture riding in the Harley; a biker on a chromed, blue trike with a four-year-old boy clutching a huge rabbit in the sidecar.

That night, Jason, Rita, and Chester went out to dinner at the Western Sizzlin restaurant. The emotional emptiness Chester felt each time he "came down" was being restored. He talked with Rita about her life; was she was happy? Perhaps for the first time in their life together they really talked.

Chester took his son and ex-wife home, thinking about what might have been. Once in bed, he lay awake and dreamed of how being reuniting with his son and Rita would be.

But now it was time to get on with business. His cash supply was getting low. He needed to find a way to generate cash. Once again, he contacted the Banditos. They were happy he was back in town. Chester had learned how to turn a fast buck with them.

He also needed a regular job for additional income and an honest front for his illegal activities. Besides, he was tired of sitting around all day. His biker buddies worked during the day and he had nobody to hang out with. He noticed a huge construction crane close to where he was staying. His cash was "tearing up" (running low), and a laborer job would suit him fine. His union card permitted him to work anywhere in the U.S. He applied for a carpenter's position at the site.

The job superintendent needed experienced workers and immediately put Chester to work. Chester's brother Vernon and his cousin had been also looking for a good paying job and Chester helped them hire on with the construction crew.

A second cousin of Chester's who lived in Jackson told him about a duplex apartment available in town. Chester's motel rent was rapidly depleting what little funds he had, so the three laborers went to check out the duplex.

The small, two-bedroom duplex contained a bath and kitchen. It would fit the trio's needs exactly. Chester couldn't know it then, but the duplex would begin his journey down the road to Parchman prison.

The duplex quickly became a place to crash after a night of partying. The three went there to clean up and get to work quickly. The apartment's convenience would turn into a liability in just three short weeks.

The place provided another convenience. Chester had brought some good smoke (marijuana), and the upper knippanol, with him from California. He began to break it down and sell it from the apartment. The duplex provided privacy.

Riding with the Banditos provided Chester a source of income from his drug stash. Local bikers bought some of the LA dope. They always stayed on the lookout for good smoke and for a downer after staying high all day.

The Mississippi members still respected the LA prez. The quality of drugs he sold them provided increased acceptance by the membership. Again the Banditos began to bring him into their illegal profit ventures in Jackson.

Several days after renting the duplex, Chester met his next-door neighbor. She was washing her car in the driveway when Chester drove up on the front grass. He found her attractive and provocative in the shorts she had on. She introduced herself and they engaged in small talk outside the little double-occupancy building.

Strangely, during their first conversation, she had mentioned that her boyfriend was a Jackson policeman. The cop had already asked her who owned the 1977 Mustang parked in the drive. The boyfriend wrote down the tag number and told her he was going to run an ID on the car to see if it was "hot."

Chester cannot explain why this policeman who had never met him and had no reason to suspect the vehicle was stolen should check him out. One answer to the cop's actions may have been his girlfriend. Perhaps a neighbor told him of her conversation with the stranger who had moved in next door to her. Chester had talked to her too long the day she washed her car. The cop boyfriend was just jealous, so he ran Chester's vehicle through MVI. Chester suspected his attractive neighbor might have been coming on to him in the yard, the first day, perhaps to determine if the outlaw biker might have some interest in her.

Later, in a courtroom, Chester realized her comments regarding her cop boyfriend should have been a warning. Perhaps the outlaw image of a biker was a turn on to her. But Chester knew he didn't need involvement with the law in any way because of his illegal activities in Jackson.

***

Chester and Della had been living in Jackson a month. In just four weeks, money was rolling in again. Life was good in Mississippi.

Chester still had a pound of marijuana left from the California stash. He decided to break it down for sale on the streets. After repackaging the weed, he hid it in his apartment; surely it would be safe there.

Later that night, Chester, his brother Vernon, and a cousin were drinking and smoking dope at a poolroom near the downtown Budget Inn. "Vernon had been dealing some ounces of my weed in the poolroom, and when it was smoked up, he asked me could he go back to the duplex and pick up some more. I said go ahead and I'd meet him at the lounge where Della tended bar. My brother asked where the stash of weed was hidden at the apartment, and I responded, 'Under my bed'."

Vernon returned to the apartment in Chester's Mustang. Later in the night, Chester left the poolroom and walked over to the lounge where Della worked. Just after Chester arrived, their conversation was interrupted by a phone call. Della handed the phone to Chester; it was Vernon.

"He asked if I had another set of apartment keys; he had forgotten to take his with him when he locked up earlier when he showered and changed there. I told I didn't, but to break out one of back door window panes and unlock the door through the window."

Thirty minutes after he called, Vernon returned and met Chester at the bar. They continued to party until closing time. Vernon still had the Mustang, and said, "I'm on the way home."

"I told Vernon he could sleep at Della's apartment with me if he wanted to. I planned to spend the night there. Vernon said, 'Fine with me'."

Vernon drove Chester and his girlfriend to her place. All three spent that night there, or so Chester thought.

"I woke up in the morning and looked for Vernon. Sometime during the night or early morning, he had gone. I tried to call him at the duplex but he didn't answer the phone. I needed my car and thought maybe Vernon went to his aunt's house; he always liked to visit her. I had Della drive me over to her house to see if he had been there or if she had any idea where he might be. Her place was located across Jackson, some ten miles away. She came to the door when I knocked and I asked her if she had seen Vernon. I explained Vernon had taken my car and I needed it. She said she hadn't seen him since the previous day. Where he had gone with my car, I didn't know."

His girl then drove Chester to his apartment to get his scooter. He had become terribly irritated with Vernon; he was always unpredictable. Vernon always fooled his dad into thinking he was more responsible than Chester. His dad saw him as the good one of the two brothers. His dad had favored Vernon, like when Chester and Vernon fought and Chester got knocked around if the fight didn't go Vernon's way. Every time any of the siblings fought, regardless of who had started it, Chester received the blame and took the whipping.

Chester now understood Vernon had left with his car. He didn't know that he had left town and taken the remainder of his drug stash.

Chester and Della arrived at the duplex and Chester got out of the car and started toward his apartment. He hesitated at the door as one of the neighbors approached him.

"Hey, Chester; the police are looking for you," came the neighbor's startling news.

"Why, did they say?"

"I don't know; they were here this morning and just said they needed to talk to you."

Chester wondered what the police wanted. If Vernon had not been arrested, they shouldn't know about his drug stash. Chester's unlawful activities were clothed behind the secrecy of the biker club veil and he doubted if anyone had become aware of anything illegal.

The concern about the police was quickly forgotten due to his irritation toward Vernon taking his car.

Monday morning, Chester clocked in at work and Vernon still hadn't shown up. Chester began working on a high-rise department store building at the Metro Mall. The construction company he worked for was erecting a penthouse on the top floor. He received a call from the supervisor to come down to the trailer office.

"I rode the employee elevator down to the ground and walked into the boss's office. As I walked in the office, my boss was speaking with a plain-clothes detective. The detective asked me, 'Are you Chester Johnston?'

"As soon as I responded yes, he pushed me against the wall of the trailer and locked handcuffs on me. I was being arrested for the rape of [name withheld]. My neighbor filed the charges even though I wasn't out that night.

"The cop sat me in the back seat of his law enforcement car and took me to the police station. There, they booked me on the alleged rape charges."

Chester's next three days were spent in the Jackson jail. Chester called a lawyer, James Nobles, to represent him. Nobles had represented some of the Banditos in the past.

At the time Chester was telling me his story, Nobles still practiced law in Jackson. But, even very experienced, Nobles would not be able to successfully defend Chester against the trumped up charges.

Chester knew he didn't commit the offense and felt comfortable knowing he had spent the night with Della. However, the charges were real and he would have to defend himself.

The preliminary hearing date arrived after Chester had been locked up three days and nights. Chester and his lawyer appeared before the judge in the Hinds County courtroom. Brother Vernon had finally reappeared and joined them in the courtroom. He sat down behind the Defense table.

Life contains many hidden turns during one's journey. They are never expected, never prepared for. Chester began to live through one of those unexpected events in life.

Chester thought he had an alibi preventing him being found

guilty of the rape charges. He had spent the night with his girlfriend, Della. She could testify to the fact, but strange things take place once one enters a courtroom. Chester knew this for sure. He had known some of his fellow bikers who were found guilty when they believed they had an alibi.

The charge landed him in court. He hoped the judge would dismiss the charges when Della testified where he had been. Then he would not have to go through the suffering of a trial.

In all our conversations, Chester has readily confessed that he took part in numerous illegal transactions. He acknowledges that the police in Mississippi and California suspected him of many crimes. If they had found evidence, he would have been found guilty. But he never got close enough to the events themselves for the cops to link him to them or find enough evidence to convict him. When they did, they could not connect Chester to it.

As the judge began the hearing, he read the charges and asked the defendant his plea. Chester replied, "Not guilty." The judge turned the hearing over to the States Attorney. After several questions to the victim, Chester and Mr. Nobles leaned forward in their seats when the prosecutor asked her if the man who raped her appeared in the courtroom.

She replied, "Yes."

Chester sucked in his breath as the state prosecutor asked her to point out that man. She looked down at the Defense table, then her finger pointed behind Chester to Vernon, seated in the visitor's section.

The State's lawyer quickly jumped out of his seat and requested the court stenographer to record the victim had pointed out the defendant. Just as quickly, Mr. Nobles jumped to his feet and protested she had not pointed to his client. Several family members in attendance that day all agreed that she hadn't. In truth, she had pointed out Vernon, sitting in the visitor's section.

Chester's lawyer pleaded with the judge to correct the record, as the female neighbor pointed out the younger brother, not the older one. The judge flatly refused. After a discussion at the bench between the state's attorney and the judge, he ruled again that the victim had pointed to Chester. The judge's ruling would stand.

Chester looked for Della among the visitors in the courtroom; She had not come. His alibi didn't show up.

Chester still maintains his innocence of the Jackson rape charges. False accusations by a local policeman's girlfriend may have been a result of a plan by terrified politicians to get Chester in prison, out of the way. No doubt the check scam had been lucrative, but also was dangerous for the state lawmakers. Several well-known individuals had been involved. Bikers and bankers who cashed the checks in New Orleans had to be added to the list of those fearful of Chester and the other matters he had knowledge of.

Some of the check-writing lawmakers were associated with law enforcement. Chester's association with the outlaw bikers wasn't a secret to the local police. Who knows; perhaps both the police and politicians became afraid of Chester snitching on them.

In addition to the check scam, there was a law enforcement escort service provided for the Banditos on their drug runs in the state. Both actions probably petrified the local politicians when Chester was arrested.

But the final result was that Chester would stand trial for rape. Because Della didn't show at the hearing, Chester's alibi evaporated. Vernon was not about to confess to anything. Soon Chester would be found guilty.

CHAPTER FOURTEEN

FREEDOM LOST

I felt it before I saw it!
I saw the tension on the faces
Of those around me who never saw it
. . . and on the ones who had
. . . it has an aura.
I've seen the effect it has
On those who've seen it up close and personal
It has that chemotherapy effect on people
(you know they've experienced something
And do not want to experience it again)
. . . but they do
. . . they have to.
It holds family trees by the roots.
It makes you hallucinate by giving you the
Illusion that it's too big, or too slow
To catch you when you run . . .
. . . but it can
. . . and does-
. . . then tightens its grip.
It lives, it breathes, it's not prejudiced;

It accepts everybody . . . every color
. . . young or old.
Its name is Parchman;
You'll know it before you see it;
Don't let it get its hands on you
. . . you might not get away"
Burkie, #44670, Unit Twenty-Six

C hester's trial for rape lasted two short days. The verdict was based solely upon testimony, not physical evidence. Who was telling the truth, the victim or Chester? The State presented her as a dishonored female raped by her neighbor. Chester claimed he was not her rapist.

The next-door neighbor to Chester and his brother had been taken to the hospital after the alleged rape. She was examined and samples of bodily fluids taken. Tests were supposedly run on the rape kit; however, the forensic DNA evidence and all corresponding reports had disappeared when the trial began. Chester had hoped Della would appear in court and testify that he had been with her all night. But they had separated after a vicious argument. She thought her man was seeing someone else and she had thrown him out, so she would not testify.

The jury had to decide between his word and hers. His panel of peers found in favor of the victim and he was sentenced to forty-five years in prison. He was a biker warlord and she was the girlfriend of a Jackson cop.

The roughneck biker lost.

***

The landscape along Highway 49 from Jackson, Mississippi, to Parchman Prison has changed little in the last fifty years. Now a work farm, the land once was part of a historic plantation. Inmates were brought from Jackson jails and made to work there for the agricultural estate owners in the 1800s. The money for the inmate's wages was paid to the State. When the state legislature became aware of inhumane treatment of the convicts on the huge farms, the state voided the labor contracts. Some years later, the state purchased the 22,000-acre plantation and turned it into a prison work farm.

Then and now, Parchman sprawls across five square miles, 22,000 acres of farmland in the middle of the Mississippi Delta.

The Mississippi Delta region is shaped topographically like a huge bowl. Flowing hills covered with majestic green trees form the rim on the north, south, and eastern perimeters. "Old man river," the mighty Mississippi, borders the western side. It is table flat farmland stretching as far as the eye can see.

Only two things have changed in the Delta since the seventies. One is the cash crop, no longer "king," sovereign of the Delta. Gone are the seeming endless rows of white cotton. Today marshy, green rice fields separated by serpentine dikes have supplanted the king.

The second change is manpower, now provided by workhorse diesel engines. No longer are thousands of workers required to work the land. No more masses of humanity breaking ground, planting, and chopping the planted mounds. Absent and silent, the long lines of Afro Americans who worked in the fields, men and women who labored in the delta sun clearing weeds with hoes or picking cotton, dragging long burlap bags behind them.

One of the Parchman officers related to me that she hired out to pick cotton at about age thirteen. Her mother fixed her a lunch. That morning, she pulled her long burlap sack and picked until the sun got up high and hot, ate her lunch, and walked home. Today, pickers have been replaced by the tractors, combines, and engine-driven cotton pickers.

There are few four-lane highways in this farmland. Mostly,

roads are narrow asphalt roadways connecting each town. These roadways are arrow straight, with brown dirt passageways running away from them.

In the years when cotton was king, clusters of small, frame, tenant houses dotted the landscape of fields; some were painted in bright reds or blues, and some proclaimed their age with cypress gray.

Today, most of these unpainted shotgun houses are gone. Some are still left beside the new highways of the delta. Now, modern technology of machines and knowledge have replaced thousands of workers and sent them to the towns or cities. There is no longer any need for the workers' rundown homes.

As a traveler rides through the delta, it is commonplace to see huge machines lumbering across the fields or slowing down traffic on the narrow roads. The steel giants are tireless when called upon. They work all day and into the night. After dark, their headlights provide a spooky sight in the fields. The lights appear to be without form, like ghosts of another time in the dusk.

This modern landscape was what Chester observed as he rode in the back of the MDOC van transporting him to Parchman in 1978. He rode and watched, hands handcuffed and feet shackled in chrome chains and bracelets. He still wore his denim pants and leather jacket, the style of biker apparel.

On arrival, the Hell's Angel clothes would be turned over to the penitentiary property clerk. The prez had been retired by a judge, and he left his scooter in the hands of a man who, years later, would say he never had it.

The prison van passed through Ruleville, Mississippi, on to Drew on Highway 49, then ten miles further, they pulled under the front gate of the dreaded prison farm.

The State Prison entrance easily identifies itself to those unfamiliar with what lies behind the front gate. On a high metal overhang at the prison entrance are the words "Mississippi State Penitentiary." A small frame building to the side provides shelter for the guards. The gate itself is made from two large white iron pipes. Attached to the end of pipe is a red stop sign. The officers will raise the gate of iron pipe for approved visitors or stop anyone they don't recognize.

The van carrying Chester passed over a set of railroad tracks and stopped in front of the guard shack. A security officer looked inside the vehicle and waved it on.

Then, as now, the warden's house was located to the left and behind the front gate. It is a long, low red brick ranch style home. The Administration Building is to the side of the warden's residence. Here, in the red brick administrative facility the warden and his power bosses have their respective offices. This one-story edifice was the control center of Parchman when Chester first arrived.

The van carrying Chester moved forward down Guard Row, or Highway 32. Left and right are modest white frame houses. These structures provide housing for prison officials and some officers. The grass is kept neatly cut and trimmed by prisoners. There are flowerbeds in the front of some and others have vegetable gardens, tended by the residents. These people attempt to bring some beauty to an otherwise dismal surrounding.

The state van carrying Chester slowly passed the frame houses for a half a mile, and then turned right into a circular gray gravel drive. Parallel to the driveway is a low white brick building. Its entrance is hidden from view by the shadow of a metal roof covering a long concrete porch.

New prisoners are taken to the A&D, or the Admittance and Diagnostics Building. Here, they are processed into the penal system. Their "free world" clothes are exchanged for white denim pants highlighted with a blue stripe down the side, and a cobalt colored shirt bearing the inmate's name and ID or MSP number stenciled in black over the breast pocket. Black, high top work shoes are supplied to each man.

Striped pants, shirt, and high top work shoes are the standard clothing issue for each new inmate. The clothing is for work, dress, and sports on the yard.

When the necessary forms are completed, the new inmate is taken to his assigned camp.

Unit Fifteen is the A&D, or processing camp. It was to be Chester's new home for a minute. Camp Fifteen is an open dormitory style housing building. Chester and the other arrivals at Parchman are each assigned a bunk in a row of double-deck, steel bunks. Little did they know what lay ahead. The bunks, or racks as the inmates call them, line the building's walls, with one row running down the middle of the area. Each bunk has a thin, pale green mattress rolled up on its end resting on a steel springs. There are no springs in the bottom of some racks, but soon the offenders will learn these will be the only rest they will get.

A yellow tiled shower area is at the end of the building wing. To the side of the showers is a separate room with white sinks and porcelain commodes. Both areas are completely open. They afford no privacy. Each new inmate must adjust to his loss of freedom. The newest prisoners will not find seclusion anywhere at Parchman. They eat, sleep, shower, and do their personal business out in the open.

The camps are oppressively hot in the summer and bitterly cold in the winter. Many of the tiered, roll-out windows are broken and lack screens. These cracks provide a variety of insects access in the summer and permit entrance to cold driving winter wind. Gaps between the concrete floor and door bottom are an invitation for rats and snakes.

When Chester entered the housing, an uniformed officer accompanied him. The guard assigned Chester his rack so he could keep count of his inmates. The camp guard ordered Chester to make his bed at once, with state-issued sheets and a single blanket. He is instructed that "Lights out" will be at ten o'clock. Wake up call will come at six a.m., followed by breakfast.

It will take some time for the Chester's digestive system to get used to the prison food. The prisoners are not required to "go back," as chow call is referred to, if they don't want to. This phrase comes from officers yelling "Going back" for each area or zone when time to eat. Many inmates begin their stay at Parchman skipping the day's first meal. Soon they learn the long hours of fieldwork or wherever work they are assigned to demands some victuals be eaten to give them the necessary strength for the day.

Eggs and bacon are a rare delicacy. Breakfast usually consists of cooked cereal, hard toast or biscuit, and coffee. But the food is hot and the supply plentiful.

The county or local jail has provided Chester an introduction to life in the state penitentiary. However, at Parchman, when the sun begins to sink, the sleeping zones fill with men coming in from work, and a troubling fear begins to grip the newcomer. The terror is of the unknown and the uneasiness of attack.

The prison new arrival has never lived on the streets in some form is not prepared for life in this jungle. Men locked up with you are serving various sentences for a variety of crimes; armed robbers, thieves, murderers, sexual offenders, and con artists sleep beside and shower with you. All have followed some criminal path to prison. Prisoners might be killed for a gold chain or a few dollars; others can be hired to shank, stab, or beat another inmate down for a package of cigarettes. A carton of store-bought smokes is the going price of a man's life.

No Hollywood production I have watched truly depicts what prison life is like. The film, *The Shawshank Redemption*, uses a homosexual rape event as the hero ex-banker's motivation to complete his time and find his dream. However, in the two-hour drama, rape only occurs once. In real prisons, this scenario is played out many times in one night in the lockup. Rapes and robberies are the result of hundreds of angry men, many who will victimize others when restrained only by a handful of officers.

***

Chester arrived at Parchman in 1978, and "the farm" has a long, and mostly inglorious history. Once a vast forest and thick tangle of brush and vines, it had been cleared by inmates and four hundred Polish immigrants at the turn of the century. The trees were manufactured into barrel staves. After the land was empty of timber and underbrush, the fertile black soil began to produce the cash crop of the delta, cotton.

Years before, a small hotel and some stores were located close to the entrance to the prison. Most old timers do not remember the location.

The landscape outside the MDOC van riding down Guard Row was separated by a blacktop highway dividing the north from the south half of the farm. The road is shown on maps as County Road 38. Narrower roads break off at ninety-degree angles from the main road, leading to the twenty-five camps around the prison. Many metal buildings accommodate factories or serve as warehouses for manufactured prison clothes or processed vegetables on both sides of the road. The prison industry print shop and vocational school are close by the front gate, accessed by Highway 38.

Housing facilities, camps as they have been called for years, dot the landscape all across the farm. They are laid out following the old delta farm sharecropper design. In times past, owners of the vast plantation had erected wood frame shotgun houses to accommodate the sharecroppers. Their homes were located on the border of the field they tended. When Parchman became a penitentiary, low brick buildings provided shelter to one- to two hundred convicts were built to replace the single-family dwellings.

Work camps are still close to the fields, providing quick access for the men living in them. Technology has replaced some of the hundreds of convict field hands with tractors and other farm equipment, but convicts are still used to gather the vegetable crops.

The "long line," one hundred inmates, moves through the crops in a straight line. They work with backs bending to the breaking point, as they plant, hoe, or gather the harvest of cabbage, okra, beans, and corn. The vegetables feed the hungry inmates; cotton, feed corn, rice, and soybeans are the main plants grown to sell.

All the inmates work except for "locked down" inmates, those held in cells twenty-four hour a day, or those sick or disabled.

Even today, only two of the units boast air conditioning. All camps are heated, but the icy delta blasts of winter rip across the open land into the sleeping areas through window cracks and crevices. The chill sends the inhabitants under cover of blankets on their racks.

To an inmate living in general population, his bunk is his home. Whether sleeping on the top or bottom of the green steel beds, his rack is his "space." Some beds have a built-in locker for the inmate's valuables. Cigarettes, canteen cakes, crackers, and canned tuna or salmon are locked inside. Others have a gray metal locker beside the bed. In prison, the inmate's bunk or rack is also his safe zone. Occupants spend most of their free time on their rack. They read or write letters and listen to music on their earphones in the home space. All prisoners must be on their rack for all body counts.

Each general population camp is built with a dayroom equipped with a television set. The guys here love to watch "soaps," talk shows, or sporting events while sitting on metal benches. *Beat the Clock* is the most favorite show, as the men bid and yell right along with the contestants. Some units have specially made metal tables with four seats attached. Inmates sit and talk or play cards and dominos for hours on the tables

Security guards watch the inmates in the zones or living areas from glass-enclosed control rooms to insure order is maintained and maintain their safety.

Each facility is equipped with a kitchen and dining area where the men are fed. Those who labor in the fields are delivered sandwiches and a beverage at noon. Here the workday begins with a wake up call at four o'clock and ends at 1700 hours, or five o'clock p.m. When an emergency arises, such as an early frost threat, the men will pick beans or whatever until after dark.

Men in "lockdown," or maximum security units, are confined in a six by nine foot cell. A bunk and toilet are the only facilities provided. Meals are brought to the cells by "floor walkers," who are trustee inmates. The most dangerous convicts are allowed yard calls outside or in a dayroom only as security guards decide to give it to them. Cells are arranged in rows or tiers where the men cannot see their neighbor. However, mirrors positioned just outside their cell allow them look at their neighbor next door when guards are not watching.

Prisoners are creative people. They can overcome most obstacles after a time to think out the problem. Food, coffee, cigarettes, and notes are conveyed from one cell to another by means of a "Cadillac." These convict inventions are made by rolling up a bath towel with shoe laces or strips of cloth wrapped around the towel. The inmate holds one end and throws the transport vehicle down the corridor, as the cord unrolls like a kite string. An empty Skoal can is attached to the other end, filled with tobacco or coffee or whatever the inmate wants to send when a request is made. The snuff container with the requested items, slide down the tier's floor to whoever has made the request. Once the "Cadillac" is emptied of the requested item, it is retrieved back down the hall.

One day as I visited on death row, the delivery intended for a guy close to where I stood came up a little short. I probably broke the law, but the sender hollered, "Hey, Chap; could you give it a little kick?" which I did to complete the delivery. I guess the men regarded me as one of them.

Work in the fields or at one of the manufacturing units is welcomed by most inmates rather than spend the day in close confinement. A job outside the camp confines is a relief from the petrifying nights spent in the unit. But the labor is hard and the guards demand maximum effort. An old convict explained the attitude. "Pick two hundred pounds of cotton daily, grab your rack at night, and keep your mouth shut, and you won't have any problems at Parchman."

Night is the most frightening time; roving gangs move through units, preying on weaker offenders who are locked in. The most outrageous acts are committed after lights out. In the dark is when new, weak arrivals are threatened with becoming punks or being robbed of their canteen by stronger, older prisoners. Darkness covers gang power moves. Extortions don't work in daylight. Other men confined may come to the rescue or a guard may pass, and lockdown is the penalty. Shanks, or "tools," are used to rob a gold chain or fancy ring.

Gangs totally run the units at night. Most illegal activities are carried on because guards are not on the tower or have been paid to look the other way. Zone "bosses" pay off officers to allow them control of inmates housed in their area.

Rising to the top of the power structure requires strength and ruthlessness. Gang leaders have no fear and openly recruit into their gang or organization. Prisoners conceal shanks under their clothing or in the bedroll. Water, boiled with sugar added, is kept within arm's reach. An inmate either sleeps under the protective watch of his associates or tosses all night, expecting a midnight visit and praying for the morning sun. Fear is an ever-present companion at Parchman.

The prison cemetery contains the remains of some inmates who went to sleep on a given night and never woke up the next day. Weathered bones lie under the dark, delta soil in the Parchman fields. Those shot or stabbed while working in the fields, years before, were hastily buried where they fell and their names quickly forgotten. A twenty-two year resident told me a story of digging a foundation for a new unit and, after several skeletons were uncovered, the location of the edifice was changed.

"V day," visiting day, is looked forward to by all prisoners. Offenders create lists that identify family or friends they want to see. Only those approved by MDOC are allowed past the front gates, and these are carefully searched before entering the grounds. Officers look for money, drugs, or other illegal items. Some contraband items find their way into the prison hidden by the family or friends. They conceal drugs and other forbidden items in any cavity in their body. Some use unmentionable body parts to escape discovery. Any person found with contraband items is promptly arrested and taken to the Sunflower County jail.

Once the visitor passes the search area, they ride a MDOC van to the prison camps. The dining halls are where visiting is allowed. Years ago, families would bring boxed lunches of roasts, hams, fried chicken, and potato salad to have lunch with the inmate they came to see. V day is the only day of pleasure in an convict's week.

Married inmates are allowed conjugal visits. Each camp is equipped with small private cells or sections called "tonks." The name was applied by inmates years ago, and is taken from the term "honky tonk." These quarters contain a bunk, sink, and a toilet. Before "tonk rooms," married inmates hung sheets around their bed for privacy with their wife.

Any time an offender gets out of line or a riot "jumps off," security staff members will use "necessary force," to restore order. "Necessary force" is anything security deems required to regain control. Fights, or involvement in a riot, result in an inmate being sent to the "hole," immediately. Offenders breaking minor, non-violent policies receive a RVR. The inmates call the RVR's tickets, like a speeding ticket. One doesn't go to jail, but will have a visit or some privilege taken. Rule violation reports, written by security officers, are sent to the Disciplinary Department. The Disciplinary Committee reviews the offense with the offender and hands out whatever punishment they deem necessary.

In addition to fearing other inmates, prison holds additional dangers. Mother Nature provides trials of her own year round to the man locked away. Brick walls and windows offer little protection from the throngs of insects living around the fields. Flies and gigantic, blood sucking mosquitoes swarm through each summer. Inmates are awakened at night by the stinging bugs. It is fairly common for sheets to be covered with blood from the attacks. Snakes, rats, and skunks are also abundant in the delta and occasionally enter the inmate's quarters. The fortunate convict will detect a snake before the snake finds him. Some snakes are harmful and others will just cause the inmate to harm himself.

Camp chow is described by offenders as, "just food." Meals are greasy and usually unseasoned. At harvest time, fresh vegetables are served with cornbread, a welcome addition to the diet. Coffee is served in the morning; tea or fruit drinks at other meals.

This is the life Chester was introduced to upon arrival.

***

The only law in a state prison is the law of survival. There are two choices under this system: one, be a man and survive by force with your fists or a shank; and two, in prison talk, "grab a man," meaning become someone's "punk."

Old hands are always on the lookout for a new arrival to rob or satisfy their physical appetites and submit to servitude. When a new prisoner chooses to become a "girl," he will be protected by his partner. The "punk" will even be given presents and treats from the prison canteen. His guardian will spend several hours daily at the weight pile, toning and enlarging his torso. Bulging muscles discourage attacks and make him more attractive.

One day, I was kidding a small but muscular Christian inmate at the weight pile about his exercising. I reminded him of a Bible passage,, "bodily exercise profits little."

He looked up and quickly responded, without missing a curl, "Right, Chaplain, but this ain't Sunday School."

I laughed at his quick-witted response.

There is only one way to prevent becoming a "punk," or being beaten down: fight! Chester was not a tenderfoot to warfare. The Mississippi river fronts, battlegrounds of Nam, and street battles in LA taught him about combat. He had survived all his past conflicts. Now he knew he must fight again to survive nights filled with muffled screams and cries of violence.

Chester finished his first meal there and returned to his rack. Chester and some Rankin County jail acquaintances rolled and lit a joint. The group stood behind the row of double bunks out of sight of officers who sat behind a wooden desk outside the fence separating them from the inmates.

Each night after supper, the security team relaxed and sat around talking or reading newspapers. They cared little about what occurred inside the fence as long as each head count showed all prisoners accounted for; body counts occur every two hours.

Chester remembers. "We had just lighted up a joint and passed it around. Each of us had one pull when a big dude 'stepped' to us from behind the bunks and requested a hit on the marijuana."

The oversized intruder was not known to any of Chester's Rankin County friends. But as a friendly gesture, they handed it to him to welcome him into their group.

"This guy didn't pass it back. Instead, he stood and smoked the whole joint himself. It was clearly an act of disrespect. I got in his face, told him not to ever smoke my dope like that again," remembers Chester.

The intruder, who had been locked up many years, towered over Chester, but his size gave him a false sense of superiority. This instinct machismo almost instantly cost him his life. "He said, 'Hey punk, you don't know who I am? I'm boss hog around this place.' I told him if he fooled with me, I was going to change him from a boar into a sow."

The combative boss hog ruled the camp and thought he was ready to defeat Chester's challenge. However, Chester had faced many such oversized bullies during his rise to president of the outlaw club and was not impressed by this one.

"The dude bull rushed me and I dodged, and I just began to throw my hands as fast as I could. I kept on until I had beaten him down to the floor. See, you just act crazy and swing until the guy goes down. Acting crazy is the only way to survive."

During the conflict, blood and spit flew everywhere. Loud grunts and curses broke the silence of the zone; there are no rules governing the conflict. The fights are a single round, ending when one man cut and bruised and can no longer rise from the floor.

The guards casually waited until the battle was over. They believe there is no reason to risk injury to them by entering the zone and stopping a fight before it is over.

Once Chester knocked the top man off his feet, he beat his opponent's head and face while sitting over him. Prison fights don't last long. Fear motivates the inmate to fight as hard and fast as he can until his opponent is senseless. "You just throw your hands until the other guy quits. You put fear into everyone. That's the only way to get respect."

When the guards finally entered the compound, the beaten boss hog told them they had been playing. But the hog no longer headed the pigsty. He lost his position of supremacy on Chester's Opening Night.

***

Parchman has always been a battle ground, with enmity between convicts and "police," the nickname for guards. Also, inmates never get along; there is generally strife within the population.

Before the civil rights movement, it was normal to confine a small number of whites with two hundred or more blacks. A long time Parchman resident told a lieutenant interviewing him that, when he first came to Parchman, one camp would have two hundred blacks and only twenty white residents. He claimed eighty or more of the black offenders had gang affiliations. One either protected his property or lost it. A man had to scrap when outnumbered.

Once inside the state penitentiary, a prisoner had to be fierce and tough to "hold up." The only means of survival was fighting, keeping one's honor and manhood. Those who are weak, or not affiliated with a gang, are in grave danger.

During the prison's earlier days, many fights occurred while working in the fields between laborers. Then, trustees, men who had earned the position, carried rifles, or were identified as shooters. They kept the inmates from running and maintained discipline on the "zones." Back then, convicts could be shot when attempting to run. Those killed were buried in the fields where they fell. The murder was hidden by falsely reporting an inmate had escaped. Men working under the blazing delta sun found that tempers often flared and fights started over nothing. Forgotten troubles flared up out there and the scrap was on.

Once Chester rose to prison "shot caller," he was often challenged for his position. His fast hands and combat prowess, combined with his strength, defeated all challengers. He sent all those who sought his position bleeding to the infirmary to be sewn up.

Chester explained. "Then [in the late 80s and early 90s], I had a macho image. It was before I was a Christian. It didn't matter if you measured six foot five. I would run into you and not think anything about it. I didn't think nothing about going up against anybody. To me, it was a challenge to see who could throw faster and harder than the other."

Chester talked about being outnumbered by race or organization. "When you are put in a situation where you are outnumbered, you have to "hold up" [stand the test]. You know they are going to test you, and there will be six or eight when they do."

I asked, "How do you hold up?"

Chester replied, "You knock them up side the head, or hit them with a lock in a sock, or throw sugar water on them."

I didn't understand about sugar water;. "What is sugar water?"

"You heat water and dissolve sugar in it. When the scalding water on is thrown on someone, the sugar makes the water stick to the skin. It will take the hide off anyone. Then you throw shaving power on the burn and it will 'set them free.' Conflicts will send you to the hole, but you have to do it."

The punishment for fighting was thirty days in the hole. At times, you had to fight or die, even if you lost all your privileges.

In the past, prison officials dehumanize inmates to keep them in line. They believed that, if they whipped them, or locked inmates away long enough, they would not resist authority. That worked with some. Others became as vicious animals cornered by walls and fences. They hunted in packs to survive. The hunt ended when fists or shanks determined winners and losers.

Chester had learned how to become a winner. Shoot meat from the legs of the opponent, or beat him down with fast and savage hands. Chester rose to the position of "shot caller" using the bloody bodies of the defeated to reach the top.

***

Chester's relentless and early knockout of the well-known inmate boss hog did not go unnoticed by inmates or Parchman police. Word quickly got around concerning the ex-biker from Jackson with a quick temper and fast hands.

However, his "beat down" of Camp Fifteen's boss quickly moved Chester to Camp Four, located on the back side of the farm. Then, it was referred to as a "throw away" camp, for men the prison officials considered to be non-redeemable. They believed these men would never stay in line so they were moved to a camp with repeat offenders, incorrigibles, and unrepentant discipline cases. "Throw away" camps confined inmates who would not be disciplined under normal prison control. All "tough guys" from anywhere on the grounds got sent here.

Each housing wing at Camp Four is an open dormitory type area. The living section of Camp four was similar to Camp Fifteen. Red brick walls formed the perimeter of the dormitories. Bunk beds lined both walls, with a third row down the center of the area. All work camps had been laid out identically.

Each unit had an outside entry gate beneath a brick guard tower. An armed guard holding an automatic weapon was stationed on the tower, three shifts, or twenty-four hours a day. Anyone desiring to enter waited until a white, three-gallon bucket was lowered on a rope, into which all car keys must be deposited. The tower guard also controlled the electronic latch on the entry gate. Nobody could enter until the man in the tower checked IDs.

One hundred and fifty feet across the yard was the entrance to the building. A concrete walk led one to the door.

Once inside, visitors were stopped by a security officer at a desk. Any non-security personnel were stopped and logged in. The security guards maintained a log, listing the name, purpose of visit, and time in and time out of all visitors. They also kept a roster of all the offenders housed there. At the far end of the open administration area was the camp kitchen. Between there and the control area, gray metal tables were arranged for inmate meals. All two hundred men in the camp ate three meals there daily.

Chester received his unofficial welcome from some of the security tough guys while sitting in the dining area. Several of the higher ranking officers had built a reputation for toughness and keeping inmates in line, especially the new arrivals were who considered "bad actors."

Some of the wardens enjoyed riding high-spirited horses close to the prisoners in the field and elsewhere to intimidate them. Even today, guards dressed in Levis and dark blue shirts ride on horseback, watching inmates in the fields. The high riders position their horses on the exterior of the fields, moving around, shouting orders to any inmate who is not working to their satisfaction. Each of the riders is armed with a carbine and is prepared to shoot any convict who dares to run. Few workers attempt flight.

Before federal judges issued stern guidelines concerning penitentiary operations, convicts were severely beaten and living conditions were more deplorable than after federal decrees. Prisons depend on federal funding to operate, so the Mississippi corrections operations cleaned up their back road whippings and cruel treatment of inmates.

The practice of controlling offenders with armed riders on horses dates back to the early prison farm existence. Then, horseback was the only method of cross-country travel. Most of the horses ridden by security were large, spirited cutting horses that could stop or go instantly upon command. Now the K-9 Unit is in charge of the horses and dogs used for inmate control. K-9 officers saddle and mount their horses when a prisoner hides or runs into the fields, to be hidden by towering crops across the 22,000 acres.

Some inmates will lie down in the field hoping to escape if the officers do not miss him when they count before they leave the fields. K-9 officers are identified by their forest green and black camouflage uniforms. They are the only guards armed with carbines and handguns. K-9 officers are a tough, disciplined lot. All are prepared to respond to any dangerous prison situation at a moment's notice. K-9 is the crack security force at Parchman.

Chester had not yet met any mounted riders on the farm, but he had only been locked up for three days. Nevertheless, the top prison bosses were an informed and intimidating bunch and had heard about the tough biker from Jackson. To intimidate tough guys, they would ride their mounts into a riot, using the snorting and prancing steeds to ram inmates away from each other until the scrap was over. The presence of the huge horses and riders took the steam out of the prisoners and the conflict was soon resolved.

Chester still clearly remembers the Parchman staff welcome he received at Unit Four. He had been at the "throw away" camp for a couple of days. It was evening, and the call to "go back" had been issued by the guards. The inmates were enjoying their Thanksgiving dinner.

Normally the chow hall is rather quiet, because little talking is permitted by the police. But, on this holiday, rules were relaxed; the men were laughing and talking in the chow hall. Tomorrow was a visiting day and the men eagerly awaited their families and the festive mood of Thanksgiving had developed, brought on by holiday food and anticipation of the packages they would receive.

On holidays, some of the hostility and loneliness of prison life is momentarily forgotten.

As the men were eating their turkey and dressing dinner, the double front doors of the building suddenly burst open, and in rode several prison bosses on horseback. They rode past the control desk and into the dining area. Their nervous horses were being held in tight reign, and the horses' hooves created a clatter on the concrete. Suddenly, the captain, a notoriously hard prison disciplinarian, shouted, "Where's the tough biker from Jackson?" The high-blooded staff horses pranced among the metal tables, causing prisoners to dodge or be knocked out of their seats.

The head of the posse kept on with his mocking questions. "Where is the "bad ass" biker who thinks he's so tough?"

Chester, his arms covered with outlaw tattoos, stayed in his seat, his dinner on a tray in front of him. He didn't want any problems with the police, as he knew stirring up trouble with the administration was not the way to do his time at Parchman. In 1978, Parchman was a mean, dark prison and nobody wanted the security force fighting against them.

The riders on horseback continued to ride through the chow hall, horses snorting and men yelling. Their dramatic entrance was intended to scare and intimidate the men of Unit Four. As they moved the inmates around with their prancing horses, they uttered threats and curses. Their horses towered over the prisoners, creating fear in many of them.

When the biker they were looking for didn't stand up immediately and identify himself, the questioning turned personal. "Come on; let's see who you are. You're 'sposed to be so bad, stand up. You raped some woman in Jackson, so you must be weak." They continued their verbal abuse.

Chester could only take so much abuse and attacks on his manhood. Finally, his pride kicked his temper into gear. The comment about being weak was more than his tough image would bear. He sprang from his seat and bull rushed the posse's ringleader, knocking him from his horse.

The other riders quickly dismounted and formed a circle around their leader and his adversary. They would not immediately join in the scrap. Chester and the captain rolled on the concrete floor, punching, kicking, and screaming at each other. Neither the warden nor Chester could claim victory that day. Once the official wasn't winning the brawl, the remaining officers began to hit the biker with long, wood batons. Finally, Chester was knocked down and blows began to rain down on his body, until he lay motionless on the hard floor.

The officers called security and a van was dispatched to pick up the biker who had just received his first of several Parchman attitude adjustments.

"Attitude adjustments" are a common occurrence at Parchman. Another inmate told me the captain who came looking for Chester was famous for administering hard and brutal discipline. He was one who believed unruly prisoners had to be taken "to the back road."

Taken to" the back road" was the phrase describing when an inmate was taken from his cell to a deserted road back of the prison, where cries couldn't be heard. There, he was beaten with a "black Annie" until he "got his heart right." A black Annie was a four-foot, black leather strap with a wooden handle used for attitude adjustments. Many men were sent to the infirmary by "Mrs. Annie." There were times a repeat offender was about to get out of line and the captain would come for him and administer corrective measures. Strange as it may sound, some prisoners actually welcomed and expected the whipping to keep them in line.

After his rough welcome, transportation arrived and took Chester to Unit Seventeen, a maximum security camp. Chester left bruised and bleeding, but with no serious damage done. The captain and his men, several of them with bloody scrapes, stood and watched as the biker from Jackson was supported by two guards to the waiting van ride to the prison hospital.

The captain now knew that the tattooed Jackson biker would indeed be a force to be watched in the future. The best medicine for a incarcerated tough guy was to be locked down twenty-four hours a day, with meager food and drink until he decided to conform to prison rules. Little did he realize it would be years before this inmate decided to conform. It would not be the harsh Parchman discipline to change him, but an introduction to a man who lived and died almost two thousand years ago.

CHAPTER FIFTEEN

THE "TAKE DOWN"

Parchman officers are often summoned to restrain inmates by force. They may respond to a riot, or a prisoner setting his cell on fire, or other activities upsetting the order of the prison. Their cruel action is called a take down. Guards attack with batons and shields until the inmate or inmates are on the ground, with handcuffed hands and feet. If the prisoner fights back, the situation sometimes gets out of control.

Prison populations are comprised of three types of inmates. There are punks (those abused by the stronger prisoners), gang members, and men. Chester proved his manhood from his first day at Parchman. Proving one's manhood on a regular basis often results in many trips to the hole, as maximum security is called.

The regulations of the penitentiary declare any person caught fighting will be sent to the hole. Yet contrary to prison rules, the inmate system of conduct is, if you don't fight back when attacked, you are a punk. Nevertheless, security officers don't investigate the reason or who started the fight. They don't care, for the most part, who won or lost, unless the loser is "hooked up" with security. All fighters are quickly transported to maximum security for thirty days or more. The police will use whatever force necessary to take control and move the prisoners there.

An inmate who had been once confined to the hole later testified for Chester at his trial. He described maximum confinement here as hell on earth A volunteer chaplain serving the inmates at Unit Thirty-Two also testified and agreed with the inmate's description.

The hole is hated because prisoners housed there have no privileges. They are not permitted a radio, a TV, tape player, or any electronic piece of equipment to help pass their time. The food is always cold, and ice-cold water is not provided during the sweltering summer heat. Electric fans are not allowed even though the buildings are not air-conditioned. Inmates "locked down" receive time to shower twice a week, if permitted by security. Yard call, lasting thirty or forty minutes, is given when officers decide to award it.

Lockdown cells are secured with steel doors constructed with bars, and a slot built in the bottom to pass an inmate's food tray through. Each tier is constructed with cells along each side of the building. A block wall separates the two rows. In this facility, the prisoners cannot see other inmates living beside them or across from them. Carrying on conversations is difficult.

MSU's worst hardship is the noise and the smell. Men yell and scream twenty-four hours a day. Continuous sleep is impossible. Many who are locked down continually use curse words. Some prisoners use their black, high top boots to beat on a stopped-up stainless steel commode so someone will fix it. Others do it simply to cause a disturbance. The cubicle's toilet is only available to the occupant. Those housed there continue to use it even when it won't flush. The odor of waste material fills the cell and then drifts down the hall; it becomes unbearable. No inmate has refuge from the din and the smell.

The environment of solitary confinement builds pressure on the occupants, until finally one "goes off," as the inmates refer to going crazy.

Chester suffered a take down 1979. His beating was extremely severe. Chester had been on the farm for two years. Starting with his fight his first day and the Thanksgiving incident with the mounted officers, he had constantly been in conflict with prison officers and staff. They considered him a troublemaker. But they had lots of experience dealing with his kind.

He had been serving time in the hole at Camp Twenty-Four the day of his take down. Now he headed the Aryan Brotherhood at Parchman and was considered by the prisoners as top man, or "shot caller" at Parchman.

A Parchman sergeant recalled Chester from his earlier years. "Chester use to get out of line once in a while," he said with a sly smile on his face. A captain who knew Chester before his con-version described him as "real tough customer," who had made a tremendous change in the last few years.

The unit administrators had moved Chester from A to B building. They had not given him any advance notice. The officers arrived at his small cell and ordered him to pack up. When they returned, Chester had packed his possessions in his blanket, tied up the corners, and looked ready to move.

The guards put handcuffs on him and led him down the tier of cells and out the doorway into the large courtyard. The trio walked the short distance to the adjoining building. The guards locked Chester in his new cell quickly and removed his handcuffs.

Chester began the usual housekeeping chores when moving into a new "house." He cleaned the sink and commode and swept the floor. Neither florescent light worked, so Chester stood on his steel locker and twisted them until they lit up. Next, he put sheets and a blanket on the thin mattress of his metal bed. As best he could, he prepared his new cell to be his home.

On Saturday, eleven days later, an officer called his name right outside his cell. Chester asked him what he wanted and the officer told him to pack up because he had to be moved.

Chester's anger began to flare. The guards moved inmates they disliked to harass them. Besides, it was Saturday, a day when the inmates had freedom from movement. Chester asked him why he had to be moved again, since he had just got there. The guard replied it, "None of your business, earlier pack up."

Chester became enraged, as he had cleaned and arranged the small cubicle into a livable condition only to be told he was leaving. Chester decided not to play along with the harassment. Chester spat out his reply, "You come in here and I'll juge [stab] your ass."

The guard left to find more officers to assist in moving the reluctant prisoner. The guard knew Chester's reputation and more officers would be required to get him out of his cell. He wanted no part of attempting to handle Chester alone.

The officer reached the control area and reported the disturbance. One of the lieutenants there, accompanied by a sergeant, went to Chester's cell. The lieutenant, who had been there before unlocked and opened the steel door and stepped inside the six by nine area. He asked Chester why he resisted being moved. Chester replied he had just got there and there had been no reason to put him somewhere else so soon. The ranking officer replied he could move him any time; he didn't need any convict's approval.

Chester became livid with rage but agreed to be handcuffed for the move. Once he had been manacled, the lieutenant decided to "straighten" [correct] Chester's attitude. He sneered at Chester and asked him if he had ever been slapped by a black man. Chester responded that he had not. All at once, the lieutenant slapped Chester across the face with his open hand. He didn't wait for a reply; he stepped back into the hall, slammed the steel door shut, and locked it.

Chester saw the incident as a challenge. "You don't let them ask you have you ever been slapped by a black man and then hit you. I had to stand up for myself."

Chester sat on his rack and simmered, his blood boiling. Shortly thereafter, Chester heard more men returning. A sergeant with a very large stomach accompanied the others to assist in the transport.

They followed the procedure manual and ordered Chester to stand back from his cell door. The solid steel doors had a small window slit near its top. The officers did not take time to look within. The made a serious mistake; Chester had prepared himself for their return. Chester had armed himself for the conflict he knew would come when they returned.

He had climbed on top of his locker and removed one of the four-foot fluorescent light bulbs from the fixture. When one of the guards unlocked the door, the top officer entered first. Chester broke the fragile light bulb across his forehead and the leader staggered backwards, bleeding. Immediately, the sergeant rushed past his leader as he fell back, only to bear the brunt of Chester's anger as the broken end of the bulb was jammed into his portly stomach. The sergeant went back, bleeding from his stomach wound.

As the officers recovered their senses, Chester waited for their second attack. Instantly, the loud yells of pain from the invaders summoned more back-up to the scene and they all rushed into the cell behind protective shields. Their wooden batons swept through the air seeking the body of the resistant prisoner. But Chester had become a fighting frenzy, fists flailing and feet kicking out as he stopped their rush.

What began as a simple inmate move turned into a wild and angry free-for-all.

The battle seemed to last hours to Chester and his adversaries. Within a few minutes, Chester had been beaten to the floor and chained, hand and foot. The assault troops jerked and dragged the bleeding prisoner across the courtyard into the administration building. Their take down had been successful.

Now would begin the real punishment phase of Chester's basic training in prison discipline. Chester needed an "attitude adjustment." They had taken him down; now the time had arrived to "beat him down."

The administration building contained a room especially prepared for dealing out extreme punishment. Its walls, floor, and ceiling had been painted bright red. The room had block walls on three sides and a heavy metal fence across the front, away from inquisitive eyes and ears. The room aptly was called the "Red Room."

Once Chester had been secured in the Red Room, the attending prison officers mockingly challenged him to fight now. They jeered and began to strike him again with their oak wood batons. He got kicked in the head and ribs with steel-toed military boots.

For a little, while Chester lifted his handcuffed hands and arms to shield himself as much as possible. He was too proud simply to lie down and take the beating. Finally, he slumped down on the red concrete floor. He could no longer defend himself. Too many guards had taken turns beating and kicking him. He lay on the floor semi-conscious, unable to ward off the blows and out of breath.

But the "beat down" continued. His body rocked with each drop kick and the impact of each baton as he lay on the red concrete. During the "attitude adjustment" phase, the angry lieutenant kicked the fallen convict and inserted the toe of his cowboy boot completely into Chester's mouth. The boot removed all of Chester's lower teeth. Finally, when Chester stopped moving, the attitude correction mercifully ended. He lay on the floor, silent and with blood all over his face and body.

"Contain and control" are the officers' academy instructions.

Antagonism was their motivation to beat Chester. Now, with Chester unconscious on the concrete, their obligation required them to keep the beaten inmate from dying. The watch commander called the prison hospital, and within minutes, a prison ambulance arrived. The hospital attendants loaded Chester onto a stretcher and rolled him from the Red Room into the hall of the administration building.

As the gurney carried Chester out, Unit Chaplain Raymond Lankford arrived at the front entrance. Looking back across the years, the chaplain's actions are amusing now. The chaplain stopped the hospital attendants to identify the inmate. Langford had been unable to recognize the swollen and bleeding inmate, and asked the officers the name of the inmate. One officer replied it was Chester Johnston.

Instinctively, Chaplain Lankford bent down over the semi-conscious form on the gurney. He knew Chester well. In a display of compassion, the chaplain tenderly opened one of Chester's swollen eyes with his fingers. The head religious man looked into the bloodshot eye and inquired, "Chester, Chester, is that you?"

Chester responded in a whisper through humbled, bloody lips, "Yes, sir; it's me."

Today, management methods have been changed at Parchman. Federal court judges have exercised their authority over all state penal systems. Federal courts have issued orders to stop excessive force in prisoner punishment. The old Red Room is still at Unit Twenty-Four, but now it's painted battleship gray. Now it is a storage area.

Once, one of the officers involved in Chester's beating proudly pointed out the Red Room location to me. He described how the room had been painted its bright red color. Next, he smiled and asked, "Chaplain, do you know why we painted the room red?" Even though I knew, I responded "No," and he grinned, saying,

"So when Internal Affairs came to investigate they couldn't find any evidence of excessive beatings. The red paint hid the blood." The officer chuckled and walked away.

After the prison doctor examined Chester at the hospital, the following injuries were listed on his medical chart: broken jaw, many lower teeth missing, shattered eardrum, bruised groin, three broken ribs, and multiple lacerations and bruises.

Years after, Chester filed a federal law suit demanding $550,000 dollars from the State of Mississippi for the cruel punishment he received that day. A federal judge proudly awarded him a judgment of $7,000 dollars.

CHAPTER SIXTEEN

THE ROAD TO LIFE

The Bible states, "God is not willing any should perish, but that all would come to repentance." The word *everyone* includes a fierce, lawbreaker like Chester Johnston.

Marvelously, God's grace forgives all sin: past, present, and future. God's forgiveness is available anywhere at any time. Such is the love and grace of God. Some sinners find God in the middle of a terrible battlefield, others in the quiet of a chapel. Chester Johnston met God in a prison hospital at Parchman penitentiary. The year was 1980.

After Chester's beating by prison officers, he recuperated in the hospital seventeen days. His jaw remained swollen from the repeated kicks that removed all his lower teeth. Baton blows left bruises covering much of his torso and legs. Today, a scar over his eye still reminds him of that horrible day.

We know God has different ways of dealing with His lost children. No way did God plan the attack, but He used it to give the prison warrior time to reflect on his life.

Chester lay on the bed at the old hospital; his mind returned to the lessons his grandmother had taught him. He remembered the prayers she said with him before he went to sleep years before.

"I knew there must be a better life."

Chester had been told about God since he was a boy. He once

attended a revival close to his home and answered the invitation at the conclusion of the meeting. He met Jesus in a small country church one night. The preacher baptized him in water for the forgiveness of his sins. Like a prodigal son, he would lose sight of Jesus during much of his adult life, but Jesus never lost sight of him

Chester sent a message to the chaplain's department to request a Bible. He had never owned one in his life, but now he desired to understand more about God.

His beating had taken much of the fight out of him. Now he realized he must surrender to the Parchman officials and to God or he would die there. He had battled the system and God from the time his mother died. The time had come to give it up.

Chester compares his change from combatant to convert with the Apostle Peter's. Their transformations did not occur overnight. The disciple lived with Jesus three years, confessed him as the Son of God, then denied him. As Peter had, Chester, for the next five years of his life would trust, then deny often.

Living the Christian life is a struggle to become more like Jesus daily. Paul declared he had not attained perfection, but was pressing on. Chester's road to attain perfection had been filled with potholes, and he occasionally fell in, but he always climbed out and continued on. The road toward God is a road traveled in trust.

Once back in Unit Twenty-Four, Chester continued to read the Bible and attend worship services. He began building a foundation in Christian living. Parchman has never been conducive to Christian living; in addition, Chester's old ways died slowly within him.

The new convert found that pride died gradually. His gradual change would enable him to leave behind "buck" (prison alcohol), marijuana, and cigarettes. Complete surrender was the most difficult step to obtain victory.

Chester described his oftentimes rocky Christian journey. "I didn't always stay in the middle of the road; sometimes I got around the wrong crowd. I still thought I had to hold up for myself. I had to keep my macho image for protection. Once somebody became a Christian and went to volunteer services, others thought you must be weak. Living in the general population and having been in the game, somebody always wanted to take your position of calling the shots. You can't just lay it down; there was a challenger around who wanted to beat you. You were not going to let anyone hurt you."

The gradual change in Chester to become like Jesus was observed in Chester's actions. He no longer retaliated when someone got in his face. "When challenged, I always pulled back before I did something drastic that I would regret. I realized God had his hand on my life, especially when I quit fighting the system."

Chester learned that pride is the enemy of self-control. "I had to pray for self control. When confronted by arrogant prison officials, I had to put my hands in my pockets and learn to chill my hostility. I found I didn't have to prove myself any more."

Over the following years, Chester's change baffled prison officials. They knew how to handle the fighter, the rule violator, but they didn't comprehend how to cope with the new Chester who had given up fighting and cursing.

"They got in my face to see how I would react. If you told them you loved them, they thought you had to be crazy and wanted to send you to Doctor Russell [prison shrink]."

His beating by prison guards became the genesis of Chester's journey toward heaven. He would continue, on and off, his journey until December 28, 1981.

On that cold December day in 1981, inmate Jorge Simmons almost ended Chester's life with a twelve inch, needle sharp tool. The attack returned Chester to the prison hospital. Again the hospital ward gave him time to reflect. He would see he had to totally give up everything to become like Jesus. He must empty himself of pride and his position as "boss." His Lord asked him for surrender.

***

Since his incarceration in 1978, Chester has met many of the Parchman inmates. Some on the free world streets; others convicted outside the Jackson area. Several, like the 'hog" at Unit Fifteen had been met in combat.

Throughout his first three years at Parchman, the ex-biker made enemies as well as friends. Chester fought his way to the top of the white Aryan Brotherhood and they all proclaimed him as their leader. The "ABs" were tough, white warriors covered with their organization tattoos. They provided protection to white inmates against the black gangs, the Vice Lords, Black Gangster Disciples, and other street groups.

One of Chester's friends from the streets later became his enemy. He was Jorge Simmons, who later stabbed Chester from behind. An honorable foe attacks from the front, a cowardly adversary from the rear. Simmons attacked from behind.

"Shooter Jorge" Simmons was another notorious Parchman inmate. He has been involved in all types of scams and schemes since being imprisoned in the 1975. He had been incarcerated at Parchman three times. After completing each sentence, he had been paroled back into society. Today, after being released three times, he is in jail once again. Shooter Jorge is described by Mississippi's justice system as a habitual criminal.

There are many consistent criminals in the Mississippi prison system. Some are held in high esteem by fellow inmates, but not Jorge. Most people who have met him, on the streets or in prison, know he is a snitch and a traitor.

In the prison social system, a snitch is on the lowest rung of the inmate community ladder. They are considered lower than a punk, a man who sells his body doing homosexual acts for protection or favors.

After Chester was convicted of rape in 1978, he was sent to Unit Four at Parchman. There, Chester met a young man who had once stayed with him and his girlfriend, Della, for a short period of time when they lived in Jackson. The boy was Jorge Simmons. Shooter, Jorge's nickname, was fourteen years old at that time. Chester provided him a place to stay after he left home.

Chester recalls Jorge enjoyed hanging out with the Mississippi Banditos in Jackson. He never became a full member or patch holder. Simmons was assigned the role of a "go-boy," or runner for the bikers.

In prison, while living at Unit Four, and later Unit Seventeen, Chester and Jorge had hung out together. They passed long dull hours of jail time smoking dope and playing cards. Both occupations are favorite pastimes of offenders. While there, they renewed their previous friendship.

Their companionship continued until early in 1981, when Chester was told, either by investigators or prisoners, that Jorge had implicated him in a murder of a man from Shaw, Mississippi. The camaraderie dissolved immediately. By Simmons's own testimony, several of his friends knew from Chester or other sources that Jorge had been talking to the police. Chester's friends began to shun the Shooter.

Life becomes extremely dangerous in prison when one is labeled a snitch. Death crouches around every corner for all who go to the police with information. All the men carry a "tool" or shank. Shanks are metal or plastic weapons fashioned by hand on brick or concrete walls into a deadly instrument. Many guys possess two or three just in case one is discovered in a shakedown by the guards.

Some facts are clear relating to the events leading up to Chester's stabbing on December 28, 1981. Both Simmons, in his later testimony to Highway Patrol Investigator Lieutenant Bingham, and Chester, in later interviews, recall the same date. Shooter Jorge was becoming branded as an informant around the yard at Unit Twenty-Four, where he and Chester resided. Jorge was losing influence and prestige because of his snitch label.

Eight years later, before Chester's trial, Simmons told Investigator Bingham that other inmates, learning he had snitched on Chester, had caused some of his pals to stay away from him. Those incarcerated realize someone who will snitch on one friend will snitch on them to make their prison life more tolerable.

In 1981, Simmons had indeed told Highway Patrol Investigator Bingham and an internal affairs investigator some bits of gossip or testimony about Chester being involved in a murder. Exactly what was said is unknown, as the notes of the interview have been lost. Then the police inquired about any officer they suspected as being corrupt. The officer under investigation had been dealing large quantities of dope at the unit where Simmons lived. First, the police tricked Simmons into talking on a phone with an officer he knew, while other investigators listened. In a later interview, prison investigators talked with Shooter face-to-face, and Simmons inferred he knew something about a murder Chester might have committed.

Jorge still held a grudge against Chester, who had previously won a diamond ring and six hundred dollars from him playing cards in Jackson and then left for the west coast.

Chester was now the unofficial boss of the prison population. This is a fact attested to by most old inmates and officers as well. Chester was hard-hitting, and never failed to back up his role as "shot caller" after he climbed to the top of the inmate power system. I have talked with many convicts and officers who confirm Chester's supremacy.

Also true is that Chester was feared by most offenders. Whether Jorge had been afraid of him or not is a matter of conjecture.

Shooter, in the later interview regarding an alleged charge against Chester, talked as though he was not, but probably really was. His sneaky method of attack seemed to prove it.

The motive for Jorge's assault was his waning respect from prison mates. Weakness is also dangerous trait in prison, especially once men begin to avoid conversation and association with an informant. The snitch is no longer brought into the money-making penitentiary games. His money supply begins to dry up and other inmates view him as weak.

Jorge's situation had to have been growing critical. Jorge was losing face and income because he had talked to prison officials. He surely decided something had to be done.

On the evening of December 28, 1981, Chester exited his single lockdown cell to take a shower. Dining halls and washrooms are where most prison attacks occur. For some unexplained reason, Chester did not take his "shank" with him; he still does not know why.

The showers in Unit Twenty-Four are single occupant facilities. A steel door on the outside is necessary, as guards lock the offender in. Evidently, Simmons watched for Chester to leave his "house" and enter the shower stall. Then, Shooter slipped down the tier walkway from his cell.

The guards had failed to lock the shower door.

Chester left his clothes in his cell and entered the shower with a towel wrapped around his waist. Once the door closed, he hung his towel up on the door and turned on the water. Next he raised both arms to begin shampooing his hair. He was in a defenseless position with arms raised and soap in his eyes, believing the shower door had been locked. Jorge waited in the dark, empty walkway outside the shower, waiting for the right moment to attack.

Jorge's tool of choice was a screwdriver ground sharp as an ice pick. As Chester reached into his hair, Jorge struck without warning from behind, silently stabbing Chester in the long muscle across the top of the back. Chester opened his eyes and turned to face his attacker as blood shot out of his back. Chester, still blinded by shampoo and water, couldn't avoid Jorge's second thrust, which hit him in the chest close to his heart. It missed Chester's lung by an inch.

Chester wildly attempted to wipe the soap from his eyes and defend himself at the same time. His eyes began to clear and Chester finally saw his attacker. Once more, Jorge raised his tool to deliver what he hoped would be a fatal blow. He would quiet Chester once and for all. However, Chester was prepared for the third thrust and threw up his hand to ward off the killing blow. His ring finger on his left hand remains bent and bears a scar where the screwdriver entered his hand.

Once Jorge decided his attack would not achieve his goal of death, he dropped his tool and ran, yelling for help down the tier. He continued his flight a hundred yards across the yard and into the officer's control area in the Administration building.

Chester, naked and with blood streaming from three wounds, was in hot pursuit, chasing his attacker across the open courtyard. Guards restrained Chester when he reached the dining hall. Immediately, they took him back to his cell and waited while he dressed. They called for an ambulance and Chester was taken to the hospital and stitched up.

From that night until today, Chester and Jorge have had nothing to do with each other. Later, Shooter told officials he and Chester had made a truce. True or not, I don't know.

Jorge had bragged about how tough he was. If he had been, he would have met Chester in open combat, not hid and stabbed Chester from behind.

During Simmons's prison stay, he would rise to the status of number one money scam artist at Parchman. In this role, he would regain some of his lost respect, but the prisoners never completely trusted him again.

The man stabbed and bloodied from behind in a shower would later recommit his vow to another person who would become his brother forever. The man's name is Jesus Christ.

After the stabbing incident, the officers returned him to his cell, number 64, and one commented, "You sure are lucky." If the man was describing God's providence, he was "on the money" in his assessment of Chester's wounding. One inch to the left by the shank and Chester would have been dead.

His being stabbed would be the second highway sign to get him back on the road of life. He described this event as "selling out."

"After the guards left, I lay on my bunk, broken like you know. Suddenly I just cried out; my spirit was broken. I said, 'If you are the God Grandma and all have been talking about, have mercy on me and accept me as I am.' I got on my knees to pray and I heard a voice saying, 'Chester Jordan Johnston, you're not a desperado any more, so just serve me.' I got up from the floor and looked through the door slot, but nobody was there. I was alone. I knew God had convicted me with His Spirit."

Chester would still fall from the narrow path of perfection once in a while. However, his desires for his old habits continued to be fewer and further between. The biggest change Chester found in his life was when he did sin, a feeling of guilt convicted him.

Chester lengthened his Bible study time using correspondence courses. He became active in the volunteer worship services.

God was preparing Chester for the greatest test he had had to face far in life. Without God working in him, he would have given up, when, in 1989, he was charged with capital murder.

Years later, Simmons referred to Chester's conversion as a sham being run on prison chaplains and officials. The entry of Jesus into Chester's life is probably the only thing saving Jorge's life. Jesus surely saved the life of Chester Johnston.

CHAPTER SEVENTEEN

SHATTERED DREAMS

T he eight years following Chester's stabbing and his committing his life to Christ seemed by Chester's old principles uneventful. He no longer fought to hold his prestigious position as "shot caller" or boss of the Aryan Brothers and all of Parchman. Most of Chester's life had been filled with conflict, external and internal discord. When he decided to live God's way instead of the warriors, he finally found peace.

Chester Johnston, # 44467, became a model prisoner, a fact that prison officials would never believe.

The most outstanding event during this span of time was Chester finding Cindy. Cindy, who later married Chester, became the greatest joy and peace he had ever known, other than Christ. He always refers to her as "my beautiful wife." Truly, Cindy is beautiful in appearance and in spirit. The story of their romance is the earthly crowning jewel in Chester's living toward his eternal crown.

Cindy tells of the beginning of their relationship in 1989. "It began with putting an ad in the paper. I don't know why I decided to do this, except my girlfriend from work, Jo Blaney, thought it would be fun. I was trying to put behind me ten years of an un-healthy relationship, so I said, why not."

As she remembers, the ad read something like, "37-year-old white, female looking for a 35-45-year-old while male. Prefer one who likes music, kids, softball, and quiet times." A post office box was acquired in a nearby town for the ad's return address.

Quickly, the PO box was filled with fifty to seventy-five responses. In the first batch of letters was one from Chester Johnston. "A sketch he had drawn drew my attention and his words caught me." Chester talked about being a Christian and asked Cindy not to judge him because he was in prison.

Cindy thought about writing back at once, but decided not to. Her intellect told her there would be many problems in a con-nection with a man in prison. She concluded a person incarcerated was completely different from her existence in the free world and she was unfamiliar with prison existence. Cindy was smart enough to recognize a "hooking up" with Chester would be a difficult road to travel.

So she waited!

Besides, Cindy had her share of family problems. Shortly before meeting Chester, she was devastated when learning that her sixteen-year-old daughter, Heather, was pregnant.

Cindy read Chester's letter to Heather and saw Jason, Chester's son, had a birthday. It was in a list of family members and important dates in the letter. Heather recognized the date because she had once dated Jason. Heather exclaimed, "That's Jason's dad." Obviously, Heather told Jason, who in turn advised his dad.

A few days later, his second correspondence arrived addressed to Heather's mom.

Perhaps the fact that Heather had been friends with Jason brought Cindy the courage to write Chester back. So she took the first step in their relationship writing to him. "I wrote back and waited for a response. I remember driving all the way to the post office in anticipation of receiving another letter. When I opened the box and saw his handwriting, my heart did a little skip."

Cindy confesses to being somewhat vain at the time. How a person looked was important to her. She admitted to wanting a man in her life with a good heart, but if he wasn't good looking, he didn't stand a chance. "I remember holding Chester's letter in my hands and praying he wouldn't be bald. When I opened his letter and saw his picture, I realized God had a sense of humor. Not only was Chester bald, but he had arms loaded with tattoos."

God not only has a sense of humor, but a plan for lives dedicated to Him.

As Cindy began to read, she found an attraction to the writer; he had been a biker and now was a born again Christian. Chester, having been converted, shared his Lord with others.

As Chester wrote, he began to share his knowledge of Jesus with Cindy. In a few weeks, Cindy made a commitment to Jesus, as Chester had done in the hospital years before. They didn't realize it then, but they built their relationship on the solid foundation of Christ. The impact Chester's Christ has made on so many lives for Christ put Cindy on a collision course with Jesus also.

At once, Cindy and Chester rushed headlong into a relationship. "We didn't consider how fast we were moving. I know I did not. I talked to everyone about him, and I guess I was immune from reality by the feelings I was experiencing for him." She was so blind she did not notice the stares of confusion on everyone's face around her. "My family thought this was just another phase I was going through, but as our bond continued to grow, I was practically disowned by them."

Cindy did not realize then that God was, in her words, "pruning me," so she would perfectly fit in His plan for her life.

As the ties with her biological relations grew distant, she found a new family, the Christian friends of Chester that she met. They supported her and Chester in this mad romantic ride they both had embarked on.

To Chester, Cindy had become his "Beautiful lady." His words flattered her and his physical attraction and outlaw "rep" roped her in. In just two weeks, they talked of marriage.

Chester and Cindy started running ahead of God.

They made plans to meet at a weight lifting contest Chester had scheduled to participate in at Natchez. It would be their first face-to-face meeting. Chester wasn't a regular competitor, but he got added to the prison's team.

Cindy and her personal friend Jo drove to Natchez for the contest. "We arrived and entered the building where the competition was going on; we could not find Chester. I finally asked someone his location and they replied he never showed up to get on the bus. I didn't realize it then, but our whole life was about to change radically."

At the same time the Parchman weight lifting team was competing in Natchez, Chester was being accused of murder at the Internal Affairs building at Parchman.

Cindy drove back to Jackson, and as she walked into her house, she heard the phone ring. Cindy rushed to answer it and the operator announced the call was collect from Chester. "He was crying and I realized something bad had happened. He told me he, Vernon, and four other persons had been charged with a thirteen-year-old murder. I don't remember anything else except writing down a few names he gave me to contact. I promised him I would get him some help."

Cindy hung up the receiver and cried, tears for shattered dreams, and of an unfamiliar situation she did not know how to handle. She also wept because of a sudden uncertain future.

Suddenly, her romantic ride with her outlaw biker she had never seen had come to an abrupt stop.

In July of 1989, daughter Heather delivered a beautiful baby girl, Jessica Renee. Heather and Cindy had already discussed plans for her and decided to put Jessica up for adoption. Chester, alone in Parchman maximum security, encouraged them to keep the new addition. Perhaps Chester envisioned helping to raise her or remembered his devastating childhood. Whatever the reason, Heather decided to keep her new baby.

In the months and years to come, Jessica Renee would become a huge part in their lives.

Cindy soon began to learn that God helps us best when we don't know how to help ourselves. At times when the future appears difficult, God simplifies it.

Chester was "locked down" awaiting his trial in MSU and visitation seemed impossible. So Cindy continued their relationship by mail. "I was constantly concerned about Chester's mental state in lockdown. I tried to write as many letters as I could. I quoted scriptures, encouraging him to hang on. My family got tired of seeing me walk around the house with a pad in my hand. If I got the urge I wrote; some days two or three times."

Letter writing was their only method of communication. Cindy had calculated the enormous cost of prison collect phone systems. The expense of phone calls far exceeded her money to spend; her phone was disconnected.

Finally, arrangements had been made with the prison visitation department and Cindy would see Chester for the first time. It was now October of 1989.

Cindy remembers the day. "I was very nervous because I knew what he looked like from his pictures; his appearance would not be a problem. We had shared a tough emotional battle with his murder charge. Even without phone conversations, we exchanged a lot about ourselves in our letters. I got up at three a.m. to begin dressing, and left home before the sun came up. Never having been to the delta before, I began to think I would never get there.

When I arrived, I discovered how big Parchman was. Chester was wearing a yellow jumpsuit the first time I saw him. His handcuffs, attached to a waist chain, limited his movement. I remember thinking, 'Why is this necessary?' We would talk through a wire mesh opening. Every component about the visit was strange and very emotional for me. He sat down and smiled and that brought me back to reality."

Chester looked very handsome to Cindy, in spite of the chains and prison jumpsuit. Now Cindy realized the person she had been corresponding with was real. "As I drove away from the prison after our first visit, I believed I would fight his court battle with him, stand with him, regardless of the outcome."

***

The day Chester was to meet Cindy in Natchez, Mississippi, Chester had learned the State of Mississippi had a dreadful surprise for him. The State Parole Board was reviewing his case file each month and Chester prayed for freedom. He longed to return to society and he had been led to believe his release was close at hand.

On June 23, 1989, he was served with an arrest warrant for the murder of Ralph Edwards.

Chester vividly remembers what happened. "I was about to leave Parchman and compete in a weight lifting contest in the free world. The transportation officers were coming to pick me up. Sergeant Irons was the duty officer that day. He received a phone call advising him, as he said, to 'hold Chester in,' or keep him at the unit. Irons called me into his office and said to return my athletic gear to my locker and return to the control area. I was not going to the contest."

Chester did as ordered, but when Chester returned to the security area, Internal Affair Investigators and K-9 officers stood waiting for him. One of the investigators ordered him to "grab the wall," lean up against the wall with hands and arms extended above his head.

Chester obeyed the order without resisting.

Immediately, he was handcuffed and restraints locked on his ankles. He inquired as to where he was going, as they had shackled him hand and foot. The investigators remained silent and did not answer his question.

Chester was loaded into a white state van and taken to the small frame building of Internal Affairs two miles across the farm. Chester recalls his arrival. "When I walked in, prison investigators and policemen were crowded everywhere. The office space was crawling with them. They led me down the hall to the office of the Director of Internal Affairs and closed the door. First, the detectives advised me of my rights and asked if I understood them. I replied I did and they all began to ask me questions about where I had been on June third, 1976. I was unaware that was the day a man named Ralph Edwards was killed. I said I didn't know, as the day in question was fourteen years ago. A lot had happened since then. Next, they inquired if I killed Ralph Edwards or if I had any information about his murder. I replied that I didn't know Ralph Edwards and certainly didn't kill him."

After being questioned regarding the murder for four hours, Chester was put in the back seat of a State Highway Patrol investigator's vehicle and taken to Indianola, Mississippi. There, he appeared before a circuit court judge, who formally charged him with murder and robbery. The victim was a man Chester claimed he had never met in his life.

What Chester could not imagine then was a plot to incriminate him in the Edward's murder had been building for almost a month. Clark Foster, a casual acquaintance of Chester's from years past, had been arrested for arson in Sunflower County. In an attempt to plea bargain, he volunteered to give the sheriff a killer in an unsolved murder.

The same investigator who had interviewed Jorge Simmons years before, Lieutenant Bonham, began to build his case. In the absence of physical evidence, he would construct the case on the testimony of Clark and Toni Foster, with Vernon and Sherry Johnston. Chester's own brother soon would turn on him and name Chester as the killer, whether true or not. Chester's dream of freedom quickly turned into a nightmare of new charges. Now he faced capital murder charges and a possible death sentence.

**

Once Foster related his story, state and highway patrol investigators went to work to reopen the murder case. They recorded his testimony. Next, the detectives must locate Toni Foster, who lived in a neighboring state. They would travel twice before getting the corroborating statement they sought from the ex-Mrs. Foster.

On the first trip, Toni's attorney didn't allow her to say anything. The second time they came prepared with a document of immunity from prosecution. Then she was willing to meet and tell her side of the story to the investigators.

Toni returned to Mississippi only once, to take the witness stand in an Indianola, Mississippi, courtroom. Although arrest warrants had been prepared on four counts of robbery and murder, she would never face a district attorney in court. Clark also was given immunity on his four charges. The arson arrests from when he was caught red handed would later be dismissed.

F. Lee Bailey once called the type of testimony from the Fosters leading to Chester's conviction, "bought."

The gathering of information leading to Chester's arrest warrant was typical of many police investigations today. Without physical evidence, the charges are grounded on snitch testimonies, obtained with a promise of a lighter sentence to the one who testifies. Generally these types of unsubstantiated interviews are scary and unjust. Innocent men sit in prison, some on death row for years, as a result. A few of them create newspaper headlines upon release decades after their convictions, when the real perpetrators are apprehended or DNA evidence points to someone else.

Clark Foster's story to the sheriff came a day after his arrest. It led to Chester's arrest twenty days later. His was a typical jailhouse testimony to avoid punishment.

Additional testimonies had been acquired from Vernon Johnston, Toni Foster, and others in the next twenty days after Clark Foster ratted to the sheriff. Each one of their stories conflicted with Clark's original account to dodge prosecution.

When Clark Foster was arrested in 1989 for burning his uncle's mobile home to the ground in Shaw, Mississippi, the police had known he was the arsonist. The Shaw police had been acquainted with Clark for a long time.

In 1976, Clark had been an eighteen-year-old biker aficionado. Chester remembered him as a tall, stocky young man who wore his hair down over his shirt collar. Clark wanted people to think he was really "bad," a Bandito patch holder, but he wasn't. He had never been more than a small time punk.

Clark's arson crime could result in serious prison time at Parchman. Nobody wants to go to Parchman. So Clark decided to offer Sunflower County Sheriff Ned Holder information of a fourteen-year-old unsolved murder to avoid Parchman penitentiary.

Clark's personal history section in his arrest record states he was a known drug user, a coke head. Even so, the county sheriff, with the State of Mississippi, would buy his story. Knowing his story was obtained from an arrested arsonist and habitual drug user, they still believed it. Soon, using Clark's story, they began arrest proceedings that could possibly execute or confine Chester for the remainder of his life.

Foster's testimony concerned the murder of Ralph Edwards, also a resident of Clark's hometown, Shaw, Mississippi. When he was murdered, Mr. Edwards managed the Areo gas station in Indianola, Mississippi. Daily, he drove the same route to and from his home to work. Early on the morning of June 4, 1976, Edwards was found dead in his car in a cotton field off County Highway 448. He had been killed with a single gunshot in his head, behind his left ear.

The police learned that Ralph closed his station around seven in the evening of the June third. His bookkeeper testified he had brought the day's cash receipts to her at the store where she worked and then left. She was the last known person to see Mr. Edwards. Fourteen years later, Clark Foster related his account of the crime to the county sheriff.

Jack Sessums was sheriff at the time of the murder. He and his group of investigators arrived at the death scene the following morning. A law enforcement team found Mr. Edwards' car fifty feet off the road in a cotton field. Broken glass was located in the dirt and weeds on the shoulder of the road. Investigators assumed the glass had come from the driver's side window, which had been shot out. They determined Edwards' car left the roadway, ripped through a barb wire fence, jumped a drainage ditch, and came to a stop in a farmer's field.

Mr. Edwards' body was still in his vehicle, slumped over the steering wheel, with the driver side door open when the investigators arrived. His pants pockets had been turned inside out and several coins lay on the ground just under the vehicle. The sheriff's team recovered a .25 caliber bullet from the car. Few fingerprints had been found and taken from the inside of the car. All had been sent to the FBI lab in Washington, DC.

Nobody, then or now, has ever been matched to the prints from inside the car. The fingerprint memo read "assailant unknown." Fourteen years later, the message was ignored in light of Clark Foster's story.

No one's, much less Chester's, prints had matched when a comparison was made.

Fourteen years passed and the sheriff still had no suspects.

During the investigation, the shells, a .25 caliber pistol, source unknown, with the fingerprints, had been sent to the FBI lab. The FBI attempted to match the spent bullet found in the car and the one lodged behind the forehead of Mr. Edwards with the pistol found, but nothing matched. Later, another .25 caliber pistol was sent to Washington, but again, no match was found between it and the murder bullet.

All this time the case remained unsolved.

Enter Clark Foster, sitting in the county jail on arson charges. Foster had lived in Shaw, Mississippi, off and on all his life. Shaw is a small town located in the Mississippi Delta, with five hundred residents. Foster had known Ralph Edwards for years. At the time of the murder, Clark was eighteen, and married. His wife was twenty-one-year-old Toni.

She allegedly had been his "rap partner," or partner in crime, in robberies in Texas, Louisiana, and Mississippi. Very little is known about her. She claimed Chester and his girlfriend forcibly moved in with her and her husband in Jackson. Chester admitted having met her once or twice, once when he and Della lived in a motel in Jackson. Yet, even Vernon Johnston and his wife Sherry claimed to know nothing about her.

Two years after the murder of Mr. Edwards, Toni divorced Clark on grounds of habitual cruel physical treatment. During the trial, the only fear she mentioned was the accused, Chester Johnston. Her husband was a 250-pound, known wife beater, but the fact never came out in court.

As weak as the connection with Chester and the Fosters' was, the investigators are offered a murder suspect by Clark in an old murder case. His suspect is Chester Johnston, then a resident of Parchman. Foster names Chester as the shooter in the Ralph Edwards murder.

The story Foster tells the sheriff is a mixed up and long-drawn-out story of the events the day of the murder. His story identifies his wife, Chester, and his girlfriend, Chester's brother, Vernon, his wife and two children as being at the scene when Edwards was shot. Allegedly all the adults had some involvement in one way or another. Foster related a yarn, saying they had gone together to Indianola, Mississippi, to find a potential robbery victim.

He stated that the initial plan was to rob Edwards. Chester's girlfriend was to hang around the service station where Edwards worked and get friendly with him. When an opportune moment arose, she was to grab the money from the cash register and run. She had waited there for several hours, then decided the plan would not work. Supposedly, the rest of the gang sat in two cars and watched the target from down the road the whole time the girlfriend was at the store.

Later, when Vernon was questioned, poor Vernon could barely remember the story and he forgot the made-up time line. Earlier that day, the Fosters had come to his house, about twenty miles from Indianola. Later in the afternoon, they all, with Chester and his friend, drove to Indianola with robbery on their mind. Supposedly, Chester's friend entered the store when they got there. By contrast, Vernon's wife testified they had left her house just to go for a ride.

Foster also claimed Chester, who had never met Edwards, picked out his station to rob. Clark claimed Chester was angry when their plan failed and suggested they kill Edwards in retaliation upon his return to his home in Shaw. After murdering him, they could then take the day's cash receipts.

Foster maintained Chester thought up the murder plan to kill Edwards while on his drive home. But Chester did not know where Edwards lived, so how could he plan it? The truth was Foster lived in the same town as Edwards. Edwards had resided in Shaw all his life. In other words, Foster wanted the police to believe that Chester, who didn't know Edwards or where he lived, had thought up the plan to rob him on his way home.

Still, the State determined Foster had nothing to do with the planning, even though only he was acquainted the victim and his place of residence; Chester wasn't.

There are more problems with Foster's tale of murder. After Chester's girlfriend failed in her attempt grab the cash receipts and run, the rest of the gang, in two cars, decided to wait until Edwards closed for the day to commit the robbery. As Vernon's wife tells it, they have two young kids in the back seat on a stifling hot summer delta day. Their vehicle, admittedly with no air conditioning, had to be roasting hot and kids irritated at being confined in a hot car for hours. In the statement of Sherry Johnston, Vernon's wife, she stated the children acted irritably. Yet, Vernon and his wife wait for the robbery to take place throughout the afternoon and into the evening, as Clark tells it.

Vernon's story also differs in when the gang of toddlers and adults went to Indianola. He stated they all went to Indianola after he got off work at five or six o'clock. His story omits the children in the back seat, hot and hungry, probably asking every five minutes, "When are we going home?"

Foster's account was after waiting and sweating through a June afternoon and evening for Edwards to close up, all six robbers do not see Edwards leave. Somehow, Edwards removed the cash from the register, locked up, got into his car, and drove off before any of the waiting criminals realized what was happening.

The stories of the gang members differ about the account concerning the late waiting. Foster claims when they discovered Edwards had disappeared; Chester yelled HE was going to kill Edwards when he went home. Even though Foster's tale to the sheriff was an ambitious attempt to absolve himself of two crimes, it was also extremely ambiguous. If his chronicle had been scripted for TV, it would have viewers falling off their seats in laughter. Anyone can see the inconsistencies in their stories.

During her examination at trial, Mrs. Foster was asked the age of the two Johnston children. She replied she did not know, but simply stated they had not been teenagers. Then she added they seemed old enough they didn't have to be carried. The children's were actually four months and two and one half years of age. Hello! Toni, a four-month-old child, could walk? How could she be so wrong about the children ages? Possibly because she had not been supplied the answer beforehand, had never seen the children, but feebly tried to answer an apparently easy question?

Foster confirmed he owned the .25 caliber murder weapon used to kill Mr. Edward. It did not belong to Chester, as Vernon testified (with the promise of a reduced sentence). He testified he had seen Chester with two pistols the afternoon of the murder, Chester had shown them to him.

Again, at least if the Fosters are to be believed, Vernon is incorrect as to the ownership of the murder weapon. They acknowledged the gun was theirs!

The supposedly non-rehearsed testimonies of Clark and Toni did not agree concerning much of the events of the day. The details of the day's events did not add up. The pistol purchase was another. Clark stated his .25 caliber pistol was purchased from a pawnshop and given to Toni for protection. Toni remembered differently. She said Clark told her he traded a friend another weapon for it.

The friend who owned the .25 caliber weapon worked as a guard at Parchman. Not only was he a guard there, but in 1989, he had a confrontation with Chester. He claimed he went to Chester's cell to tell him to pack up for a move. Chester responded cursing him and threatening to "juge" (stab) him if he did not get away from him. Strange that this officer would play a role in accusing Chester. Stranger still that the supposed murder weapon would be acquired from a Parchman guard who had great animosity toward Chester.

Clark continued his history of the .25 caliber pistol. His testimony was he had given it to Toni and she had always hid it in her purse since its acquisition. In contrast, Toni was hazy regarding who had the pistol in their possession. She testified that she had it sometimes, and at other times, Clark kept it.

The inconsistency of the two stories continues to widen. Clark says Chester stole Toni's pistol from her purse during the day of the murder. Toni could not remember how Chester came into possession of her weapon. Both the husband and wife agreed Chester fired the pistol into the Edwards vehicle, killing the service station manager.

Yet, as laughable and inconsistent as the Foster's stories appear, the investigators believed it all.

Clark finally ended his gristly murder tale. He told he drove his mother's car and Vernon was driving Chester's vehicle out Highway 448, a dark and lonely road to Shaw, to wait for Mr. Edwards. Just before dark, Clark says he yelled, "There he goes," as he saw a green Plymouth traveling down the two lane highway toward Shaw. As Edwards passes them, Chester, as Clark tells the story, is in the front seat madly waving the murder weapon and pointing it at Clark, who is driving the car. Chester commands Clark to pursue the prey, because he was going to kill and rob him.

Throughout their individual statements, both Fosters testified they wanted no role in a murder plot. Later both gave testimony that Chester had threatened them with death if they did not comply with his murder plan.

Toni said the only reason she and Clark took part in the crime was to get Chester and his girlfriend to move out of their apartment. Mrs. Foster's statement was that Chester had no money and Clark promised when they got funds from the robbery, the outlaw and his female friend would leave. Vernon told investigators that the reason Chester said he and the crew went to Indianola was to recover some money from a man owed him there. It's hard to believe a high level drug distributor/construction worker needed to commit robbery to acquire any cash at all; more likely, it was a small-time biker "wannabe."

The crime time line is another part of Clark's story not corresponding to the testimony of the others. He said the party was in Indianola all afternoon and they waited for Edwards to close up just before sundown. (Vernon's wife stated she, Chester, Vernon, and the kids left her house just before dark to go for a ride.) Arcola is almost an hour's ride from Indianola. In early June, the sun would have set by the time they reached there.

Another factor not fitting is the differing stories regarding the identification of Mr. Edwards' vehicle. Clark surely knew it; both he and Edwards lived in Shaw, a town of a couple hundred people. No one saw the automobile when Edwards left the service station. What better way for Clark to avoid a murder and robbery than to simply not identify the victim's auto when he saw it pass. He didn't do that. Clark admitted he yelled, "There he goes."

During the trial, Chester's lawyer concluded the defendant's case by saying that Clark Foster killed Ralph Edwards when he yelled, identifying Edwards' auto as he traveled toward home, regardless of who fired the shot. The prosecutor continued, saying Ralph Edwards would still be alive today if Foster had kept quiet. That fact is undeniable.

Foster said the robbery took place on a dark road as they chased Edwards with Toni and Chester in his car, and Vernon, his wife and children, and Chester's girlfriend some distance behind. As he told it, once they came to a wide enough place in the highway where they could pull alongside Mr. Edward's Plymouth, Chester waved the pistol at Clark and ordered him to draw even with Edwards.

Yet here is another inconsistency in Clark's story. There is no confirmation Chester had ever been on Highway 448, only Clark. If this part of his story had been true at all, only Clark would know a wide straight place in the thoroughfare to move alongside Mr. Edwards in the darkness.

Clark and Toni, originally co-defendants with Chester, testified Chester leaned out the car window and fired into 'Edwards Plymouth. The Plymouth careened from the roadway and into the adjoining field. Once in court, the State attempted to solidify their case. Vernon's wife, who allegedly sat in the rear of the trailing auto, testified she saw a flash like a cigarette lighter in the car ahead of them. If it is possible to see a lighter flash from the back of a car tailing another at a high rate of speed on a winding road, then her testimony is plausible and adds to the evidence. Still, it's difficult to believe.

Next, Toni said Chester ordered Clark to stop the car. Clark slammed on the brakes of the chase car, bringing it to sudden halt. Allegedly, Chester opened the door of his vehicle and disappeared down a bank in the direction of Mr. Edwards' car. Toni testified she saw the overhead light of the victim's car come on in the darkness and believed Chester opened the door of the green Fury to rob the driver.

By contrast, Sherry Johnston, Vernon's wife, testified she saw a shadowy figure in the darkness from in back of the second car. But where was the car she was riding in located? Was it stopped or moving, close or far down the road when she saw the figure in the dark? We will never know because the question was not asked.

If the Fosters' tale is true, then Chester must have had a sixth sense telling him the fleeing driver was dead or unconscious. The night was pitch black, so dark a farm worker who lived close by later testified he could not see anything from beyond his front porch. Chester certainly could not have seen through the darkness of the cotton field fifty feet away and known the store manager was dead. He learned in Viet Nam to approach the enemy with caution. He would have determined if the driver was armed and waiting in his car to kill his adversary. Surely a trained and battle tested veteran such as Chester would not charge an unseen enemy in the dark. But the Fosters said he did.

Toni swore Chester reappeared by their car as quickly as he left. She swore Clark pleaded for Chester to return his pistol. Toni said Chester replied that he had thrown the .25 caliber pistol and a nickel-plated revolver found in the victim's car into the grass on the opposite side of the highway. She remembered Chester also threw a bloody shirt used to wipe his fingerprints off the Edwards car into the weeds bordering the field.

The story may be true. Yet the facts are no bloody shirt or abandoned pistols had been ever found at the scene. Extraordinary that none of the physical evidence pointing at Chester, as detailed in the Fosters' story, was found, although Toni said the killer discarded them at the crime scene.

Clark Foster concluded his story: When Chester returned from the victim's car, he threatened the couple with death if they told anyone what had happened. Then Chester jumped into the car with Vernon and the other family members, children and all, then sped away.

Toni concluded her story much like her spouse; when Chester returned to the car, Clark asked where his pistol was. Clark did not want the murder weapon traced back to him. Chester allegedly yelled that he threw the pistol away, and made the last of his death threats to Toni and Clark. At least they agreed on the last part of the story, that he told them to keep quiet or he would return and kill them. They also agreed both cars fled the dark crime scene and disappeared into the night.

To add creditability to the story, Clark told investigators he and Toni visited a friend's house in Shaw after the robbery-murder. They were so distraught by the night's events that they needed consoling. Neither the husband or the wife they supposedly went to visit remembers the a drop-in from the Fosters.

Without hard-core evidence, the investigators, fourteen years later, believed the Fosters' story rather than Chester, who swore he was not there.

Chester would learn later that Jorge Simmons renewed his acquaintance with Lieutenant Bonham after Clark Foster told his story. Simmons added information to his original snitch statement of 1981. In the mind of Bonham, at least, Simmons had provided enough information in 1989 to point an accusing finger to the murderer of Ralph Edwards. He named Chester Johnston.

Nineteen days after Clark Foster told his story, Investigator Bonham returned to Parchman to interview Jorge Simmons once again.

During his 1989 interview, Shooter Jorge told the police that Chester dealt drugs in prison, but kept the penitentiary police off his back by snitching to the area warden. Jorge continued; the only way Chester was able to keep his canteen operation was by alerting security about illegal activities.

Jorge Simmons's final payment for selling out his friend in 1989 was a gold ring. In 1989, the reason Shooter met with prison investigators was to recover an eighteen-carat ring supposedly stolen from him. He told Bonham and other 1989 detectives that the ring belonged to his daddy, which made it special.

However, those investigating quickly became more interested in other ramblings of Shooter Jorge besides his problem about his stolen ring.

At once, the eager witness began to talk about the Edwards murder. Subsequently, he would ramble from accusing to denying Chester's involvement in the murder during his interrogation. He did make enough accusations about Chester to supply Investigator Bonham a suspect in his fourteen-year-old unsolved murder case.

During their previous interview, Jorge talked about why he had stabbed Chester earlier. He alleged Johnston told inmates he had snitched, given him up. This truth must have seared Shooter's pride. Yet, Chester had told the truth to fellow prisoners about talking to Bonham. Jorge had made a vague statement in 1981 about the highway, linking Chester to the Edwards murder. Again in 1989, Jorge faced an inquisitor who probed and led his witness until Shooter Jorge gave up Chester once again.

The transcript of the meeting reveals how Simmons was led by investigators to name Chester as the killer. In the opening of the dialogue ultimately condemning Chester, Bonham inquired of Simmons exactly what Chester told him about the Edwards murder.

This is the transcript account.

Simmons: "I don't actually know that it's true or not," referring to Chester's bragging about killing Ralph Edwards.

Bonham: "That's what I want to know; just exactly what he told you about that."

Simmons: "To be quite honest with you, I can't even remember."

Read the words of this prison snitch again. "I can't even re-member." So he either remembers, or not. But Bonham continues relentlessly in his search for information to link Chester to the Edwards killing. After asking the same question three times, later in the interview he again asks, "You don't remember him telling you that he did it?"

Simmons: "Yeah, something about it."

One minute, Jorge can't recall being told, then he does remember. This is unadulterated snitch information that has landed many people on death row.

As Jorge's memory returns, Bonham continues in his attempt to nail Chester.

Bonham: "Do you think Chester's capable of doing something like that?"

Simmons: "Oh yeah, sure he is."

Bonham: "I don't ever quit looking at it [the murder] and I mean that."

The investigator shows how important finding the killer has been to him over the years. Investigators are promoted based upon convictions.

Simmons: "I believe he done it, but it ain't no concern to me."

From this point on, Jorge now remembers several of the people Chester supposedly said was with them the fateful night of Ralph Edwards' death. He recalls Chester's girlfriend and brother Vernon as being there; however, he never mentions Clark or Toni Foster as being part of the crime, although they alone could identify Edwards.

Additionally, Jorge not only gave Chester up on this occasion, but several penitentiary officers and inmates as well. And if Jorge thought the dialog would never be published, he was wrong. In just one interrogation, Jorge gave information on eight individuals that could incriminate them all.

It's the truth; Chester branded Shooter as a snitch and the police record proves he had been.

The next day, the sheriff prepared arrest warrants for Vernon and Sherry Johnston, as well as Chester's girlfriend. The charges against each defendant were murder, conspiracy to commit murder, robbery, and conspiracy to commit robbery. Of the six people charged in the crime, only two, Chester and brother Vernon, would ever face a jury of their peers on the charges.

Curiously, Chester's girlfriend was never questioned. The only person who possibly could collaborate or collapse the State's case never gave an official statement. The police scheduled her to come to the police station, but she never showed up. Again and again, the police scheduled to meet with her. She never met with them or offered one word of testimony, yet they dropped her charges.

Chester was flabbergasted when served with the warrants the day he was to meet Cindy in Natchez. He has affirmed from the day of his arrest until today that he did not kill Ralph Edwards and had never heard of him prior to his arrest. Moreover, he hardly knew the Fosters.

Later, prior to the trial, an ex-FBI agent would attempt to clear Chester by finding information of Chester's whereabouts at the time of the murder. Inquiries were mailed to former employers, the IRS, and other sources, but nobody kept records for fourteen years. They requested Chester's father and stepmother try and remember his work record, but no records existed proving where he had been. Too much time had slipped by.

Chester had lived a life on the run, riding with bikers, transporting drugs. When he needed an alibi, his past had closed in behind him. Chester got dealt a hand of aces and eights, the dead man's hand. Living in Mississippi, all the cards were stacked against him. Rather than the State being forced to prove him guilty, he was put in a position to have to prove himself innocent.

Fourteen years after the act, with all physical evidence missing and with faded memories, Chester could not provide himself with an alibi.

Chester's shock over his arrest subsided slowly. His bitterness and anger became replaced by an urgency to prepare for a fight for his life. His door to freedom had been slammed shut. Part of Chester's spirit died then.

There comes a time to dismiss shock, wipe away the tears, and to begin a battle to live. Chester would be forced to return from a spiritual grave to continue living. The first item on his agenda was to employ a lawyer. Chester had no money to engage one, having been locked up for eleven years. So the court filed an order requiring the state to provide funds for his defense. Initially, the court appointed an attorney who told Chester the State was not providing adequate funds for him to continue the case. He needed to spend a lot of time on Chester's case and required more money. Chester had him removed and another lawyer appointed.

The court decreed one thousand dollars be given for a legal defense, and two lawyers were engaged. The first attorney was Pascal Townsend of Drew, Mississippi. Mr. Townsend was well known and respected throughout Mississippi for his legal prowess. He had borne the weight of many trials on his slim frame. Under his thin gray hair was a brilliant legal mind. The second member of the legal team was Jim Sherman, from Indianola.

Chester began regular meetings with his defense lawyers at the penitentiary. The small visitors area made it difficult to discuss his case. But if Chester would live and possibly regain his freedom, they must make the best of a thorny situation.

When Clark Foster was arrested for arson in early June of 1989, he wasted no time getting the attention of the Sunflower County Sheriff, Jack Sessums, with his overdue story of how Ralph Edwards died. After he acquired a "deal," plea bargain, from the authorities, he implicated five more people in the murder scheme.

But his accusations pointed mostly toward Chester Johnston. Foster stated Chester planned it and had been the killer who carried out the plan and fired the bullets into the car and body of Ralph Edwards. In return for his testimony, Foster would never face a jury of his peers for arson or his role in the death of Mr. Edwards, even though his testimony would not be used in the trial against Chester. It seems evident the State was afraid to put him on the stand. In contrast, Chester's attorney preferred to cross-examine Clark's damaging lies in front of the jury.

Clark's story began Chester's road to conviction, but for one reason or another, he never appeared in the courtroom.

***

Fourteen years after the murder, Clark's story presented the

State with difficulties. No matter what information Chester's attorneys came up with, they could not dent the case against Chester and Clark's story.

Chester's lawyers found a fellow inmate of Foster's in the county jail who discredited Clark's story completely. The cell partner was Victor Hurns, and he swore his story to be the truth and that Foster had lied. In September of 1990, Victor gave an affidavit that in June of 1989 Clark had returned to his cell bragging he would soon be turned loose. He boasted he told the sheriff about a crime committed fourteen years before. Clark bragged he got himself out of his involvement in the crime by putting another guy in it.

After his discussion with the sheriff, Foster said to Hurns that he would get a lighter sentence. Foster continued his swaggering talk, saying he once killed a guy named Ralph Edwards. He had passed him on the Shaw road, turned around, pulled up beside Edwards, and shot him.

Certainly, the account told to Hurns is a more plausible story than the one he told the police. Foster related he passed Edwards going home, and flagged him down. Most likely, the killing happened as Clark related to Hurns. Since Edwards had been acquainted with Clark, it is likely he would pull over on the side of the road to wait for someone he had known all his life.

Foster supposedly turned his car around and drove up to Ralph's car and shot him through the side window. Then, taking whatever Edwards had of value, he pushed the car over the side of the road, down the embankment, and into the field, with the ignition in the off position.

Law enforcement believed they had their murderer. Clark had named Chester Johnston to authorities in the Edwards' death. They had no time for another version as told by another inmate. They just wanted a conviction.

During the Defense presentation, Hurns would take the witness seat to offer his testimony. As quickly as he sat down, the assistant district attorney for the State silenced him with a motion. She argued Hurns statement contained hearsay evidence and was therefore inadmissible before the court. The judge quickly agreed and Hurns left the courtroom. The court never heard Hurns testify that Clark had lied.

The state requested and received a grant of immunity for Toni Foster. They called her lawyer and said she would be released from any responsibility in the crime if she testified for the State. Toni would be permitted to tell her version of the crime story without fear of prosecution, even though she, by her own admission, participated in it.

Mrs. Foster's statement alerted the defense lawyers; they noticed the minor inconsistencies of Toni's narrative compared with her ex-husband's account of the night long since past. One glaring discrepancy was the acquisition of the murder weapon by Clark Foster. As mentioned earlier, Clark stated he traded for it with a Parchman guard, yet Toni swore under oath that Clark told her he bought the weapon at a pawnshop.

They also differed on who had possession of the gun. Toni could not even remember how Chester supposedly had taken the weapon from her. It was in her purse or not in there, or she didn't know who possessed it on the night or how she lost it.

Clark's story of acquiring the pistol was that he purchased it and it was registered, therefore legal. However, Toni's account was Clark acquired an unregistered, unlicensed weapon from a Parchman guard. In court, her statement wasn't favorable to the State case and would not be presented.

Clark did not want to be seen as having an illegal gun, so it became a hot potato. He surely didn't even want the pistol to have been in his hands after he acquired it.

Another contradictory point in the Fosters' accusations had to do with Chester's supposed behavior during the chase of Mr.

Edwards. Clark said Chester pointed the handgun at him as he drove and Toni remembered Chester just waving the gun wildly. Minor points, yet why did their stories differ?

Preparing for the trial, Chester's lawyers discovered from Toni's statement to Mississippi investigators and her testimony in court that she appeared uncertain of when and who changed the plan of robbery into murder. She firmly testified Chester had first presented the scheme to shoot Edwards. However, she couldn't remember hearing Chester say it. She simply said that, after the Edwards car left the service station, Chester became angry and decided to kill Ralph. But remember; they said they didn't see it leave.

Chester and his lawyers had an abundance of work to do. They must review the statements of the former husband and wife and the other State witnesses. There was more data in the case to be discovered than simply the Fosters' charges against Chester.

Chester's attorneys requested the discovery evidence from the district attorney. By law, 'all the States data and the State's witness statements must be turned over to the Defense term. The defense lawyers made a written request of the DA for the evidence file, now fourteen years old. They had been stonewalled by the DA's office. Finally, after filing a motion for the file to be turned over, they made a remarkable discovery. The existing evidence file, with fingerprints, and the recovered bullets and pistols supposedly associated with the murder had gone missing. Crime scene notes and pictures had also disappeared. Even though the file had been locked in the sheriff's safe for many years, no one on the staff had any idea where it might be located. The defendant's team quickly filed a motion to dismiss all charges on grounds Chester could not properly defend himself without the original evidence from the crime scene.

The court ruled against the motion. Judge Davis ruled the evidence had little effect on Chester's ability to defend himself and ruled against the Defense, most likely a first in Mississippi jurisprudence history.

Some of the State's documents had been received. The DA supplied the statements of the Fosters' and the letters and replies between the sheriff and FBI in 1976 and 1977. The autopsy report was also provided. A letter from the State about Toni Foster's immunity was given to them

With all the missing evidence, the defense attorneys quickly saw they did not have sufficient time to properly prepare Chester's defense, so they filed a motion setting aside the trial date of early 1990 until a later date. The court granted this motion.

Filing a motion for a special *ex-parte* hearing had been an additional task facing the defendant and his lawyers. This action, too, would be denied by the court. The defense attorneys then appealed to the State Supreme Court, and were denied again.

One other important matter disposed of by Chester's lawyers was making Chester's trial separate from the five other defendants. At the time of Chester's indictment, the other adults known to be at the crime scene, as testified to by Toni and Clark Foster, received the same charges of murder and robbery. To date, only Chester and his brother Vernon would ever be brought before the bar of justice for Mr. Edwards' murder.

In hindsight, this move to separate the other defendants may have backfired on Chester. Trying all of them at one time would have brought them into the courtroom together. On cross-examination, all their statements under oath would be compared. Also, the inconsistencies with their previous statements and corroborating testimony could have been reviewed. With the fear of a guilty verdict facing all of them, a crack in the ranks began to appear. If the division had continued, the truth might have come out. If just one conspirator had cracked, the whole truth may have come to light. No doubt the others indicted believed Chester should take the rap alone, and he did.

Many other Defense motions were filed; the court denied them. They are part of the preliminary proceedings preceding all trials. Chester submitted to a mental examination, requested by the State. They hoped to eliminate insanity pleas. Chester, after being examined, was demined to be mentally sound.

Yet, hindsight is always perfect. We can't know how the case would have turned out with different circumstances and untested decisions.

In spite of all his new enemies, Chester had acquired a powerful new ally in his life. The lady he had met in response to a lonely hearts ad continued to visit him. They continued their relationship while he waited in MSU for his trial.

Cindy continued to visit Chester twice a month until he moved to Unit Thirty-Two, a new lockdown unit. Now the visitation schedule was cut back to one visit a month. Cindy never missed a V day, except when she had her nursing license renewed.

"I'm not going to say I didn't get weary of the traveling. Sometimes I even questioned why I kept doing it. But during my little time with Chester, God had become so real in my life, His strength kept me going."

In addition to the stress of a prison relationship, Cindy experienced financial problems at home. She was raising two girls and a granddaughter on an insufficient income. "Sometimes we had very little food to eat. I spent much of my time down on my knees in prayer. And all through this period, my relationship with Chester and our relationship with God continued to grow."

Cindy attempted to keep Chester from knowing about the financial difficulties at home. She didn't want to add to his worries. He had become her best friend.

Somewhere along the journey, she had fallen in love with him. Cindy had made the decision to stand by her man. The hard times made the bond between them stronger. She learned more and more about her man and his loving heart.

"One day, I received a check for two hundred and fifty dollars from Chester. Chester had sold his TV and sent the proceeds for us to live on. Chester thought about us all the time and did all he could to help provide for us."

Chester never asked anything in return for his acts of kindness. All he wanted from her was her love. Feeling a part of a real family for the first time provided him an escape from the murder charges he faced.

In turn, his preparation for trial stayed constantly on Cindy's mind. God developed His plan for the lives of Cindy and Chester as they grew deeper in love. And through all the difficulties, they learned to trust Him more.

CHAPTER EIGHTEEN

LIFE OR DEATH

Within the order of Judge Davis for Chester's trial is a statement that the judge considered the case unusual. This is because fourteen years separated the murder from the arrest and trial of the alleged killer. There were other extraordinary circumstances in the case identified by the judge. Perhaps the most unusual one had to do with the role Lieutenant Jesse Bonham played in the Edwards murder investigation.

The account of Chester's trial is incomplete without considering this element.

Lieutenant Jesse Bonham served as the Highway Patrol investigator in the Edwards case that culminated in the arrest of Chester. Bonham had served the State for twenty-two years, ten of them as an investigator. His first involvement in the Edwards' murder case came in 1981 when he interviewed Parchman inmate, Jorge Simmons.

The details of Bonham's first interrogation in 1981 are rather vague. Apparently, his first questioning had been directed toward another inmate involved in a money scam Simmons had knowledge of. During this interview, Shooter Jorge, as he was called, mentioned that an inmate, Chester Johnston, had bragged to him about killing a man on the road from Indianola to Shaw, Mississippi. Why the discussion turned to Chester's bragging is not known.

The investigator's story would change in his court testimony from what he said in his June 20, 1989, conversation with the informant, Shooter Jorge. On the witness stand under oath, Bonham stated he had information from Simmons regarding an incident involving Chester and his girlfriend in 1981. However, in his 1989 meeting with Simmons, Bonham told Jorge he had never mentioned Chester's girlfriend. Shooters reply had been that he had indeed told the investigator previously about the girlfriend.

After the 1981 interview with Jorge, Bonham sent the informant's statement to the then sheriff of Sunflower County, Jack Sessums. Apparently Sheriff Sessums wasn't able to tie Chester to the murder by fingerprints from the crime scene or other information from the investigation. The sheriff replied to Bonham's letter by sending handwritten notes, six or eight photographs, and a couple observations to Investigator Bonham. By his own admission, Bonham said he found no leads or ties from the sheriff's information to Chester then.

Officer Bonham's investigation remained in the file for eight years, until Clark Foster was arrested for arson. Lieutenant Bonham was contacted after Foster told his wild story that involved six people in the Edwards murder, four adults and two children. The investigator learned Foster had named Chester Johnston as the trigger man. This information now put Bonham back on Chester's trail.

The lieutenant testified during the trial that he had been given a suspect in 1981, provided by Shooter Jorge. His memory of Simmons' statements conflicts with the recorded transcript of his interview with the informant. This transcription contains many statements from Jorge Simmons which differ as to exactly what Chester told him about the murder. Jorge also waffled regarding whether or not he actually believed Chester's bragging, which is how he supposedly overheard the murder story.

The truth according to Chester is that he never told Jorge he had committed the murder. Later during his interview with Bonham, Jorge stated he overheard Chester bragging to some other inmates that he had actually pulled the trigger. Jorge never revealed who the fellow prisoners had been, probably out of fear of reprisal. Furthermore, none have ever been interviewed by Investigator Bonham with reference to Chester's braggadocio statements or the death of Mr. Edwards, not before or since the trial. Unusual investigating, if Bonham had been searching for the truth!

In addition, on the witness stand, Bonham, when asked if he had ever confronted Chester with Shooter's story concerning bragging that he had committed the murder, replied he had. The next question to Bonham by the assistant district attorney was, "Did Chester say anything?"

Bonham replied, "Chester had not answered any questions about it."

The next question was, "Did he refuse to answer or did he deny Simmons' accusations?"

Bonham testified that Chester had denied the story.

Mississippi limits the use of snitch testimony. The law is on the books for good reason. It is there to prohibit "bought" testimony that unjustly condemns a man or woman. Simmons never told his story in the courtroom as a State's witness. Perhaps the State had been fearful Shooter would damage their case in front of the jury more than he would help it. Yet, his snitching was the foundation of murder charges filed against Chester eight years later.

To correctly appraise Jorge Simmons' testimony, one must know Jorge's background. Jorge has always been a rough looking character, with an extremely dirty mouth. I personally spoke with him on one occasion and listened to him on an emergency phone call where it seemed he thought his vulgar talk would cause people to fear him. Vulgarity is used as a tool of intimidation by some. His arms and torso are decorated with tattooed penitentiary art. The tattoos are of the biker genre. Simmons loves to loudly boast about the money he has made, in prison and out. At fourteen, Jorge lived with Chester and Della for some time.

From an early age, Jorge became involved in several minor crimes. He confessed to being an accomplice in a robbery, supposedly with Chester. He also admitted breaking into and robbing homes. Jorge has been convicted of felony offenses against the State three times and is at the time of writing in prison. His MDOC record identifies him as a "habitual criminal" and insures he will stay there for twenty-five years.

During one stint in Parchman, he was the ringleader in many money order scams. Money order scams occur when inmates have contact with someone in the outside world who supplies orders to them with a face value of one dollar. The amount of the money order is then erased by a chemical process and changed to a much higher amount. The highest dollar value change was $702.00. Some inmates are experts at this. Later, the document is smuggled into the free world and cashed by an accomplice and the ready funds returned to the inmate.

Another ruse is when inmates contact an unwitting person in the free world and cultivate a person there using the U.S. mail until they can be trusted. When the time is right, they tell a sorrowful story requiring the free world Clark to send a wire transfer. The sender has no idea they are sending funds to a Parchman prisoner.

In the eighties, the Parchman inmates had so many money scams going on that the governor ordered a full investigation into them. As a result, dozens of prisoners were taken to maximum security units for their roles in duping the public. Shooter Jorge had been the acknowledged king of money order scams.

I personally heard him tell his sister during a phone conversation that he would kill her if she did not retrieve some of his money and get it to him. This is the man who implicated Chester in the murder of Ralph Edwards. Shooter had not been exactly a tower of truth.

After Bonham learned of Foster's story to the sheriff, he wasted no time in driving to the Bolivar County jail and interviewing Clark. He listened as Clark related his story, naming Chester as the Edwards assassin.

Less than twenty days after this meeting, Bonham returned to Parchman to renew acquaintances with his old informant, Shooter Jorge.

Bonham guided his stool pigeon throughout the conference to get the information he wanted. The dialogue seemed to indicate Bonham already knew what he wanted, but wanted Jorge to confirm them. Had the lieutenant searched for the truth or simply made an attempt to encourage Simmons to accuse a killer?

At the start of their meeting, Bonham attempted to clear the air of a prior problem with Jorge. The predicament stemmed from Chester in 1981 learning Jorge had snitched on him to Bonham regarding the Edwards murder. Jorge had been labeled a snitch around Parchman. So he figured Bonham or someone had leaked who had implicated Chester. As previously stated, Simmons suffered a lot of grief when the word got out. Investigator Bonham had to soothe this problem over before Simmons would cooperate.

Lieutenant Bonham believed Simmons shanked Chester; as a result, word leaked around the prison from their interview. Jorge denied that the snitch references had been the reason, but nonetheless, he stuck Chester three times in a shower. Jorge also told the investigator the stabbing had been related to another incident, but Simmons had been lying.

Once the air cleared in the interview, Bonham directed the conversation to the Edwards murder, using a direct question to

Jorge regarding Chester's role in the killing. Jorge replied, "I don't actually know if it's true or not," then added, "To be quite honest with you, I can't even remember."

Bonham continued to press his informant, asking, "You don't remember him telling you he did it?"

When Jorge doesn't respond as he wants, Bonham changes the direction of the interview by telling Simmons how interested he is in convicting Chester on the murder charge. "I don't ever quit looking at it, and I mean that." It seems strange Bonham cannot get the case off his mind when he never played a role in its investigation back in 1978 when it occurred.

In response to the investigator's obsession concerning the case, Jorge says, "I think Chester done it, the murder."

Later in the interview, Jorge is asked by Bonham what Chester received from the robbery. Jorge said he had been told a couple of money sacks. Nowhere in anybody's testimony is any mention made about sacks of money. Bonham should have known Shooter lied.

Feeling successful thus far, the patrol investigator leads Jorge to get additional corroboration. "Did he [Chester] say anything about a pistol?"

Shooter suddenly remembered Chester said something about a .357 magnum; the only person involved in the case mentioning a .357 magnum pistol was Chester's brother Vernon. Where had Shooter got this information? If Bonham had become more informed about the case, he would know Jorge scammed him when the mention of this caliber pistol did not match the weapon used in the murder. Still, Investigator Bonham continued his line of questioning.

Later, to encourage Jorge to assist him in closing the case, Bonham says to him, "Frankly, I've never stopped thinking about that, and I would like to finish it out, you know finish the case."

And finish the investigation he would, with probably the wrong man on trial.

During this consultation, Jorge made the following comments regarding Chester's culpability. "I never believed it [the shooting], to be honest with you, and he never came out and honest and truly told me he had done anything." Then toward the end of the meeting, "Just for a fact, I really don't know if he done that, see."

Strange testimony indeed, still never brought out in the trial.

In Jorge's defense, he did not know Bonham's tactics for this interview. It became the origin of the charges brought and the eventual conviction of Chester for capital murder.

Immediately after his 1989 interview with Simmons, Bonham was added to the murder investigative team. He rushed to Alabama to quiz Toni Foster. The scent of his prey was getting stronger and he did not intend to lose it.

Under cross-examination during the trial, Bonham had been questioned about his original trip to Alabama. He testified that Toni's attorney related enough to him then about Toni's knowledge of the crime to be assured she had first hand knowledge about it.

As mentioned, Bonham received a grant of immunity from the Mississippi District Attorney, absolving Toni from conviction. Once obtained, he quickly returned to Alabama to get her story. When Toni had finished telling her story, Bonham hustled back to Mississippi. He interviewed Vernon and Sherry Johnston both on the same day. They had since divorced, with Sherry living on the Gulf Coast and Vernon residing in Arcola, Mississippi. After these interviews, he had arrest warrants made out for all six of the conspirators: Chester, his girlfriend, Vernon and Sherry Johnston and Clark and Toni Foster.

Although Toni testified that she'd had no contact with her former husband in fourteen years, their stories generally seemed to match. Lieutenant Bonham stated under oath that he had not discussed any of Clark's story with his former wife. Did their stories tell the truth about contingency plan years before, when they committed the crime, maybe without Chester? Or better yet, had they talked on the phone before the Jackson investigators returned the second time?

One of the many arguments between the State and Defense attorneys centered around the highway patrol investigative file. A brown binder supposedly contained all the notes of Lieutenant Bonham's work. However, no record of his interview of Jorge Simmons or Chester Johnston in 1981 existed. These records were not delivered to the Defense team.

Additionally, no record exists in Sheriff Sessum's file of Bonham's contact concerning Chester as a suspect in 1981.

Unusual record keeping!

Lieutenant Bonham has served the state of Mississippi for many years with outstanding service. Without question, he had an unquenchable craving to solve this case. Could this be a need for the truth in Chester's case? Perhaps! Be sure and don't forget Chester's protection agreements with the highway patrol and his beating of the state official who attempted to shake him down.

In conclusion, we know that, in 1981, Bonham didn't play a role in the investigation of the Edwards case. Then he received Chester Johnston's name from an infamous jailhouse snitch. When Clark Foster had been arrested 1989, Bonham rushed to interview Clark, and then renewed old friendships with Shooter Jorge. From there, he went to Alabama to acquire Toni's damning story.

Lieutenant Bonham took her story, the snitch testimony of Shooter Jorge, and Clark's story, refuted by inmate Burns, and arrested Chester Johnston for the murder of Ralph Edwards. The arrest led Chester to an Indianola courtroom.

***

Chester's trial for murder lasted just four days. Two days had been spent in *voir dire,* the jury selection. The trial documents were identified as the State of Mississippi versus Chester Johnston. The State's star witness would be Toni Foster. All other witnesses, except Sherry Johnston, would present no evidence pointing toward Chester.

The Defense really had just one witness, Chester Johnston.

The State of Mississippi's lead prosecutor was Mrs. Hallie Gail Bridges, Assistant DA. She opened the State's prosecution case by calling the daughter of Mr. Edwards. The only information she added was that her father managed the Areo service station in Indianola.

Next in line came the cash register clerk from the station, who added that Ralph Edwards was at work the day of the murder. She also remembered a young girl left by friends and Edwards gave her something to eat and she stayed there all afternoon.

The bookkeeper followed, and testified that Edwards delivered the day's cash receipts to her on the night he had been killed. None of the witnesses said they had seen Chester or any of the other people arrested in the murder.

The State began to build its case by establishing a sequence of facts.

The DA then called the investigators who first arrived at the crime scene. All they could relate was the scene appearance that day and describe the evidence they found. The physical materials found were the two .25 caliber bullets and fingerprints taken from the dashboard of the vehicle Edwards had been driving.

The crime scene investigators all agreed no weapon had ever found, in or near the scene. They could not recall a bloody shirt being retrieved near the site, which negated Toni's testimony. No suspect or suspects had been discovered in the past fourteen years. All the physical evidence gathered, bullets, fingerprints, and photos, didn't provide a suspect. The conclusions of their testimony? A murder had been committed. No physical evidence found at the scene tied any defendant, much less Chester Johnston, to the scene, much less the crime.

The prosecution continued their case, calling the coroner. He summarized the pathological report he had performed. He concluded that Ralph Edwards was killed by a .25 caliber bullet entering his head behind his left ear and lodging in the front of his skull. The information he provided was that Mr. Edwards had been shot and died. That was all the DA needed from the coroner in her march toward what she hoped would end in a murder conviction. Their plan of attack was proceeding as planned.

Next, the Assistant DA called its star witness, Toni Foster. Her information was presented under a grant of immunity from prosecution. She had been charged, like Chester and the others. The case Chester was being tried for, which could put him away for life or possibly result in an execution, she was exempted from. Still, the State's purpose for their star was to point the finger of guilt at Chester. Toni took the stand with no fear of incrimination to herself. Furthermore, the State would not call her husband because their stories might conflict, and they would have.

Her story on the stand matched what she had told investigators in Alabama when they first met. They had just planned to rob Mr. Edwards' station t to begin with. Once this strategy failed, Chester suggested Edwards be killed and they take his money. Toni swore under oath that she and Clark never had been a part of any scheme to kill anyone. To hear them tell it, Clark and Toni never wanted a part in a murder.

The cross-examination by the Defense failed to knock any large holes in Toni's carefully laid out story. Moreover, during the cross, the court would exclude any reference to her husband's drug use on the day in question. She admitted in her original statement that Clark had driven on back roads because he was smoking marijuana.

Even though she had been positive Chester had used her pistol in the killing, she did not remember how Chester took the weapon from her, only that he had. Her testimony put Chester at the crime scene and placed the revolver in his hands. She alone placed Chester in jeopardy of losing his life in the gas chamber. One major incident marring the stories Clark and Toni told to investigators did not check out. They both swore that, after the murder, they drove around crying because of what had occurred. Finally, they went to the home of one of Clark's drug smoking friends for consolation in Shaw. The highway patrol investigated the supposed visit, interviewing both the husband and wife the Fosters said they visited. Neither recalled Clark and Toni coming to their house that night.

This fact was dismissed and never presented to the jury by the Defense.

Taking the witness stand next for the State was Vernon Johnston's wife, Sherry. Her story related to the events leading up to leaving for Indianola and what she saw from the vehicle trailing Chester and the Fosters on the night Mr. Edwards was killed. She told her version of the night, testifying the six adults, complete with children, left her house close to dark. From the time she left her house until the firing of the pistol, she offered no corroborating facts of anything else. She only reported seeing a flash in the car ahead and concluded Chester had shot Ralph Edwards. When asked by the assistant district attorney if she had been promised anything for her testimony, she responded no. The State's lawyer asked, "Have I told you to say anything about that night?"

Sherry responded, "Only it would not be used against me."

Vernon's wife fulfilled her purpose for the State's prosecutors. Toni pointed to Chester as the murderer and Sherry had confirmed it. Husband Vernon did not take the witness stand. The Defense would be able to shoot holes in his version of the murder. Rather than call him themselves, later they concluded he would just lie and further confuse the situation. So Vernon never came into the courtroom.

Finally, the State called its "big gun" in the case, Lieutenant Bonham. He related his interview with inmate Jorge Simmons and how he provided him with the suspect in the Edwards case.

Probably because of the possible damage to the prosecutor's case, Shooter Jorge wasn't ever called to the stand. The state didn't want him anywhere near the courtroom. His story could be ripped apart by the Defense counsel and the DA had no room for cracks in their fragile case.

There was no point in the Defense calling Jorge, either. A liar and a proven snitch would not help their cause. The prosecutors had their killer on the statement of a thief, money order con man, and proven liar. In addition to Shooter Jorge, they had two women who admittedly were involved in the commission of the crime.

The State rested its case after calling Sheriff Ned Holder to say he had no idea where the missing evidence file with the bullets, guns, fingerprints of crime scene photos had vanished to. Judge Davis ruled with a straight face; in his opinion, the missing file would not affect Chester's case. With those materials gone which possibly would exonerate Chester, he appeared guilty.

The missing evidence file became more important in Chester's appeal than in the trial, but it could have been the key to the Chester's defense. The chain of evidence had been damaged by the change of sheriffs during the fourteen-year span from the crime to Chester's arrest. The 1976 sheriff, Jack Sessums, said the file had once existed and the evidence, prints, and pictures had been put into the evidence safe. His successor, Sheriff Ned Holder, testified that he did not ever remember seeing the guns or bullets in the safe. The conclusion of both sheriffs was that, evidently, the file of evidence had been misplaced or lost.

The suggestion of the Defense was that perhaps the file had been conveniently misplaced or removed.

The State's case in a nutshell had been that Ralph Edwards was alive the day of the murder. He closed his station and delivered the daily cash receipts to the company bookkeeper. Toni Foster swore Chester had been the man who killed Edwards on his way home after they had stalked him all day. Vernon's wife, Sherry, saw Chester fire the pistol from the dark back seat of the trailing car. Investigators went to the scene and found some physical evidence, which later disappeared. The service station owner is dead, and so Chester had killed him. Weak or not, this was the complete State's case.

If there was any humor during the trial, it came from a witness called by the Defense. The witness was a black man named Manuel Bryley. He had been riding his bicycle home from Shaw, Mississippi, on Highway 448 after visiting his girlfriend on the night of the murder. It had been late when he got ready to leave, so his lady offered to give him a ride home. When his bicycle wouldn't fit into her vehicle, he declined her offer and peddled off into the night.

His vivid description of his subsequent bicycle accident in the darkness, dumping him in a water ditch and covering him with mud, brought roars from the courtroom audience.

Manuel continued his testimony, saying later the same dark night, after he arrived home, he went onto the front porch, which was close to the murder scene. He was enjoying a cup of coffee. That night, he didn't know Ralph Edwards car with Ralph dead inside was in the field across from his house. He did remember seeing a pickup truck stop on the highway and the driver get out and stand in front of the headlights. Next, the driver disappeared, walking into the darkness toward the field where the Edwards Plymouth Fury was found the next day. Thirty minutes later, so

Manuel said, the pickup driver reappeared, got into his truck, and drove off into the night.

The point of the Defense was to suggest someone other than Chester had killed Ralph Edwards and returned to the scene. Could the real killer be the man Manuel swore he had seen in front of the pickup? If not the killer, why was he there on a dark, lonely night for thirty minutes? Half an hour is much too long for a rest stop.

The State's prosecutor ridiculed Manuel's story and dismissed any other possible murderer other than the defendant. Humor would be all Mr. Bryley would bring to the jury and the courtroom.

The defense made a point about the missing evidence file. Chester would have used the evidence against the State and gained acquittal. However, the judge ruled against the plea of the Defense.

Some testimony conflicted with Sheriff' Sessums, regarding no murder weapon being found. The sheriff stated under oath that no weapon had been found at the crime scene. However, one of the female clerks employed at the Sheriff's Department had a different recollection. She stated the sheriff told her a weapon had indeed found there. Supporting her claim was a document from a Cleveland attorney who represented the Ralph Edwards family in an insurance suit. He also swore in an affidavit that the sheriff told him there was a weapon found at the crime scene.

The Cleveland lawyer became involved in the case when the Edwards family sued their insurance company, claiming Ralph had been involved in an accident some time the day he was killed. The attorney remembered his discussion with Sheriff Sessums when the murder trial was announced in the papers. His notes confirmed his recollection the sheriff had told him a weapon had indeed been found at the scene.

However, the assistant DA would object to his statement as

being hearsay evidence, and the court would uphold her objection. Again, the jury must disregard the faulty memory of the sheriff.

There is one other bit of information regarding a weapon being found at the crime scene. I have been told by a man who knew Vernon, Chester's brother, that Vernon had been threatened if he didn't testify against Chester. Vernon had been told by the police that they had a .25 caliber pistol with his fingerprints on it that had been used in the murder of Ralph Edwards.

In both testimonies regarding the weapons found that conflicted with the State's presentation, the jury chose to not believe the testimony that would favor Chester.

When Chester took the stand, he continued his denial of being the assassin of Ralph Edwards. On the witness stand, he asked permission of the court to speak to the Edwards family there. Receiving permission, he told the Edwards family he felt sorry for their loss and that he did not kill their loved one. His words did not sway the jury.

Chester's story was he had known the Fosters when living in Jackson. The knowledge of them happened to be a far cry from Clark and Toni's description. Chester dated a girl who was employed as a night clerk in a local motel. He also had a job there as a part-time maintenance man. Chester told the jury how, one night, he returned to the motel and his girlfriend told him about a disturbance reported in the Fosters' room. She suggested Chester investigate to see if things were okay.

So he went and knocked on the Fosters' door. The door, partially open, enabled him to see Toni crying. Obviously she had been beaten up by her husband, Clark, as he was the only other person in the room. Chester suggested she go to the emergency room and get checked out, which she did. The ER doctors discovered she had suffered a miscarriage from Clark's beating.

Because of the incident, the motel owner asked the couple to leave the next day. This event was never mentioned.

Chester's testimony about Clark causing Toni's miscarriage pointed to another inconsistency of Toni Foster's statements. Toni had testified Chester and some of his friends moved into their rented apartment against her and Clark's will. After several days, he and his girlfriend refused to leave. Toni said the reason she and Clark had gone along with the robbery plan was so Chester might get some cash and move out.

Chester testified that the only time he had any contact with the Fosters had been at the motel. To his knowledge, they never lived in an apartment.

The defendant had been asked if he had an alibi for the night of the murder. He reiterated how he had tried to establish his whereabouts on the night fourteen years ago but had been unable to. He had even employed a former FBI agent to secure the information from former employers. With no data found, the door to the past got slammed shut.

Chester attorney attempted to bring out another set of events relevant to his innocence. A trio of people were arrested on robbery charges in Jackson, Mississippi, close to the date of Edwards' death. Prior to their arrest, they had been seen in the Indianola area. One woman involved, from Greenwood, Mississippi, just twenty miles from the Aero service station, would be questioned. The trio was arrested for service station hold ups.

During the trial, the cash register attendant at the Aero station testified a young woman had been hanging around the station on the day of the murder. A scenario somewhat like the Fosters' story. She remembered that the girl had blonde hair, not long brown hair. The vagrant girl spoke to Mr. Edwards and told him someone she had been traveling with had put her out in Indianola. The cashier said the girl sat outside on the concrete island until late in the afternoon. Someone picked her up and she was not seen again. It was the only single girl she remembered seeing.

Clark and Toni stated their alleged robbery plan was for

Chester's girlfriend, who had long brown hair, to go to the station and attract Edwards and then rob him at an opportune moment.

The three arrested in Jackson had kidnapped a young couple in Jackson, forced them to rob a clothing store, and later released them in Alabama. Next, the three persons returned to Mississippi and robbed a service station near Jackson and forced the owner to accompany them. The service station operator had been blindfolded and threatened to be killed. The trio went as far as shooting at him; however, the bullet missed.

Chester still believes this trio of kidnappers and robbers may have played some role in the Edwards murder case. One other strange twist is that Janice Hawkins, the daughter of Ralph Edwards, identified the girl in the Jackson robbery as the same girl she had seen in the Indianola service station the day her father was killed.

The State never investigated the incident Chester mentioned in their rush to judgment. The DA blew the incident off when the defendant raised it.

Chester had little else to offer on the witness stand. He simply stated his innocence, yet his words fell on deaf ears in the jury.

With no alibi, Chester was unable to forcefully defend himself. Yet few of us remember exactly where we were that long ago. In addition to the FBI agent's search for an alibi, Chester's family was questioned for letters or documents to prove Chester was somewhere else; however, none were found.

There was testimony and evidence contrary to Chester's guilt.

The Fosters owned a .25 caliber pistol. It allegedly wound up in Chester's murderous hands. Either registered or traded for, it was traceable. The Fosters could jeopardize themselves by leaving the crime scene without it.

Even though reports said the Fosters were involved in similar robberies, those facts would not be heard by the jury. The reports were not allowed as evidence. The fact that Clark Foster was a constant drug user and probably was smoking marijuana the day of the murder was not permitted to be heard by the panel of twelve.

The testimony of Victor Hurns, who heard Clark Foster boast of framing Chester, never had been admitted by the judge. The testimony of Manuel Bryley, in a word, had been laughed out of court. So the case went to the jury on the story of Toni Foster against the denial of the defendant, Chester Johnston. As lawyers say, it had been just a shouting match, and the State shouted the loudest.

The State offered its closing arguments. A murder had been committed. The victim had been the object of a crime beginning as a robbery turning into a death. Everyone involved in the conspiracy, except the killer himself, wanted to leave Indianola and go home. Everyone was afraid of Chester, so they continued with the plan.

Chester's wise old Defense attorney said, "It was her word against Chester's, and she was very strong in her testimony."

The prosecuting attorney opened the case for the State saying she would prove Chester Johnston was guilty of the crime he was accused of. She concluded with the same statement. Toni testified that Chester was present and he alone wanted to rob and kill Ralph Edwards. Chester took Toni's pistol and, as she swore under oath, he pulled the trigger. His former sister-in-law confirmed the fact from the back seat of a car trailing the murder vehicle in the dark. Mrs. Bridges rested her position.

Jimmy Sherman led the Defense in the closing arguments. He summarized the case briefly, pointing out the holes in the State's case.

P.J. Townsend, the picture of the typical Faulkner southern lawyer, gray hair and a baggy seersucker suit came next in closing for Chester. As he arose from his chair at the Defense table, the jury must have seen him as a stereotype from a Hollywood courtroom scene. All his delta wit and trial wisdom would not rescue his client this day.

Townsend reminded the jury that none of the fingerprints were Chester's. He explained that, if Toni's statement about Chester approaching the vehicle and opening the door were true, he would leave fingerprints there, yet none were found. Toni Foster also that testified Chester turned off the headlights and cut off the engine. The Defense attorney asked the jury, if he had, where were his prints in those places? The FBI reports where unmistakable; no prints found were Chester Johnston's. Toni also testified that Chester wiped the car clean with a bloody shirt; no shirt was found at the scene. No blood type matching Chester's was recovered. Hard to believe? The State and the jury did.

Attorney Townsend's most compelling point came from his closing words. He directed the jury's attention to the fact it had been Clark, by his own admission, who turned the gang's attention to a green car traveling down the road to Shaw. Only Clark knew it was Edwards. Clark said, "There he goes."

Clark's identification had been like a starter gun firing to start a race. Both the cars carrying the wannabe robbers took off. Townsend concluded his thought, saying, if Clark had not said, "There he goes," Ralph Edwards would probably be alive today.

In his instructions, the judge reviewed the proposition that Chester was presumed innocent until proven guilty and Chester did not need to present at defense to prove his innocence.

Evidently, all the collective mind of the jury needed in their search for the truth regarding the murderer of Ralph Edwards was one woman's testimony. This was all the evidence necessary to prove Chester's guilt.

The jury deliberated seven hours before returning with their decision, "Guilty beyond a reasonable doubt." A jury of eleven women and one man failed to hear a man's pleading of innocence. A victim trapped by fourteen years of faint memory and the testimony of one women who would never be called in front of the bar of justice for her actions on the day of murder. Never tried, even though she admitted she was present. A panel of twelve local residents returned, single file with eyes on the juror ahead of them, to the court. The Foreman read the verdict. "We, the jury, find the defendant guilty of murder."

The final tally of the jury panel in their search for the truth regarding the killer of Ralph Edwards rested solely on Toni's word. The missing evidence, the holes in the State's case, and conflicting stories under oath, were ignored. Chester Johnston was guilty.

The only trial phase remaining was the sentencing. Now all the participants in the trial would wait to see if the State of Mississippi would permit Chester to live or sentence him to die.

***

Cindy had attended the proceedings from the beginning. "I sat there and listened to the prosecuting attorney paint a picture of a person I didn't know. I couldn't believe they were talking about Chester. I didn't believe the Chester I knew would kill anybody. The man I loved was kind and gentle. Oh, I knew he had been a rough biker and had a warrior background, but not a killer."

Cindy didn't stay for the trial's sentencing phase. She had endured all the pain of the trial; she left before the sentence came down. "I watched, I listened, and I couldn't believe what had happened in the courtroom. I had been taught to believe in the end justice would win out. Before, I had full confidence in our judicial system; now I became appalled by the Prosecution's performance. I felt betrayed by our system and began to fear for Chester's life. When I heard the judge read the verdict of guilty, I thought my whole life was going to end."

Cindy remembered that, when his verdict had been read, Chester's head went down briefly. The deputies took him away at once. Cindy cried until she ran out of tears; she was done crying. She knew she couldn't stay for the sentencing phase.

"I didn't think I could stand another blow." Cindy was close by Chester's side throughout the trial. "He always included me in every decision regarding his defense. I don't know how much help I had been. I did everything I believed possible."

***

The court had already inquired about the jury panel's sentiment regarding the death sentence or life without parole. This had been established during the *voir dire* phase of the trial. A number of potential jurists had been examined by the State and Defense attorneys. The State felt positive this panel would not hesitate to give a death sentence to the defendant.

Chester's defense team would have to make a valiant effort to save Chester from the gas chamber. Their plan was to put several witnesses on the stand who would testify to the outstanding work Chester had done in assisting other people since his conversion in 1981.

To which the State would reply, "Jailhouse religion."

"Jailhouse religion" is a term used to describe those who, upon being locked up, quickly affirm their faith as Christians. They believe life will be easier once they do so. These are those who put on a facade of Christianity when they find themselves behind bars. Most often, it is a practice of inmates in local and county jails. It seldom happens in prison because men and women who announce themselves Christians are severely tested for their faith.

It became imperative to show the jury that Chester's life was worth sparing. The Defense prepared witnesses who were called to state Chester's redeeming qualities. He would also be called to witness about the faith he now had. If the witnesses failed to paint a portrait of change in the ex-biker, the gas chamber awaited.

The Defense's plan was for each one to relate their personal knowledge of the change in the ex-biker's life.

Virginia McBride was a retired Parchman tour director who spoke on Chester's behalf. She knew Chester for many years, by his record and his reputation. Her description of the old Chester was a troubled inmate as well as a roughneck. She testified that much of his earlier prison time had been spent in MSU. Virginia continued by telling how her relationship with the defendant matured.

Mrs. McBride began to visit with Chester in the lockdown unit. The Parchman guards were beginning to see a change in Chester, also. Soon she put in a staff request to have Chester moved to another camp, so he spoke to school tours when he completed his punishment time.

Seeing him on a daily basis, she noticed a change in his attitude. The change came partially from Chester realizing he was having an impact in lives of the young people he spoke to. Some of them were delinquents, as he had been years before. Chester related to them and they found an ally in him; therefore, they listened and believed his message.

Mrs. McBride outlined the essence of his presentations. In her words, Chester told the kids, "Prison is a dumping ground of society." Chester related first hand what living in the dumping ground of society was really like.

As Chester became more proficient in his speaking abilities, she escorted Chester on trips off prison grounds. Now he had the opportunity to speak to school students and civic club members. These visits included three visits to a Delta State Sociology class.

Chester's grades for his work in schools were high. Mrs. McBride related how "teacher after teacher told me they saw conduct changes in young teens who had given them trouble. We had eight thousand kids tour the prison each year and more requests had to be turned down." Many who met the ex-biker testified by letters written to him about how he had helped them change their lives. She still has many of the letters.

To rebut Mrs. McBride's testimony, the assistant DA asked about Chester's violent behavior when first coming to Parchman. The retired tour director was questioned about his tattoos and where he got them. Mrs. McBride responded that he told the young people he had them done when a gang member and now wished to have them removed. The inquiring DA attempted to lure Mrs. McBride into discussing Chester's activities with motorcycle gangs, but was unsuccessful.

The State's attorney could not budge Mrs. McBride in her assessment of the positive character and beneficial service of the new Chester

Mr. Townsend's final question on redirect to Mrs. McBride helped to sum up her feeling toward Chester and his impact on others.

Mr. Townsend: "Do you feel his life is worth is worth saving?"
Mrs. McBride: "YES."

The next character witness for the defense was Hollis Allred. He served as a Church of God lay preacher, and preached as a volunteer at Parchman for sixteen years. His work had brought him into contact with the defendant for the past eight years.

Brother Allred described Chester as one of the more outgoing inmates. Chester assisted him in conducting services, handing out literature to other guys attending, and giving his testimony. His witness described how Jesus had changed his life.

Mr. Townsend concluded his round of questions, asking, "Do you have an opinion as to whether or not Chester Johnston is a Christian?"

The witness's response was, "Using the principles and standards of the Book, I would say he is."

The DA turned her attack on the statement toward the false

label of Christian she believed Chester wore. Her redirect was as follows:

DA: "Mr. Allred, are you familiar with many inmates who have become institutionalized?"

Allred: "Yes, ma'am."

DA: "For quite a while?"

Allred: "Yes, ma'am."

DA: "And they learn how the system works, don't they?"

Allred: "Some of them do, yes, ma'am."

DA: "And they learn how to get along and how to take advantages in the penitentiary system?

Allred: "Some of them try."

DA: "And a lot of them learn how to do that, don't they?"

Allred: "Oh, some of them learn to do that. That's the reason you have got to have the ability to discern between the two."

Obviously the DA was attempting to tarnish the defendant's Christian image. Preacher Allred shot her down by stating one must have the discernment to know between real and actor.

Later, the DA attempted to compromise Chester's Christian testimony in the redirect with his sister. The younger sister described her relationship with Chester before and after his incarceration. She related how, as a young man, Chester felt the call to become a minister. Then he forgot all his grandmother's teaching about God. Pat offered that the basis of her reasoning that Chester had changed was because of their phone conversations since he went to prison. Then, he talked about the church, family, and his mamma and daddy.

Her opinion to the court had been that Chester was very bitter when first going to Parchman. Later, he changed and spent his time helping those in prison with him.

One occasion, she remembered he prayed that he would not harbor bitter feelings toward the people who unjustly sent him to prison on his rape charge.

The DA objected at this point that the sister's testimony was self-serving hearsay. The DA's objection was overruled.

When DA Bridges had her chance at Chester's sibling, she attacked with added vengeance. She didn't want any "goody two shoes" image of the defendant to impress the jury. It seemed she was out for blood, Chester's.

The sibling witness was questioned about Chester's use of marijuana. She replied she never saw her brother use drugs. The DA changed course for a moment, asking about the children's formative years, what church they had attended, and so forth. The sibling answered her questions honestly. She described their life growing up together, going to church, and Chester doing well in school.

Then the DA returned to the defendant's drug use. She asked if the witness was aware Chester smoked marijuana in 1968. She replied, no, she was not.

After being unsuccessful in attempting to damage the sister's testimony, the DA changed course once again. She asked if the sister was aware Chester listed no religion on the prison admittance form. She replied she was not; however, at the time it was a correct and truthful answer. Besides, it had been years ago and she was discussing his life after his conversion.

Once again, Mrs. Bridges changed her style of attack. She delved into Chester's ability to assume responsibility. Did Chester's accept responsibility for his past criminal actions? Did he ever tell her he accepted responsibility for his charges? Had he attempted to blame his rape charge on brother Vernon? The assistant DA fired one question after another at the distraught sister.

Chester's sister had broken down in tears when first taking the stand; now, she had prepared herself for the State's offensive. This time she held her emotions in check.

Attorneys are taught early in law school never to ask a question you don't already know the answer to. Mrs. Bridges, in her zeal to damage Pat's testimony, forgot this lesson. The sibling witness held herself together, saying Chester maintained he had been wrongly accused of rape. As to the part about brother Vernon, she never heard any discussion regarding blaming Vernon ever.

Each time the Defense called a witness, the district attorney attacked Chester's image as a Christian. To receive a sentence of death from the jury, the DA had to tarnish his image. She failed even to tarnish the picture of the converted man on trial for his life.

The jury heard how Inmate Johnston provided other services for Parchman inmates. In 1989, Chester completed a "Heads Up Literacy" program from TV's Pat Robertson. Chester knew many Parchman inmates who had not learned to read nor write. He decided to take his newly acquired skills and use them to make other people's lives fuller.

During his trial, Chester told of one of his experiences of teaching prisoners there to read. He and his pupil had sat down in the prison yard for a learning session. The man wanted to learn to read, but when other guys came around, the student would close his alphabet book. It embarrassed the illiterate inmate for others to know his deficiency. Chester taught him to read and write, along with many others.

The *Clarion Ledger* carried an article complete with a picture of Chester and his pupil, Johnny Grey. Johnny had not learned to read or write before entering a literacy program sponsored by the Sunflower County Library. His teacher during his confinement in the hole was Chester Johnston. He discarded his whittling and picture frame making to become literate.

Illiteracy is a contributing factor leading to crime. When Johnny left Parchman for a new beginning, he had a better chance to stay off the streets and out of jail because of the tools Chester taught him.

Later, Chester would meet evangelist Pat Robertson when he delivered a certificate recognizing Chester's teaching skills. Chester's teaching was one more service offered to his fellow inmates and people in the free world since Jesus changed him.

Chester had continued to improve himself in other life areas during his time at Parchman. This was also brought out during the sentencing phase of his trial. From 1982 through 1985, Chester took college courses from Coahoma Junior College and Mississippi Delta Community College. His study courses included history, social studies, English literature and composition, and psychology classes. He sustained a high grade point level while enrolled. Not bad for a "throw away" inmate.

Chester's statement told the jury how he prepared himself for legal work to assist himself and other inmates. He enrolled in and completed a paralegal course with Southern Career Institute. He then used his legal skills to advance his and other inmates' legal battles.

***

The sentencing instructions would be more tedious than those of the trial phase. This phase would be more difficult on they jury. They must decide whether or not he would forfeit his life.

Judge Davis issued the following instructions to the jury panel. To proclaim a sentence of death, they must find one or more of the following circumstances existed:

- The defendant actually killed Ralph Edwards Junior
- The defendant attempted to kill Ralph Edwards Junior
- The defendant intended the killing of Ralph Edwards Junior to take place.
- The defendant contemplated lethal force would be employed.

The judge continued his instructions, summarizing the aggravating circumstances that must exist in the case for the jury to issue a death sentence; if Chester had been previously convicted of a felony using violence, or if the present offense had been committed while attempting to rob Mr. Edwards or was committed for pecuniary gain. If either of those aggravating conditions existed, the death penalty must be declared.

A number of additional sentencing orders were read to the jury. The panel of twelve might be merciful and not require a death sentence. If they believed the present character of the defendant would redeem him or if they felt sympathy for him, they might spare his life.

The jury returned with a sentence of life without parole.

***

Their scale of sentencing is somewhat strange, compared to their finding Chester guilty of pre-meditated murder. If they actually believed Toni's story, all of the circumstances requiring the death penalty to be invoked were present. Death had come to Mr. Edwards during a robbery. With those facts, the jury had no choice but to return a sentence of death in the State's gas chamber. Yet they chose to issue a sentence of life imprisonment to Chester.

Perhaps they found some shred of mercy for the ex-biker. I'd rather believe they searched their respective hearts at the real moment of life or death and wondered if the weak story of Clark and Toni was actually true. Perhaps, as they held the life of a man in their hands, the State's evidence was contaminated by a reasonable doubt. We will never know for certain. What is known is the jury sentenced Chester to remain at Parchman for the rest of his natural life. He would continue to live in a world where life had little value and a man had to fight for what little he possessed.

Even with the efforts of the State's prosecutor, the jury had seen the light of change and value in the life of the man they had convicted. Their sentence, life, but not death.

The State's Attorney and others who see Christian offenders as fakes fail to realize Jesus begins His work within all converts, free world or prison converts. No longer must a convert depend upon willpower to change; one can lean on God's power.

Few people who know Chester today and know the fiery trials he has endured would argue that God has not changed his life. None of the young people who have met him question the fact. I have worked for over twelve years in the prison ministry field. I have met inmates and seen their lives change, and I have seen a few who attempt to run a religious game. Just look for their fruits and listen to who they proclaim in their lives, the Lord or themselves. This will tell you who they serve.

I have also learned the most difficult place in the world to live a Christian life in is prison. Many inmates shun and turn their backs on anyone professing Christ, regardless of previous friendships.

Jesus changed lives in His earthly walk among men. He healed the sick, restored sight to the blind, lifted men from a sick bed to walk, and called his best friend back from the grave. He did so by touching lives. This is what Jesus called "fruits." Words can be spoken in hypocrisy, prayers offered vainly, and the Bible read and quoted. The test of a man's conversion is found in the changed lives of those he has met.

The testimony of those who came to his side during the trial proved Chester Johnston, through Christ's power, had aided men through God's strength to change lives. On judgment day, no other testimony will be required.

CHAPTER NINETEEN

THE REAL STORY?

E ver since the OJ Simpson case drew national attention in newspaper headlines, defense attorneys have begun to use a strategy devised by OJ's lawyers called the "Dream Team." This defense scheme was perfected and useful when there was an absence of alibis or evidence. The Defense created an alternative story about what happened for the jury to weigh against the other side's presentation. Following is an example of a different story of that night.

After Chester's guilty verdict, largely the result of lies and mis-information, a scenario of what possibly happened the night in question, using the same testimonies of all the original defendants, very well could tell a different story and result in another conclusion.

Analyzing all the evidence and interviews points me to a much different conclusion than the jury found. Also, when one considers the data and testimony never heard by the jury, it surely could have raised a "reasonable doubt" verdict. Reading the trial manuscript, the interviews, and the other case information several times paints a different picture of the night of June 3, 1976, than the one presented by the State. Admittedly, some of their argument is only what they wanted the twelve men and women making the decision of "guilty or innocent" to hear about what went down that night. Two sources contributed information not heard in the courtroom, Victor Hurns and Manuel Bryley. Their statements most likely would have raised questions about the prosecution's case; however, it might have come out. It could have assisted Chester's defense, or refuted the State's charges. Either way, the jury never heard their stories.

A possible murder scenario is a synthesis of all the information available, and additional information given privately that never reached the courtroom.

My picture of the events of the night Edwards died takes note of the loopholes and fallacies in the stories of the other people admittedly there. Compare Toni's story to her husband's. The first question raised concerns the purchase of the pistol, and who had possession of it the fateful night. They differ in the story of its purchase, who had it prior to the night on the highway, and where it was before the robbery-murder. Moreover, the narrative the Foster told investigators concerning the day's events from start to finish does not match Sherry's or Vernon's.

Sherry never mentions having seen or been with the Fosters that afternoon, nor did she mention them visiting her on the day in question when testifying. The Fosters claimed to have been at her house the previous day, but Sherry doesn't remember it. Both Fosters admit to having taken a part in the crime, yet listening to Sherry's statement when questioned separately, the Fosters are not present. Surely if her version were correct, she would mention Clark and Toni Foster.

Sherry only remembers Chester being in the car ahead of her. She couldn't recall if Chester was driving or not. Her first account to the police is that she saw a flash, like a Bic cigarette lighter being lit. Later on, after being blatantly helped in her statement by the investigators, her description changes and becomes like "TV gunfire flashes." The two illustrations are worlds apart.

Sherry also omits all the events of the time they passed watching the Areo station in the early afternoon. All she really recalls is seeing a flash on Highway 448. She omits all the afternoon's events sworn to by the other witnesses. Her story has as its players, Chester, Vernon, and her kids, leaving home close to dark. The Fosters remembered Edwards had closed his station just before dark. Sherry doesn't recall the girlfriend trying to hustle Mr. Edwards, the afternoon vigil, or who planned the robbery.

The term "dark" is a rather critical point in various testimonies. When it's used to define time in the South, is generally is understood as when one turns their lights on after the sun sets. The Mississippi Delta summer sun sets in a hurry, around eight to eight thirty that time of year. If Sherry told the truth, they left Arcola at dark, which meant Edwards had long since closed the Areo station, around seven o'clock. If correct, that would be before Vernon and family even left Arcola. It is a thirty-mile drive to Indianola from there. Leaving their home at a much later hour would put Vernon and family arriving in Indianola after dark. The Fosters claimed they watched the station for several hours before Edwards closed. The timelines don't fit!

The State's only purpose in putting Sherry on the stand was to link Chester with the gun flash in the vehicle ahead of Vernon Johnston. More than likely, the reason Sherry forgets to mention the other afternoon's events and says they all left at dark is because she was never there.

Consider this: how many mothers would take their young children on a planned robbery attempt in the delta heat?

More doubt is cast regarding the varying validity of accounts bringing Chester's guilty verdict. Toni remembered Vernon and family waited with them as Chester's girlfriend allegedly attempted to

seduce Edwards and rob the station. Vernon swore the robbery attempt took place in the afternoon, before he and his family left home
according to what his wife said. Vernon declared he worked that
day and got in around five or six o'clock. Vernon agreed with his
wife Sherry as to the time of departure, disputing Clark's wife's
report.

Both the Johnstons said someone with them entered the service
station in the evening and bought sodas. Clark and Toni must have
forgotten this. No one would have gone into the store other than
to "case" it. That job supposedly was played by Chester, earlier.

Besides, once arrested, Sherry and Vernon's narratives are
obviously directed by the detectives to agree with their conclusion
of the event years prior. The motives of the investigators are clear
in the transcripts.

The stories of the evening's events also contradict according to
the one telling them. Vernon's tale was they saw Edwards leave
the station, so they all followed him to a bank. Investigator
Bonham interrupts Vernon's questioning, "They went to the
bank?"

Vernon replied, "Yeah."

Bonham, knowing this part of the story, contradicted the story
of the Fosters, advised Vernon, "If you are not sure of something,
tell it like it is."

Vernon then corrects his statement, "As far as I know, he went
to the bank."

Now, if Vernon followed Edwards as he testified, he would
know if Edwards went to make a bank deposit. He would not need
to be corrected by the investigators. Was Vernon really recalling
what really happened? Remember, the accountant testified that
Edwards brought the days cash receipts to her; there was no
mention of a bank. Could it be possible that Vernon and Clark
killed Edwards without the "gang" including wives and children?

Regardless, whether Vernon was adding something that actually

happened or he forgot the scripted story, neither Foster ever mentioned Edwards going to a bank. They can't seem to get together
on their stories.

There are additional situations where it appears the
investigative guys led the witnesses. Here is an excerpt from
another transcript.

BONHAM: "All right. What happened next? They came
back?"

VERNON: "They came back and they said to hell with it. We
gonna be sure he went back and made a drop."

BONHAM: "All right. Who said that?"

VERNON: "Chester. I said. 'Well, what you gone do?'"

BONHAM: "Said to hell with him?"

VERNON: "Sir?"

BONHAM: "Go ahead. I'm sorry. I didn't mean to interrupt
you. What'd you say?"

VERNON: "Chester said, 'To hell with it. We gonna go on and
do it.' I said, 'What you fixin' to do, Chester?' He said, 'We gonna
follow this guy on down the road,' and he . . ."

BONHAM: "When he said 'do it,' did he say that or did he say
'I'm gonna kill him'?"

VERNON: "He said he was gonna kill him."

Bonham supplied the words incriminating Chester, and Vernon
became his parrot.

Later in his interview:

BONHAM: "What kind of gun did he [Chester] have at that
time?"

VERNON: "A .38."

BONHAM: "You know that, or think you know that?"

VERNON: "Well, I'm positive he had a .38."

Now watch Investigator Bonham turn the words of Vernon's
testimony.

BONHAM: "But did you know he had it on him then?"

VERNON: "Did I know he had it them? The only thing I knew he had was a .22"

BONHAM: "On him?"

VERNON: "On him."

One minute, if one believes Vernon, Chester is armed with a .38, and then its a .22. Bonham's question on the topic of Chester's pistol would have misfired anyway, because Toni and Clark both testified the murder weapon was hers, or his, depending upon what day it was.

There are several omissions in the testimonies recorded by the police between the five alleged suspects in the case, far too numerous to mention. The State's attorney dodged the testimony discrepancies by only putting Toni and Vernon's wife on the stand. That limited questions the defense lawyers could ask. The lawyers had been shrewd enough to know they could limit the facts in front of the jury to only what they wanted them to hear. Legal, yes. But ethical?

It would have been highly possible if questioning leeway had taken place in the court, or all those other members of the gang testified, that there would have been numerous Fifth Amendment pleadings. They all faced the same charges. Under the cloak of immunity, the limited witnesses and testimonies would not present an opportunity for Chester's counsel to refute Toni's and Sherry's testimony.

The statements of the co-conspirators also contained information this is simply incorrect. For example, there is no place on Highway 448 within five miles of Shaw, where Edwards supposedly was forced from the roadway, where one car might pull alongside of another. I personally drove it! The highway has far too many curves and narrow stretches. There are numerous spots where one vehicle could run another off the road into a field.

Most likely, the story told by Clark Foster to Victor Hurns in the county jail was based on what actually occurred. Some of his story is true and part is simply made up.

Victor swore Clark told him the following story

Victor Hurns said he believed what Foster said in jail, that he was traveling Highway 448 on the fatal day, just before dark. I wonder if Clark passed Ralph Edwards or trailed Mr. Edwards from an Indianola bank as Vernon suggested? Could Toni have been with Clark in this version? What other reason was there for Toni to lie for him fourteen years later. Was Vernon with them during the real event? Well, witnesses told me Clark and Vernon did small time drug dealing together. You decide.

Here is what I believe occurred. Clark was traveling south on Highway 448 the evening the death of Mr. Edwards occurred. He knew Ralph Edwards because he was from his hometown and had made plans to rob him. However, as Clark, and possibly others, drove toward Indianola, he passed Edwards traveling north to Shaw. That was not where Edwards was supposed to be. Clark said he turned his car around when he saw his victim, Edwards, not that he was following him. It seems logical that, when he caught up to Ralph, he pulled alongside, with a plan to take his money, and shot Edwards through the window. Mr. Edwards' vehicle veered off the highway and into the adjoining field. Then Clark robbed him, threw his gun into the field, and left.

Another set of facts not mentioned in the trial was a lawsuit the Edwards family filed against their auto insurance company. Something rubbed white paint and put scratches all over the side of Mr. Edwards' car. The police had photos of the car with the paint and scratches. The body repairman who worked on Ralph Edwards' car days earlier said the paint and scratches had not been there when he repaired it. Mr. Edwards' daughter agreed the paint was not there the morning of the day he died.

Without doubt, a white vehicle put one fender against Mr.

Edwards' auto some time during the day of the killing. The missing paint and scrapes were visible down the length of the green auto. Remember, no mention is made of the two cars colliding in the Foster testimony during the trial.

Perhaps, when sideswiped, Edwards lost control of his vehicle and ran out into the cotton field. Maybe he sat unconscious behind the wheel of his car, or passed away. Was Mr. Edwards sideswiped and shot? Did he lose control of his auto? We don't really know how he got there. What we do know is he wound up in the middle of a cotton field, dead!

What could have happened next varies depending on Clark's account or Victor Hurns report as to what he was told in the Sunflower County jail.

Chester said Foster had a macho yearning to for the tough biker image. That would not allow him to tell a fellow inmate that he had acted in cowardice.

Synthesizing the matching parts of the stories, here is what I believe. Clark was not headed south toward Indianola the day of the crime; rather, he was following Mr. Edwards, with Toni and Vernon, from Indianola. The trio forced Edwards off the road. Clark was aware Edwards was a semi-invalid and would be defenseless, so he stopped, and he or Vernon got out of his car, and he, or whoever, slowly approached the victim's vehicle to appraise Ralph's condition. Clark was cautious, as he knew Edwards carried a pistol. Whoever arrived beside the car and saw Ralph unconscious then shot Mr. Edwards behind the ear, almost like an execution. Next, someone opened the door, emptied the victim's pockets, took the car keys from the ignition, and fled the scene. A few coins were left behind on the ground under the car. That was their only take, Mr. Edward's pocket change; not the large day's cash receipts as anticipated.

Somewhere between the crime scene and Shaw, someone threw

the .25 caliber murder weapon and car keys out of their car, and they are still in the pasture grass alongside Mississippi Highway 448.

Would Clark or Vernon been mean enough to commit cold-blooded murder? Toni divorced Clark because of cruel and inhumane treatment. Her words were that he had beaten her often. Chester still remembers an incident at a motel where he lived with Della when Clark had abused Toni. She was afraid of her husband! She stated the fact several times. Vernon also physically abused Sherry and his other wives. Was Clark cold blooded enough to murder an unconscious Ralph Edwards? Somebody was.

While serving as a prison chaplain, I heard additional information about the Edwards murder from an inmate who was locked up with Vernon when Chester was being tried. After the trial, Vernon served two more years with my informant at the Sunflower County work camp.

For some years, Vernon dealt drugs small time. The story was that a prominent Indianola resident, along with local law enforcement, had been paid off to look the other way on drug deliveries. Some of his narcotics were delivered by Chester from Jackson to Vernon. Remember, Vernon and Clark sold drugs together. Chester played the role of supplier, not delivery boy.

Before the trial, somebody in law enforcement visited Vernon and told him they had a .22 caliber pistol used in a killing with his fingerprints on it. Vernon was given a choice; he could finger his brother, Chester, or take the rap himself. Vernon chose the easy way out.

When all the evidence before the court and the additional data is considered, it most likely points to Clark or brother Vernon killing an unconscious service station owner in the cotton field. Vernon said the deputy advised him the fingerprints on the recovered pistol belonged to him. Both the Cleveland sheriff's clerk and attorney both confirmed the sheriff said they *did* recover a murder weapon at the scene. It was lost sometime during the fourteen-year interval following the killing.

Is this the real story? Right or wrong, this story is closer to the truth than all the stories the conspirators told.

The inmate in Sunflower work camp related this story to me. He and Vernon had been smoking marijuana in a work building at the camp. While they smoked, the subject of Mr. Edwards' murder was mentioned by Vernon's buddy. Clark remarked that Chester received a life sentence for Ralph's death. Vernon quickly replied that he had murdered the service station owner. Would Vernon's dope buddy be telling a lie to a chaplain? There was no reason to. The question is, did he?

What's the true story? We will never know, yet, in my mind, any conclusion that weighs all the statements, evidence, and facts is not what the jury found. If they heard all the information available to me from the police record, The Crime Book, and other testimonies, all the interrogatories of all the witnesses, etc., it very well would have been a different verdict.

As someone once stated, God invented making lemonade out of lemons. Chester's best and worst was coming.

CHAPTER TWENTY

LIFE IN THE HOLE

Once the court's sentencing order had been issued, Chester returned to Parchman. Now he would spend the remainder of his days and nights in the maximum security unit living in a six by nine foot cell.

Mrs. McBride, the Parchman tour director, described MSU during the trial. "The cells are six by nine feet, with concrete block walls and a small window. Each one is furnished with a concrete slab bed and thin mattress, and a stainless steel washbasin and commode. Sometimes the security staff will permit the prisoners to have radios or TVs. But when they are disciplined, their radio and TV privileges are taken away from them. They are allowed thirty minutes daily in the exercise yard and to take a shower, if the officers have time."

Once, she had been asked, "How do you consider the confinement of MSU?"

She answered, "I would think it would be best described as 'hell on earth.' I don't see how a person can live so enclosed, with no human contact day after day."

Later in the trial, Victor Hurn described the conditions at MSU. "The circumstances are restricted to a one-man cell, and the only time you get a chance to go out is when you are on call to go to court or when we take a shower. You are limited to three pairs of shorts and socks, no gym shoes, comb, or brush. Any visits you have are spent talking to your family on a phone through a window. Meals are served through the cell door. Yard call is thirty to forty-five minutes – ten for a shower." He would also describe living in the hole as hell on earth.

Chester would live in these surroundings for the next three years. "Hell on earth," is how Inmate Victor Hurns and Mrs. McBride, the prison tour director, described living in lockdown. This form of close confinement is as near to the old form of solitary as federal law permits.

His six by nine cubical becomes almost his total world. He eats, sleeps, reads, watches TV, and does his personal business inside fifty-six square feet. The prisoner's room is the size of a bathroom in a typical home.

The MSU inmate looks forward to two showers a week, visitors once a month, and thirty minutes exercise each day. Meals are usually cold, vegetables are like paste, meat, when provided, is hard and difficult to chew. They are not delivered on a regular schedule. One's life is paltry compared to living in a dorm type unit or on the streets.

Chester endured this monastic lifestyle for the next three years.

His years at MSU progressed into the third stretch to his road toward heaven. He started his lockdown time at Unit Seventeen, where death row was at that time. There, he became friends with Connie Ray Evans, the last man executed at Parchman at that time. When Unit Thirty-Two, the new hole, had been completed, Chester was moved over there. Unit Thirty-Two boasted over one thousand maximum security cells. Chester would call these units home for the next three years.

***

Immediately following his murder conviction, Chester's anger and bitterness returned. His mind became consumed with thoughts of bad breaks and people working against him. He began to play the blame game all over again. Nobody stepped outside his zone of responsibility for his misfortunes in life. The game included his mother's death, his father's rejection, and the inequitable trials for rape and murder he had suffered through.

In September 1990, Chester moved to the new Security Unit Thirty-Two. It had been built with the latest in prison technology for solitary confinement. Following the Attica riots, architects designed smaller buildings. The concept had been designed to prevent having a large number of inmates housed together where they could take control of a prison. Prisoners confined in smaller groups were less likely to build up a manpower force strong enough for a takeover. This premise compared to having multiple watertight compartments on a ship that reduced the possibility of large scale flooding on a ship. The watchword for prisons is custody and control.

Unit Thirty-Two is a red brick building separated into five wings. All contain single cell housing. Each wing is divided from its neighboring one by a solid brick wall inside and wire fencing on the outside. Higher fences have been erected a short distance from exercise area, restricting movement to the administration areas. Control towers loom above the grounds at each corner and in the middle of the camp. All electronic gates are operated from there. Concrete roads and walkways crisscross the open space so food and security vehicles can make their deliveries. Outside the maximum security domain is another high steel fence with razor wire rolled across the top. Escape from the hole is almost impossible.

When Unit Thirty-Two was completed, death row inmates and those serving life sentences were moved there. The gas chamber remained at Unit Seventeen. Men scheduled to die were transported a day before their execution date to the death chamber.

All the time Chester lived at Camp Seventeen, death row inmates, lifers, and men with extreme disciplinary problems had been all housed together. They only met each other while on yard call. Yard call permitted social time, and some played checkers and other's simply talked. Conversation became a rare commodity in the cells for these castaways. Outside prisoners are excited to meet and speak to their neighbors on the row. They chat constantly until the guards blow their whistles, ending yard call.

The only other face-to-face conversation on the tier occurred when a man passed their cell on the way to the shower room. The rare occasions when executions are scheduled, the condemned man is moved to the cell nearest the execution chamber. As the designee for execution walks his last steps down the tier, final goodbyes are exchanged.

Executions are the most difficult time for occupants of the lock-down units. The camp began a silent deathwatch until a stay was granted or the executioner completed his state-commissioned task.

Life seemed tough in these Spartan surroundings. Little conversation, a dismal environment, and the only people you see are men going to shower as they pass your cell, or guards. If you are to be executed, you will see the warden or a man going to the death chamber. Chester lived here; it was his home until moving to Unit Thirty-Two.

***

Once again, God visited Chester in his lonely lockdown cell. The only way to pass time at MSU was talking to men you cold not see or reading. Televisions, radios, and all sources of entertainment are banned. Once Chester gained a victory over his initial bout with anger and bitterness, he took out his Bible and began to read God's word again. The Lord came by meeting Chester daily through His Word.

Chester filled the next months in the hole with hours of Bible study. He began to receive Bible correspondence courses, which he completed and returned for grading. He learned that the more he studied God's Word, the more he learned about the nature and ways of his Father.

As he understood more about his heavenly Father, he developed a deeper his trust in Him. The Bible Chaplain Lankford had given him after his beating provided Chester with a manual to draw closer to God. He learned from the Apostle Peter to cast all his care upon Him because He cared for Chester. He never had a caring father like that before.

The study of God's word and communicating with Cindy through the mail would occupy most of his three-year stay in lockdown. Both his relationships would grow stronger during these three years in the hole.

These three years would be Chester's last ever in maximum security.

Slowly, all Chester's hard old ways began to disappear. Chester's old man suffered a slow death, but he was dying. Chester's anger and bitterness became lost in the immense love he learned God had for him. While doing time in the hole, he gained complete control over his life.

Throughout the seven years after his murder conviction, prayer was an indispensable part of Chester's life. This continued until he died. Without prayer and Cindy's love and letters, Chester would have exited MSU a defeated animal. Cindy had endured his trial and continued to stand by Chester through his three years of close confinement.

Chester's Aunt Sue called Cindy at home once the sentence of life without parole was ordered by the court, because Cindy could not bear to be there when it was made public.

It had been a bittersweet moment for Cindy. "I was so relieved his life had been spared, because the death penalty had been an option, yet I didn't know how his sentence would affect our relationship."

When Cindy and Chester met for the first time at Unit Seventeen after the trial, Chester renewed his marriage proposal and Cindy had wrestled with his offer. "I knew he loved me. Being married would give him assurance I would not leave him. Even though I knew I was marrying him for all the wrong reasons, I said yes."

God still had His hand in their relationship. So they filed a request with the Chaplain's Department to be married; however, they were denied. The Lord wasn't ready for that phase yet.

Chester was moved to Camp Thirty-Two and remained there in lockdown for another eighteen months. That became a stressful time for both of them. When God is working a plan, Satan always attempts to intervene.

Confusion became Satan's tool in Cindy's life. "I truly believed God had brought Chester and me together. I knew God would free him in His time."

Each time Cindy won these mental battles, Satan would drop seeds of doubt. Cindy wondered if she had been fooling herself about the relationship. "I came close to just giving up and telling Chester I couldn't do this anymore. Chester must have sensed my doubt because he began to talk about freeing me. Then in the same breath he would beg me not to leave him."

Chester and his lady suffered through what Cindy now calls their "wilderness experience." Short visits following long drives to Parchman begun take their toll on her. Their times together became filled with rapid emotional ups and downs with little time to enjoy the ride. Once Cindy returned to Jackson following after a visit, she found herself physically and mentally exhausted.

In 1992, Chester and four other inmates filed a legal brief requesting the Sunflower Circuit Court allow them to be reclassified in the prison system. Previously, the classification committee had ruled to improve the standing of the five men; however, each time, the committee's director reversed their decision. Finally, the court issued an order that the five inmates must be reclassified. The ruling ended Chester's monastic banishment in lockdown. The penitentiary officials moved him to Unit Twenty-Five.

Cindy remembers when Parchman moved Chester from MSU. "It seemed like a form of freedom to us. I could touch him for the first time since the trial, and feel his touch in return. That feeling felt like heaven and my faith and my spirit became renewed."

Soon Chester became reclassified to "A" custody privileges. He got the assignment to operate the canteen at his unit. A store operator must be a man who is honest and can handle money. Weekly inventories are taken and the cost of the merchandise sold is compared to the cash turned in. Any discrepancy must be reported immediately and the store manager sent to the hole.

The camp canteen is stocked with tobacco products, candies, cakes, and necessary personal items. Some canteens produce more than $2500.00 weekly in sales. This operation is called by the inmates a "catch." A "catch" is any money-making or lifestyle-improving venture. Some inmates sell hot coffee, iron clothes, or resell canteen items to those too lazy to go to the store, or at night when the canteen is closed, to make money. The unit store at Camp twenty-Five became a place for another endeavor for Chester, a ministry for the Lord who rescued him from a death sentence.

CHAPTER TWENTY-ONE

THE MINISTRY

C hester and Cindy had been praying for God to give them a ministry during Chester's time in solitary confinement. He answered their prayer. "We started it right here in the canteen at Camp Twenty-Five. We wanted to share what God had done for us with others."

Their Christian work began simply by living for Christ in front of the inmates. Running a legitimate canteen was the beginning.

Cindy remembers, "We always started our visit with a time of devotion and prayer. Granddaughter Jessica joined us when she visited. Chester prepared lunch for us when we arrived, unlike some inmates who demanded elaborate meals be delivered when their family came."

Chester knew the emotional strain of visits and wanted to make Cindy's as easy as possible. Chester and little Jessica began to bond. He was the one who insisted she be kept at birth. Then the baby girl wove her magic on Chester like only a little girl can. Cindy described the connection as, "a love between them that is indescribable."

Again, marriage returned to Cindy and Chester's discussions.

She asked Chester, "What are you going to do if you are never released from here?"

He responded, "Continue the ministry right here where we are."

This was the answer Cindy was looking for. She said yes!

Chester remembered, "Cindy wrote to me. I look back now and realize our lives had to be tested by fire to prepare us for marriage. The Bible records situations like ours in those men and women of the Old Testament. We had years of disappointments, valleys, mountaintops, silence, and even doubt, but we made it to April of 1993, our wedding day."

***

Chester and Cindy's wedding was performed at the Spiritual Life Center chapel at Parchman. Marriages could be approved and the scheduled two times a year. Those who attended were friends who had stood by Chester during the past four years and shared his bitter cups of disappointment when sentenced to life in prison. They now stood with him in his time of victory. Ministers Frank and Ruth Sherry, Dennis Wilson, and Pauline Hurd arrived to be a part of Chester's joining with Cindy.

Cindy describes the friends who gathered as real disciples of Jesus. They daily carried the cross of Christ.

The ceremony was as ordinary as one can be in a penitentiary. Volunteer Chaplain Dennis Wilson officiated in uniting the bride and groom. Later on, the new bride and groom served the cake, and pictures were taken that would be treasured in later years. Cindy threw her bouquet, and the nuptials were over.

God provided a special blessing for their ceremony. The newlyweds were selected by the Chaplain's Department to make a videotape made of the marriage. Today it reminds them of the precious time forever.

Cindy knew that, "God was in my wedding. It was so hard leaving Chester after the reception, but I knew He would somehow soothe our heartache and dry my tears."

On April 22, 1993, the Supreme Court of Mississippi ruled Chester should not have been sentenced as a habitual offender. His sentence must be changed to life with parole. The court ruling was as though God had stamped His sovereign approval on their union.

In the winter of 1995, Chester went to work at the Chaplain's Department. He cut the grass and maintained the miniature rose bushes lining the sidewalk at the building's entrance. He carefully cultivated the tiny roses and found joy in giving them to friends. The gentle beauty of the petite flowers seemed a match for Chester's regenerated heart.

Working at the Chaplain's Center gave Chester the opportunity to speak to visiting school students. He believed telling about his past and directing them to making God the author of their lives would help them to make wiser choices. The setting for Chester's presentations was the vaulted, brick sanctuary of the Spiritual Life Building on the penitentiary grounds. The audiences were groups of visiting high schoolers.

Join them and listen to a Nam vet, former biker, and "shot caller" as he tells his powerful story.

A Parchman State Penitentiary inmate named Ernest introduces the speaker. "Now I am going to let Chester talk to you."

A figure moving with the grace of an agile competitor appears from behind a square red brick column. He glides to the microphone, his upper body slightly bent forward. His carriage reminds of a prizefighter answering the bell to attack his opponent. Chester Johnston, #44464, steps behind the microphone. The purpose of these high school tours is Parchman prison's "show and tell."

Chester eyes the crowd in front of him. The visiting boys wear denim pants or Levi jeans with figured sport shirts or tee-shirts hanging outside their pants nearly down to their knees. Some wear bright colored athletic jackets decorated with patches of a professional athletic team. Many of the girls are dressed to match the boys. Jacket colors designate gang affiliations; Gangsters, Vice Lords, or local teen organizations.

The "show" is the students being in the prison setting, the flat, open 22,000 acres of farmland. They see the gray warehouses, and bleak, brick buildings dotting the landscape. They become wary, noticing the buildings are all enclosed by cyclone wire fences. All the fences are crowned with shiny, coiled razor wire. High, heavy wire gates keep residents in and visitors out.

The students realize the razor wire is continuous strands of barbed wire with small metal razors attached to it. The wire will cut a man into bloody shreds if he attempts to climb over or through it.

The "tell" on the trip is young people hearing about life in this foreboding place from men who lived for years locked up here. The speakers spin grim prison stories that occurred inside the high fences and brick walls. Hopefully, the young people will be frightened enough to think about the choices they will make in their future.

The goal of the "show and tell" tour is to scare the students "straight."

Chester accepts the mic and turns to face his audience.

The man staring at them is a formidable figure. Chester's long blonde hair flows from around his balding pate, curling slightly upward on the ends. He is dressed in standard prison-issue, powder blue denim shirt with his name and MDOC number stenciled across the pocket. Across the back of his shirt, the word CONVICT is printed in large black letters. His pants are dark blue denim, with a one-inch white stripe sewn down the side. The white stripe denotes his "A" custody level, "trustee."

Chester allows his appearance to sink into their minds for a moment. He raises his head and stares intently at the audience. They see that his arms are covered with tattoos from top to bottom, and his unflinching, blue eyes pierce the crowd.

Today, these touring high school students are from Forrest, Mississippi. A hush falls over them as Chester searches the crowd. Some of the students recoil backward in their seats from the menacing look of the tattooed convict in front of them.

"Hi. I'm Chester, number 44464." His voice is slightly high pitched, but his words flow quickly, like a tough pitchman making a quick deal.

"At one time, I called the shots at Parchman. I was the boss here. Then, I could throw my hands faster than any man in this five thousand-inmate population. Me and my fellow biker Bandito brothers controlled the inhabitants of the prison. Other inmates feared us, and the officers respected us."

The students and teachers press forward slightly in their seats to hear better when Chester questions them, "How many of you hugged your mother and daddy this morning before you left for school?" With the boldness of a warrior, he issues an early challenge. "Did you? See, I never had a mama or daddy to hug me when I was growing up. If I did, I might not be here today."

The attentive kids did not expect to hear this warrior talk about hugs and family. Chester, in prison blue, pauses to let his inquiry sink in. He has given and received many challenges in his life, and knows well how to issue it "in your face."

"See, I came from a broken home. Nobody ever told me they loved me . . . you know, 'broken homes, broken lives'."

Some in the young audience drop their heads. They connect their life, their homes, with the menacing figure in front of them. The young people stir restlessly in their seats. They understand the concept of broken homes with the edict to love their parents.

"See, my mother was a lady of the night. Do you understand what that means? She was a 'road whore.' That's what I was told!"

The kids are stunned by the convict's frankness regarding his mother. His speaking technique is coldly calculated as he begins a struggle with the students' probing for a weakness. There will be no second chances for him to reach these high school teens. He must grab them on his first attempt.

"I guess she loved me in her own way." The word love softens the audience and they rest a little easier on the cushioned pews

"When I came home from school, she wasn't here to ask me if I had a good day in school or what kind of grades I made; she didn't seem to care." His hard words and straightforward presentation are like a prizefighter's unrelenting jab to the kids as Chester seeks to reach into their minds.

Empty houses after school is the opening of weakness he seeks. Almost every student in the room knows this feeling. His verbal jabs grab their attention as they, too, experience an emptiness of love in their house, attested to by their silence.

The convict exploits his opening. "I'd come home and drop my books. I'd leave the apartment and go down the street, and run around with a bunch of guys who had big, bad motorcycles."

He drives his word with a forceful, one-word question . . . Huh?"

"I felt like I was wanted by them, like they had time for me, like I was somebody. They was my big brothers. If somebody at school jumped on me, my big brothers would go down and kick their butt. We had a big, tough family; I belonged. I was loved by somebody, and it felt good."

As Chester tells about his introduction to motorcycle gangs, his words flow faster and the tone of his voice raises.

"Then my second family started putting money in my pocket. And you know what? I could get any little old girl I wanted. See I had a moped, a scooter ,and you didn't have nothing."

Chester again strikes home when he speaks of family. His words are hard, but his love for the visitors shows through, and they identify with him.

Next he moves to the problem of gang memberships. His eyes

squint as he searches for those in the young audience who appear to be affiliated to various organizations.

"I was a big gang member then. You got gangs right here at Forrest, haven't you? You got some Vice Lords here, haven't you? Point them out. You just looked around and told me here's some in the group. You got some Gangsters, don't you? Why are you killing each other? Both of you are black." He points to himself and snarls, "You're 'sposed to hate this cracker. But instead, you hate each other."

Now all the male students wearing gang colors squirm on their seats. Their cover has been blown; they've been exposed by the ex-biker, a gangbanger who looks, menacingly, straight at them. The biker strikes a deep nerve with his reference to young blacks killing each other. Some have seen friends and family members killed on the streets.

Chester has found another weakness. The young guys are dropping their defenses. He has diagnosed how to get the guys to understand his line of reason. Females are in the group, also. They, too, might make poor choices, and end up in a state institution. He turns his attention to them.

"Now some of you little girls remember when you got mad at Mom this past weekend or over the holidays. Did she want to ground you?"

The man in Parchman blue has been moving closer to the group of students. Now, he is just a few feet away from them. As he eases toward them, he has been discreetly noticing the reaction of a young girl on the second row. When Chester asked the group how many drank alcohol, she raised her hand, with many more. She admitted she did. As Chester continued to confront the class with their problems, the chapel was filling with intense emotion. Suddenly, Chester is right in front of her; leaning over her.

She does not recoil but keeps her eyes fixed apprehensively on her questioner. As he fixes his stare on her, he captures the attention of every one of the girls in the chapel. He senses this and strips her defenses.

"Especially you; did she? Did Mom ground you?"

All present share her thoughts. How does he know about her past weekend? Who told him her Mom grounded her after a late night of drinking? She can't explain how, but he has exposed her secret.

"When you got mad, you wanted to run away from home, didn't you? DIDN'T YOU?

All the kids on the tour begin to fidget and squirm on their pew cushions. The trip they thought would be a lark had suddenly turned deadly serious under the furrowed gaze and piercing words of this ex-prison boss and gangbanger.

Chester attacks, then quickly glides away from her, and returns to the front of the group. He has seized the mind of each young girl there. Most, one time or another, had considered running away from home.

The ex-gang leader knows all about young runaway girls. Runaways are usually fourteen or fifteen years old. Close to the age of the girls on the tour. Once he and other biker gangs had posed a serious threat to runaway girls.

"Do you know what we did to little girls like you?"

The query hangs in the air, then slowly descends as he begins to answer his question. "Oh, man! You'd be my old lady tonight and his tomorrow night. Later, you would belong to the whole club. We would fill you with drugs, and you would be anything we wanted you to be."

The pained expression in his eyes and his big tattooed arms are proof he understands what he is talking about. No one, not kids or teachers in the sun-lit room doubted it.

Horrible pictures quickly pass through their minds of the young girls in the group.

"You were nothing more than a piece of meat. When we tired of you, we put you out; we sold you like meat in a market."

The romance of Hollywood biker movies and daydreams of James Dean riding his Harley are instantly vaporized by his compelling description of real life on the streets. It is a grim word picture.

His voice softens as he moves back away from his audience. "A very dear friend of mine asked me the other day, 'Chester, why did you do it?' Do you all know why? Why I took that arm and put that tattoo on here? I started sticking that needle in that vein and shooting them preludes and drinking that Budweiser and whiskey. I thought I was the meanest thing ever hit. I thought the more butt you kicked. the more respect you got. Boy, was I programmed wrong."

The balding fighter pauses. This group has been challenged mentally, and they hang their hands down to their sides. Their defenses are tired and worn down.

"Everything I did was the wrong choice. You made one this morning before your pretty feet hit the floor. You chose who you were going to serve. The bad choices I made brought me here."

He pauses so they can individually connect their choices and the dull silver prison fences surrounding them. The ugly life they are been thrust into.

"When I first got here, I had a head full of blonde hair. One inmate told me I was a pretty thing, but I was a man." He spits out the word *man*; his brow wrinkles, and his eyes are narrowed by the anger he remembers. "I hated it, them saying those words. I had a lot of bitterness in me. They throwed me in with a hundred and eighty blacks and four whites. One of them dudes came to me and said, 'I want you to be my boy.' You know what? When I hit him in the head with that two by four with a nail in it, I couldn't even find him."

The speaker's silent pause cuts through the audience. He must push a little more. Then one day, some of them will also win against the same enemy he has known, because His God will direct them.

Chester points to a case on the platform where a group of prison made shanks, or knives, are displayed.

"See those things right here? I walked around here with one of those and I ruled this place. I was the shot caller! People did what I told them to do. Some of you can't even make the choice if you are going to answer to a gang leader or not. You don't want to, but 'cause you fear him, you know you got to do what he says."

He observes one of the youthful gang members perform a childlike act. "Suck on your thumb if you want to, but if you come in here, we going to have you, too."

The reference has strong sexual overtones; the young males recoil.

"What you going to do when you get here and someone comes to you at three in the morning and puts one of those tools to your neck and tells you to 'get right'? What you going do? Huh? You going to get right!"

His attack is vicious, and his hateful words sting the faces of the high school group like driving raindrops.

"Yeah, I guess," comes the cringing reply.

"You going to become a girl? Huh? That's what you just said. You out here popping those tops and smoking them cigarettes, you're a prospect for this place."

The unspoken fear of prison rape or robbery grips the young students.

"And you, lady; what you going to do when they send you down to Rankin County, and one of those big women down there wants you. She don't want him, she wants a pretty little thing like you. WHAT YOU GOING TO DO? You don't know? You'd better know. Cause this is penitentiary. This is reality when you make choices to drink and use drugs. This is a world within a world."

The flurry of unanswered verbal blows sinks the opposition slowly to the invisible canvas. The smart looks, the arrogant walk, the gangbanger bravado of the student opponents is vanished.

What little false pride left in Chester's audience enables them to sit back one last time.

"Let me tell you what happened to me. 1981. I was taking a shower. I knew . . ." his voice rises shrilly, "I knew I shouldn't take a shower without protection. A dude hit me right here with a twelve-inch screwdriver. I turned around and he hit me right here." He points to his heart.

"What's right here? A heart? A HEART?" He teases the crowd with the question. Chester disdainfully spits out the reply. "I thought it was just a piece of meat. The third time I caught his knife right here. See how my finger is crooked? It won't bend. They took me to the hospital and patched me up. Back then, I went around like a desperado; like some of you. But, like the song, you better let somebody love you before it's too late. I almost waited too long. December 28, 1981, I fell down on my knees and asked the man who hung on that cross up here to come into this old tattooed, scarred up life of mine."

All eyes in the crowd lift to the large cross, mounted just below the high ceiling in the front of the chapel.

"I said, 'I can't handle it anymore.' The man on the cross said, 'I accept you just like you are.' You know what? It hasn't been easy for me. But I said, 'Lord, I want you to take all this old ugliness I told you about. Change me!'"

A pleading, loving voice comes from the ex-biker gang leader now turned into a servant. "Young people. Get an education. Don't hate your brother; love him. Young lady, that drinkin' you're doing? It ain't going to get you nothing but a hospital bed or worse. Gang member, be your own man. Get those drugs out of your school."

Chester turns and points upward to the cross. "Put that man in the center of your life. And don't ever be ashamed of him 'cause he'll never be ashamed of you. You're looking for something that's false. Be the man . . . be the woman . . . be what God created you to be.' He said 'I'll never leave you nor forsake you.' I love you."

The stillness of the moment is broken briefly by sobbing in the audience. All heads are bowed. No one in the chapel moves. The sincerely softness of "I love you" has completely broken every student down.

When they look up, the old warrior has disappeared. Their questions must wait until later.

The chapel rocks with applause. Parchman's "show and tell" has delivered again. The convict turned convert has won the hearts of the young vulnerable visitors. They put their hands together in appreciation.

Chester has never pulled punches in telling teens how living with motorcycle gangs and criminal activities were wrong. He admits openly he lived outside the law. He desires they should avoid his mistakes.

His powerful testimony attracted a black youth named Greg. Greg had visited Parchman and heard Chester speak when he was attending Jackson Calloway High School. Then, he was a member of the Black Gangster Disciples. His life was going in the wrong direction, then he heard Chester talk to his group.

Greg later wrote, telling Chester how he had given him courage to get out of his organization. Greg later graduated from high school and went on to Jackson State University. His education and productive life was a direct result of Chester's influence, by his own testimony.

Another testimony to the Lord's power to work from Chester's life is seen in the life of a fourteen-year-old girl in a private school for troubled girls. Chester shared her letter to him. Her name was Amanda. She wrote how she had been sexually abused at home. Like many teenagers, she left the church. Mistrust replaced faith in preachers and the professing Christians she met. Gang membership replaced church groups. Her life was filled with fights and dismissal from school. She was raped, and her mother placed her into the Baptist Home for troubled teens. Her faith in God became so weak she thought about suicide.

On her trip to Parchman, she saw the reality of God in Chester's life. That day, she found a renewed strength to live and change her life. Now she shares her story of Jesus and is his messenger with other teens she meets.

Many other stories prove the sincerity of Chester's conversion, good works motivated by a pure heart.

I was privileged to witness first hand the most amazing story of Christ's power in Chester's life

The scene was again the chapel at the Spiritual Life Center. A group of visiting junior high students had gathered there. Chester began by relating to them how tough prison was and how they did not want to come. He talked about his past, then how he was changed by the gospel. He began his closing, talking about family and love. He asked how many kids hugged their mom or dad that morning. Even the retired warrior was unprepared the response.

A slim young student held his hand up. Chester called upon him. He said that he had not embraced his dad as he left home. Chester, somewhat taken aback, inquired why. The young boy replied that his dad slapped him around a lot.

The youngster's response took Chester back to his childhood experiences. Chester had experienced the young man's pain and motioned with his hand for him to sit on the front row. Chester told the boy that, from now on, he would be the boy's big brother.

No one had better harm him from now on.

The eyes of those in attendance in the chapel turned misty.

While he was still moving to his seat of honor, another hand went up from the audience. Perhaps gaining strength from his classmate, a second male student related that his stepfather also beat him up upon occasion.

Chester moved him to the front beside his new little brother.

Emotion began to fill the spiritual life center. Nobody was prepared for the next young lady's story.

Her hand shot up from the back of the group. Chester, looking for a little emotional space, inquired, "You didn't hug your mama today?" She replied no, and Chester asked why, and asked her to stand up. Her reply silenced the room.

"My mother lets her boyfriend come into my room at night and do things to me he shouldn't do."

I was standing behind a brick column not far from the speaker. I watched as tears begin to stream down his face. Teachers and kids gasped and sobs were heard throughout the audience. Chester went toward her and led her to the front with his new brothers.

God is amazing! He gave the school kids a tattooed ex-biker to share their secret problems with. They could not tell anyone else; fear forbade it. Then the kids met Chester, related to him, and more than relating, they trusted him for protection.

Three days later, one of the teachers called and told Chaplain Padgett they had no idea the kids were being abused. That afternoon when they returned to school, they contacted Children's Family Services. An immediate investigation was started, which confirmed the stories of the children. Each story from the students revealed just how far Chester had grown as he emotionally reached out and provided strength to others.

He had truly grown since his arrest and conviction in 1989.

The Sunflower County DA and those who think Christian offenders are fakes fail to realize Christ begins His work within all converts, free world or prison converts. No longer must a convert depend upon willpower to change, but God's power.

Even with powerful presentations like these, some in the system play politics, and personal opinions exist. Somebody believed Chester should soften his speaking style. It was too offensive, they claimed. Yet the teachers and police officers who accompanied the groups declared his style was just what the young people needed. Chester became disillusioned by the negative comments. And he was told he must change his presentation.

Again frustration caused him to seek another environment. He requested a staff change in job assignment. He was given the canteen at Unit Twenty-Four to operate.

Chester had become a force in my life. We prayed and talked about the problems many times. Later, I only was with him in church services at his unit, although I constantly spoke of him as I traveler to churches and schools. I missed the relationship we had. He was not there when I prepared to go home and to join hands with me in a brief intercessory prayer. His blazing strength died a little, within me and him.

Even with his new work assignment, little of his daily routine changed. Cindy and Jessica continued their visits. He had a good "catch" in the canteen and was able to supply Cindy a little extra cash from coffee sales.

Chester was still respected by all the organizations on the farm. He no longer wanted to serve himself by the power of his fists. He only wished to surrender to God. Once, when black gang members attacked and beat a white inmate, their leaders showed up at Chester's cell. They told Chester the reason for the attack was that he had infringed upon designated territorial drug boundaries. Chester reminded them he no longer had anything to do with these activities. They replied that they still appreciated him and wanted him to understand.

In December of 1995, I accepted the position of clinical

chaplain at another unit. Once at the recovery program unit, my time was consumed by duties in the alcohol and drug program. I never seemed to find time to get over to Unit Twenty-Four and visit my Christian brother on a regular schedule.

1996 passed by rapidly for me. Chester continued to run the store at Unit Twenty-Four, and be with Cindy on visiting weekends. However, change was in the prison winds at Parchman. A rumor that the canteens would be changed to a cashless system soon came to pass. Chester was moved to Camp Twenty-Four extension. Then, he became the assistant to a free world manager.

The cashless canteen program was quickly replaced with a system where orders were delivered from central supply. Chester was without a job. He had always been able to make money with his canteen "catch." Now he had no way to assist Cindy and her family in their financial struggle. The canteen job also had helped his days to pass quickly. He felt completely lost.

Chester would be the first to tell you the accomplishments he has made came from God. Paul the Apostle wrote about his change from murderer to minister. Chester submitted to God, then the Father worked transformation through His Spirit.

There was still more evidence concerning Chester's new allegiance to whom he served. In addition to his good works, over the next six years, Chester remained RVR free. He had ten fighting incidents in the first two years at Parchman. He has not had any since he was stabbed in 1981.

The weight of evidence of his "new life" comes from people who knew him before and after his conversion. Some knew him in the old days; a few tasted his flying fists in battle. All testify of a new man. Some inmates who witnessed his change have sought the strength to live differently themselves. The same power that worked for Chester has worked for them. It's God's power of the gospel.

Yes, Chester's new man image to righteousness was slow,

gradual. It carried him through difficult years from 1990 until his death. He traveled down the narrow but straight road. He refused to turn down any old detours.

As Jesus forgave the traitor who turned him in, so Chester forgave his old enemies.

I visited him one evening after he lost his job; he was so depressed. He told me how uncertain he was about his future. Everyone he knew at Unit Twenty-Four had been moved to another unit. The drug recovery camp was being changed to provide for psychological cases. There was no place for him now, and he was searching for God's direction.

That night we sat on a picnic bench outside the unit. We discussed the governor's recent automobile accident. The light was not bright, but Chester's color seemed to be waxy and yellow. I inquired how he felt physically, and he replied "Okay," however he was experiencing pain in his stomach and back. I asked if he had been to the hospital, and he said yes, they told him he simply had kidney stones.

I left the unit thinking Chester would bounce back. He had been depressed in the past; prison does that. As to the ailments, prison food and general conditions kept one from feeling fit all the time.

Little did I realize then that he was beginning his greatest battle. Like the secret gangs that covertly attack under cover, an unseen enemy was attacking Chester from within. This aggressor would become a robber of Chester's days on earth.

CHAPTER TWENTY-TWO

HIDDEN ENEMY

I n the spring of 1997, Chester began fighting what would become the toughest fight of his life. His new enemy hid more secretly than the VC in Vietnam, and was more deadly than any biker encounter he had fought for supremacy in. His struggle was against infectious hepatitis B. The doctors in Clarksdale who examined him gave a prognosis of a 50 percent chance to live five years. Their opinion was assuming proper diet and complete medication, unheard of at Parchman.

The disease did not overwhelm Chester all at once; it advanced slowly. If Chester had lived in the free world, where diagnostic equipment and specialized physicians were available, the enemy would have been detected much sooner. Parchman doctors are difficult to schedule an appointment with. The original prison hospital diagnosis of kidney stones was changed when Chester finally moved to the hospital in Clarksdale, close to death.

Once I saw how sick Chester had become, I tried to visit him as often as possible. I had served as chaplain at the unit where he lived, so security allowed me to visit in the evenings without any intervention.

Chester never complained about the infrequent visits. As always, before my departure, he had the same request, "Brother Roger, can we have a word of prayer before you leave?" Then, as we had for three years, we joined our hands, and prayed to the God of the imprisoned and the free.

Several weeks later, a message came to me. Chester was very low and confined to his prison bunk. I went there at once. It had been some months since I had last seen him, and the change in his appearance startled me. He had lost weight and his face so very lean; his eyes appeared to have sunken back into his head. Even worse was the yellowish color of his skin.

We embraced and I asked him how he felt. He responded, "Okay," then added, "I simply don't have any energy."

I asked him if he had been eating and he replied he couldn't keep the food he ate down. He said he had been to the doctor who had examined him and diagnosed his problem as kidney stones. That had been two weeks ago and he didn't appear any better. Knowing Chester's toughness, I believed he would bounce back.

What he said next greatly concerned me. "Brother Roger, I keep throwing up all the time. Now I am vomiting blood and some of it is clotted in balls."

I knew enough about kidney stones to realize that, painful as they were, they were not Chester's ailment.

The next day, I received a phone call from one of the security officers at the hospital advising me that Chester had been moved there. Chester wanted to visit with me as soon as I could come. The chaplain over the prison medical facility gave me permission to visit there and I drove over.

After being processed through the hospital security, I went upstairs to his room. Again, I wasn't prepared for how Chester would look. An officer escorted me down the drab gray hall to Chester's ward. It was furnished with a bed in each corner, each filled with a sick inmate. Chester looked small and somewhat defenseless for the first time since I had known him. An IV in is arm provided him medication and fluids.

The doctors ran tests and took x-rays that day, but his medicine left him confused and dizzy. Out of respect, he sat up on the side of the bed when I entered. He greeted me in a voice barely above a whisper and extremely raspy. I inquired why he sounded hoarse and he replied he had thrown up so much it had made his throat sore.

After a short visit, we had a word of prayer with all the offenders in the room and I left.

I called Cindy that night to inquire if she could give me more information about Chester's condition. She had been on the telephone with the doctors that day and they were very evasive, and she had not been able to pry out any more facts other than they would run more tests the next day, and she could call them. I ended the call by telling her I would call the next day.

During the next two weeks, Chester's condition got worse, so the Parchman doctors sent him to the hospital in Clarksdale, Mississippi, about twenty-five miles from there. After three days of tests and exams, the doctors determined his ailment was a ruptured esophagus and cirrhosis of the liver. Surgery was scheduled for the next day.

The hospital security was tight around their prison patient, so I had little contact with Chester. During his stay there, a guard had been placed in his room and a second outside the door, twenty-four hours a day. Phone calls were cleared through security. The guards were somewhat bad-tempered and I did not call as often as I would have liked. I planned to be in Clarksdale for his surgery on Friday. To my surprise, when I got there, he was already in the Intensive Care Unit, as the operation had been performed the previous day. The infirmary did not notify Cindy until the evening prior to the operation, so she had been unable to reach me. When I arrived, I showed my chaplain's credentials to the security guard, who permitted me inside the small hospital cubicle. Chester lay on the narrow ICU bed with tubes running in and out of him. He smiled and raised his hand in greeting. Illness had done to Chester what no enemy had been able to do. His liver problems had put him flat on his back.

After visiting for a few minutes, Chester urged me to find Cindy and his parents, who were staying at a motel close to the hospital. I had wanted to visit with her and was anxious to meet his parents after such a long time.

I checked at the office for the room number of the Johnstons and met Cindy in the parking lot.

She wanted to talk to me before I went to the room to meet all the family. The operation had been partially successful. The surgeons had planned to implant a shunt around Chester's liver to relieve pressure, and to repair the ruptured esophagus, critical for Chester's survival.

Soon after the surgical procedure had begun, problems arose. Veins abused by years of drug use had become brittle and began to break under pressure. The OR team spent more time repairing the rupturing veins than finishing the necessary repair. Finally the esophagus had been repaired and the team moved quickly to bypass the liver with a makeshift shunt. Six hours later, the procedure still wasn't completed.

The surgeons met Cindy and advised her they had done all they could do and could only attempt the repair one time. If the graft did not hold and the shunt didn't work correctly, Chester's life would be in grave danger. Tears streaked her fresh makeup, leaving small trails down her face.

Then we went to meet Chester's family.

Cindy introduced me to everyone in the room. Chester Senior was a short, stocky man with the identical grin I had seen many times on Chester's face. In a few minutes, I felt I had known the stepmom and sister Ann for a long time. Good country people that had experienced struggles and triumphs in their life, and had overcome most of them.

I wondered if Ann bore a resemblance to her mother, Sarah Ann. Cindy thought so. A picture of Sara Ann showed almost a sister-like resemblance, proving Chester's mom was as pretty as he recalled.

In two weeks, Chester had recovered sufficiently to be returned to Parchman. He was transported by ambulance back to the prison hospital. The surgery appeared to be a success and Chester could eat solid food again. But his battle for life was far from over.

Once back at Parchman, Cindy wrote many of the top MDOC officials requesting Chester be given the diet prescribed by his Clarksdale doctors. Her pleas fell upon deaf ears. Even the head dietitian for Valley Foods, the contract food provider, would not assist.

After returning to Parchman, a prison doctor who had known Chester for years visited him during lunchtime. Chester stared at the food on the tray as the doctor entered. The dinner consisted of an Italian sausage "hot pocket," cooked apples, and mushy English peas. His physician laughed and said his meal looked good to him.

Chester invited him to take a bite of his "hot pocket." He selected a bite of sausage, and when he put it into his mouth, the doctor recoiled at the grease and spice. "You can't eat this," he exclaimed, and left Chester's room. Later, his general practitioner returned singing a different tune. He decided he could eat it, as it should not bother him.

"Go figure, as they say. "That's penitentiary life.

One week earlier, another inmate had died from cirrhosis. Unable to curb his hunger, he ate the food brought to him, satisfying his hunger but shortening his life. Chester began to survive on noodles from the canteen to supplement his diet, since Cindy and Christian Ministries could not provide him proper food.

He would continue to stay alive on snack food as long as his money held out.

***

At the close of the Civil War, the officials of Andersonville were charged with crimes of cruel and inhumane punishment due to the lack of proper provisions to the prisoners.

Early in the 1980s, the United States Federal Court began to look at improper food and living conditions in state penal systems. They did not like what they found. Overcrowding had become standard and offenders suffered from lack of exercise and proper diet. The federal investigators also found grossly unsanitary living spaces. Roaches and rats roamed prisons unchecked. State prison officials considered rodents simply another form of punishment.

The judges began to hand down orders demanding change. They wanted prison facilities cleaned up and with more attention to inmate conditions. They ordered the overhaul to begin immediately. Some states began to respond with change, yet for some penitentiary officials, federal change has been difficult to swallow. "Old ways die hard"

Cindy and all those who loved Chester Johnston were determined not to permit him to waste away in prison. Chester made many mistakes for real, but he had defended our flag and what it stood for. Our Constitution guarantees the right of freedom.

The Fifth Amendment defines an individual's rights apply even when one is incarcerated for a capital crime. It declares that an individual may not be deprived of life, liberty, or property without due process of law. Chester's friends and family believed that the State of Mississippi, by depriving Chester of food and medication that would extend his life, surely violated his rights.

To seek resolution in the State's Courts could take years that Chester did not have. Although the federal courts wrote in detail regarding correcting deplorable prison conditions, states must maintain in their corrections systems, and to confront MDOC then would be futile.

Perhaps some of the state officials who partnered with Chester and the Banditos in the seventies were still afraid of him. Maybe this is the reason he was, as I believe, unfairly put in prison in 1978 and held there until 1990. However, the officials cannot understand the code of silence Chester had lived under since he was fifteen years old. He would never change now, even to save his life

Months after his surgery, Chester, very despondent and ill, sat talking to me in the library of Unit Thirty-One. Now, no longer the prez or the "shot caller," he found it necessary to depend upon others for assistance. No assistance seemed to be in sight.

Sadly, Chester said, "You know Brother Roger, I believe I'm just sitting here waiting to die." He paused and then said, "I sometimes wonder why God won't heal me. I pray that he will, even with all the wrong things I have done."

I too wished God would repair his body now under attack.

All who loved and had supported Chester did not want him to die in prison. Regardless of his sentence, he had a right to be paroled medically. Parole is a right by law. Now, MDOC, without authority to carry out a execution, created a more devastating sentence than the original verdict received from the Indianola jury.

However, for those whose trust is in God, we have hope beyond release or death. As the Apostle Paul wrote, "For me to live is Christ, and to die is gain" (Phil. 1:21). The gain of heaven is what Chester and all other Christians live for. We know God holds tomorrow in His eternal hands. Our Father makes decisions based on eternity, not tomorrow.

Life in prison is simply not well suited to battling cirrhosis. Prison doctors and state officials were advised of Chester's situation in a letter from the Clarksdale hospital. They would never decide to give Chester a medical release, although he clearly met the federal guidelines. Cindy took his cause to the Jackson newspaper and a local radio talk show host, without success.

For real, Chester had been placed on a medical death row.

CHAPTER TWENTY-THREE

DYING WISH

The Mississippi Department of Corrections can be extremely difficult to deal with for inmates and their families most of the time. They run their prison facilities "close to the vest," even make unnecessary efforts to live by their own rules when it suits them. Of course, rare occasions arose when officials turned their heads with inmates to advance MDOC authority. Case in point, the "beat down" of Chester in his cell years before, the infamous Red Room where inmates were given an "attitude adjustment" back in the day.

Even the officers who ran a money laundering operation in the days of wire transfers, some of whom got rich, say it's just inmate talk. Well, believe what you want, but I worked at the prison daily for six years.

The lack of compassion set the tone for Chester's last days, his fight to be released before he died. To Chester, dying in prison was like the sentiment of old time cowboys who wanted "to die with their boots on." In both cases, it had a disgrace attached no one wanted to have.

Chester had won a second lawsuit against MDOC some years earlier. Motor Jorge Simmons had snitched on him concerning the

1976 unsolved murder, and also attempted to stab him to death with a prison shank, without success. Chester requested he be transferred to a separate unit, away from the wannabe bad guy, but they refused. He finally filed a suit in the courts against the penitentiary system; he won and was moved.

In 1997, prison doctors diagnosed Chester with cirrhosis of the liver and hepatitis, and gave him five years to live. This prognosis increased the need for more intensive medical care. It also intensified his urgency not to die in prison. Chester had been told he had liver cancer in March.

Cindy's comment was, "He has so much wrong with him." She had been trying to persuade correction officials to grant a medical release for her husband. Cindy was afraid his body would give out before he could be released. "I don't want him to die in there," Cindy said. "If he does get sick, I won't be able to see him. He'll die alone."

But release before his death would never happen.

After a long legal battle with state corrections, Chester was moved to the Rankin County Correctional Facility in Pearl, Mississippi. The hope was that he would receive better care there. He was also closer to Cindy and the move eliminated her tiring drive on visiting days. His living space was simply a bunk in an open style dormitory with fifty other special needs offenders. Once he arrived, plans had been made for him to become a member of the chaplain's "speaking team," going to schools and churches, sharing with young people his story and the Good News about Jesus.

His engagements continued until finally his illness would no longer allow him to travel. He felt a need to share the Lord with young people, who would provide them the lasting acceptance Chester found. His past tough guy reputation, having being the Parchman "boss" before meeting Jesus, was not without obligation. Even with disappointment, Chester would not turn away from Him now.

My last time to see Chester in this world is burned into my memory. The Parchman head chaplain made arrangements with the Pearl Chaplain's Department for me to have a special visit with Chester. Rather than meeting in a public place such as the visitor area or chow hall, I was able to visit with him in a private office.

When one of his unit officers brought him to the office where I waited, his appearance totally astonished me. I could not get over how he looked. Several inmates sang a song titled, "The Old Man is Dead." One line said, "I'm not the man I used to be." The song spoke about the sinful person he was before becoming a child of God. That day, Chester was physically no longer the man he used to be; not the imposing figure who struck fear in other inmates and visiting students. Now he appeared gaunt and drawn. His battle against cancer and liver disease had reduced his frame and shrunken his face to the point where I hardly recognized him.

There were two traits that didn't change, his strength of spirit and his wry grin when amused. We talked about a million things that day, I guess. We remembered old convicts we both had known, and some chaplains who had consistently stepped up to the plate, and a couple who did not, for inmates' rights. He told me of long days and nights battling sickness when there was no tonic for him in the prison. Some of the effects of the illness might have been alleviated if he had been in the free world. Never complaining, simply relating, as he always had. He realized then that his long battle was close to over, and he faced it with courage.

Naturally, we talked about his "Beautiful lady" God had brought to him years before. She remained that way and stood beside him throughout the whole ordeal. Her granddaughter, the one he had suggested not be given up for adoption when born, still loved him, though as a teenager, did not have much time for him. Things were better with his family who now were able to travel to visit more often in Pearl than in Parchman. They had all been forgiven and most had reciprocated to some degree.

Chester found healing in reminiscing and telling his story. As we talked about his heartbreaking experiences, the release of pain healed many wounds, I could sense his relief. Times of joy brought renewed gladness. He was becoming emotionally complete. Finally, he had left all the acrimony behind hm. He still got hurt sometimes. He continued to process his emotional wounds for healing.

Prior to his passing, Chester forgot the past and lived each day looking forward to his final, eternal home. He looked forward to happy occasions with those he loved. They became a source of delight for him. Even though baby Jessica had grown into a young lady, one day she would come back.

Chester still prayed till he died that he would walk out of prison a free man, able to come and go as he chose. It was his right to pray for it. Granted that he had committed numerous lesser offenses, he had been innocent of the two major ones he was convicted of. He had done ample time for the lesser crimes. Chester lived with the hope that his false accusers might one day step forward and confess their crimes; they never did. In contrast, they will live wretchedly with their guilt until their coffin is lowered into their grave or they find the solution Chester found.

The ex-biker and reclaimed drug abuser lived in hope of many more hours speaking to young people about life's choices. He knew some could be reached about a fuller life now and the eternity of tomorrow. The State would never grant that privilege. Chester later lived his life peacefully allowing God to call the shots. He believed God was constructing a heavenly clubhouse for him. He had built a Harley that will truly be a righteous machine.

Our visit ended much too soon, and time had come for me to leave. I prayed I would visit him again, knowing I probably would not here on this earth, He sensed it also and we joined hands as we always did when we were to be separated. One last good will wish, a hug, and he was gone.

In the fall of 2001, I retired from the chaplains service at Parchman. While I really hated to leave working with the other chaplains and inmates, the time had come to go home. We had been gone from Haleyville, Alabama, for twenty-five years. Busy with other things, considering the great impact Chester had on my life, he would cross my mind often. I attempted to stay in touch with Cindy, but made a poor effort.

In 2001, MDOC continued their hostilities against Chester for whatever reason. After nearly twenty years of enjoying the freedom of the top trustee level of custody "A," Chester once again ran afoul of the MDOC guards. A guard almost beat him to death without a reason, or provocation. Whether this beating had been a result of long standing officer hostilities or the influence of crooked Jackson councilmen who still fear the ex-biker being released, we will never know.

The narrative of the beat down and the ensuing events display the hatred of those in high places for the now wounded warrior. The event took place at the close of visitor day, October 6, 2001.

I'm sure the reason for it went back across the years to the reputation the old warrior once carried.

Here are the events of that day, October 6, 2001, which surely hastened Chester's death.

Cindy had just left the visitor area, although there were other inmates remaining. I personally know one of the remaining occupants of the visitor area; he has submitted the events as he witnessed them and I trust his story implicitly.

Immediately after Cindy exited the visitor area, Chester went to the vending machines that serviced the area and purchased some food items. As soon as the items dropped down the machine chute and Chester retrieved them, the officer over the area told him he was not allowed to take food back to his dorm and that it was being confiscated.. The officer ordered Chester to sit in a chair, took his candy from him, and began to ridicule him. The officer also advised that he could have him locked down for the infraction. Chester sat without responding and took the belittling.

When the officer ended his tirade, Chester said, "I haven't done anything wrong. Guys take food back all the time.

When Chester replied he had not done anything wrong, the officer took the response as a matter of disrespect and ordered him into the shake down line. Once in line, he leaned against the vending machine, in other words "assumed the position," and the sergeant kicked his feet wider apart. He was then ordered to remove his clothing, including his boxers. After the humiliation of disrobing in public, his clothes were thrown on the floor, and he was ordered to bend over and cough several times. The officer's actions were designed to embarrass the inmate. Finally, Chester was ordered to bend over so far as to show the officer some love. This action also was totally unnecessary, and Chester finally appealed to the area lieutenant to have the other officer stop the humiliation.

Immediately, the sergeant began to beat Chester in the face with his fists and rang blows all over his body. Weak from his liver disease, he could only cover his head. The sergeant repeatedly hit him and with such force that he broke his hand on Chester's skull. The resulting injuries to Chester were a broken eye socket, broken jaw, and cuts to his ears and eyes. In addition, his dentures were broken. Chester had literally been beaten to a pulp. When Cindy finally saw him several days later, he was so swollen she hardly recognized him.

Chester was given a RVR, Rules Violation Report, a detention notice and, sent to lockdown without medical attention and no meds for pain.

Cindy's friend, whose husband witnessed the whole event and called his wife, then called Cindy once she left the facility. Cindy had confronted MDOC before and had no fear of doing it again. She literally began to burn up the phone lines with calls. Her man had been beat down, and she was not going to stand around and do nothing. That Saturday afternoon, Cindy called Lou Davis, the head of the MDOC Ethics Committee, her State senator, the current commissioner, and the Highway Patrol Investigators. All promised to look into the event.

On the following Monday, the corrections facility at Pearl, Mississippi, was covered up with investigators from Internal Affairs, the MDOC investigative division, the State Ethics Committee Chairman, Lou Davis, and Highway Patrol Investigators, all looking for answers. The officers who were present in the visitor area were all interviewed, along with Chester. Chester's injuries were still very visible, as the beating had occurred two days prior.

Even though the reports of the officers involved differed, there was no doubt with any of the investigators Chester required immediate, professional attention and right now. It was also obvious that none had been given. Lou Davis and one of the assistant wardens escorted the victim to UMC Hospital, where he was treated at once. The attending physician examined and recorded all the multiple injuries he had suffered.

Proper medical attention and a night in the hospital wasn't enough for Cindy to be satisfied. Chester was her man and she would fight for him. An attorney was acquired and a lawsuit was filed against MDOC for the injuries sustained. A judge ordered that the security video of the incident in the visitor area be turned over, but it was never received.

When Chester returned to his unit the next day, all the state officers fell in file and began to harass him. An appeal was filed. A District Judge ordered the video recording of the event be turned over to the committee but this was disregarded by MDOC. What follows is a transcript of the court's findings.

Both the magistrate and the district court chose to believe, in substantial portion, Johnston's version of the facts. These findings are not clearly erroneous; on the contrary, there is substantial evidence in the record to support them. Johnston's testimony is consistent with both the medical records and the cell assignment lists, as well as with the corroborating testimony of Myers, Irons, and Smith. Defendants' explanations, particularly when viewed as a whole, are somewhat strained *Chester Jordan Johnston, Junior, Plaintiff-Appellee, v. Eddie Lucas, Aaron Jagers, Major Fred Childs, Barry McGrew, Robert Grayson, James Flowers, J.B. Williams, and Joe Conners, Defendants-Appellants, 786 F.2d 1254 (5th Cir. 1986)}*

Five months later, the sergeant was fired by MDOC: That was little recompense for the Johnstons.

***

Chester was permitted to return to his dormitory style living quarters, where some medical attention was permitted. His life returned to as normal as is possible living in prison. In November of 2002, Chester was ordered to submit to a urine test for drugs. He had been a trustee for years and no policy or procedure called for this class to be tested. Yet it did for him.

The prison officials had advised Cindy they were going to lose their case concerning Chester's beat down. They strongly advised her to drop the case, something she was not going to do.

In 2002, Chester came up positive on a drug test in Pearl and the officials wanted to send Chester back to Parchman. Chester was called to Internal Affairs, required to submit a urine sample, and was told that he had tested positive for illicit drugs. Cindy again called Lou Davis, who investigated the testing procedure. IA had retained a frozen urine sample from the previous test and, upon testing, returned a higher drug volume than before. That was impossible, as two tests on the same sample must return the same results. Lou Davis checked their test procedures and proved them inadequate.

Cindy obtained the assistance of a state senator and a lot of free airtime on local radio stations, and got the move stopped. But in the closing days of his life, Cindy and Chester began their last conflict with the Department of Corrections, a battle for medical parole.

Regardless of the lack of validity of the tests, Chester was busted down to "D" custody, losing all visiting, phone, and canteen privileges. Chester requested a hair follicle test to prove conclusively that he was drug free, but this was denied. Later, state and private tests proved Chester had not used drugs.

Chester's ongoing battle with MDOC seemed to boil over each time he and Cindy fought for respect for their constitutional rights. The bottom line of the false allegations inquiry was dragged out so that Chester served a three-month restriction before his privileges were returned.

Cindy, Chester, and all their friends realized Chester was finally fighting the one battle he could not win. Physically, he never recovered from the undeserved beating at the hands of the MDOC officer. But, more intense and disturbing was his mental combat, not seeing his lady for three months, and enduring the lowest custody class. All his achievements of the past years were forgotten, at least by state officials.

In March of the following year, the worst happened. Tumors were found in Chester's chest, and now there was little life expectancy left. Once again, his dying wish for release, to die in the free world, was pushed aside. Again, MDOC responded with more charges to stop his release.

On June 3, Internal Affairs discovered Chester had received money orders from people other than family members several years prior. Retaliation? Most likely! The result? Loss of privileges and a return to Parchman on June 27. That was the last time Cindy would see Chester alive. Knowing Chester as I did, I know he dropped his head in resignation and took his undeserved medicine.

One month after his move to the day, Cindy received a call while at work. The caller informed her to rush to Parchman at once, that Chester was dying. Ten minutes later, as Cindy was rushing out, another call from the Parchman Chaplain's Department came, telling Cindy that Chester was gone.

His file for release was still on the commissioner's desk. There was no concern, no recognition for the achievements of twenty years; simply callous indifference. Whatever label is attached by Mississippi prison officials to Chester's dying years and his hope for release, Chester died with dignity. The warrior was now free.

Chester died July 27, Jessica's birthday; bittersweet!

When Cindy received the phone call, it was surprising but not unexpected. I knew in the back of my mind that one day soon it would come.

CHAPTER TWENTY-FOUR

PAROLE AT LAST

On July 24, 2004, Chester Johnston was finally released from prison. A release of sorts, but not the medical parole Chester and Cindy had worked so hard for. The release was not what Chester, Cindy, and many others had prayed for. Instead, he left the Rankin County facility in prison denim blue, not funeral finery. No limo transported him away from his home; rather, an MDOC van with a plywood coffin containing his last remains. His body was taken to a funeral home where Cindy had previously made arrangements for his farewell service.

Not much of a send-off for a man who bossed five thousand inmates, and who one time rode at the head of a biker motorcycle procession. His was a procession of one.

Chester had made me promise that wherever or whenever, I would conduct his last ceremony. The promise came some time after he learned that his life was being shortened by the disease that had ravaged his body. It was a promise I would keep from love and respect.

Chester's last service here on earth was in a beautiful mortuary in North Jackson, Mississippi. Some of the family had already arrived, and Cindy was busy as always greeting everyone and making sure that my wife and I were introduced to the funeral director and others attending. After reviewing the order of service with her, we spent the remainder of the time before the service meeting family members and those we had met in the past. As time for the service drew closer, some of the members of the Kairos team that had ministered to Chester began to arrive. They would provide the most memorable part of the service.

I took my place on the chapel platform and noticed a much larger crowd than I had expected was seated there. I thought that Chester would be amazed that so many people had come to say goodbye. His constant shyness and shy smile would reflect his pride in being remembered.

Most of the ceremony followed the regular Christian funeral order of service. I remember how thankful I was that Chester would not be interred in the lonely cemetery he once tended at Parchman. He would be buried where family and friends could visit his grave, not lost in the high grass and weeds around the Parchman burial ground where it is difficult to locate anyone's marker. The only burials easily accessible there are on a low levee behind the Chaplain's building. Three were buried there during a flood. Two died of natural causes and one had been executed. Strangely, a father and his son were buried there together.

The obituary was read, accompanied by the sound of sniffles and muffled sobs. Several volunteer chaplains who brought worship teams to prison, and adopted Chester, made a few remarks. Next, I shared some precious memories of my time with Chester. Some were pleasant and some quite humorous. Yes, there are humorous and entertaining men there. I remembered Chester giving me a background bio on one of his friends I needed to visit. His name was Billy Joe and he had ridden bulls in the now-defunct prison rodeo. This night, Billy Joe had been bucked off rather rudely, so he angrily turned and ran head-on into the bull. Naturally, the Brahma suffered no ill effect; however, everyone who knew Billy Joe said he was never right after that. In my six years knowing Chester, we had seen offenders married, some with great fashion, and buried others in plywood boxes.

My remarks were followed by prayer, but the highlight of the service belonged to the group from Kairos. At the close of the service, about twenty of the members came to the front of the chapel, formed a line, and sang Chester's favorite song, "Lights to the City," accompanied by a guitar.

The song was an overture to Chester's life and the victory he had won over all those who had offensively affected his life for many years. The crooked legislators, irreverent bikers, unforgiving prison officials, and now, death. Yet Chester won in the end, proven by praise of those there, the victory message of the Kairos song, and a promise from God years before.

In this house we've built of make believe
Loved ones go long before seems it's time to leave
But we will learn how to grieve, to forgive and receive
'Til we see them there in that city

Chorus:
On that day we will sing "Holy, Holy"
On that day we'll bow down in the light
And then we'll rise and turn our eyes
To the One who's the light, the light of that city.

As words "holy, holy" of the chorus was sung, the singers would jubilantly raise fists and shout. It was a victory cry of one who had triumphed over so much and was now home.

After the song, a hush settled over the gatherers, and the service was over.

The peace many people wish for when death draws close was never afforded to Chester Johnston. Without complaint, Chester lived with continuing family quarrels, and an absence of retreat in a dormitory ward while suffering the indignities of illness. These were punishments added to the sentence inflicted by the Mississippi Department of Corrections.

Granted, he will never again ride in the wind in this world, with his long blonde hair flowing from beneath his bandanna. More likely, his hands will never reach for another shop tool or be covered with grease while breaking down or rebuilding an engine. Those days are gone and unimportant now.

Although his body was incarcerated, now his spirit is free, riding in the wind every day. Chester Johnston steers his heavenly ride with his best friend in flowing robes on the buddy seat behind. His ride had taken him into a dark valley for a minute. He has no fear, as the warrior David, because Jesus is with him. The valley is death, but he will find rest. The Harley's headlight lights up the road ahead. Never again will darkness overshadow. He rides in the eternal light. He and his partner have ridden together now for many years. The ex "shot caller" is riding in front and the true "shot caller" is sitting behind.

Today, Chester's road is wide open without end. There are no walls or bars to impede him. Chester asks, "Will you join me there?"

LEGACY

N ow that Chester is gone, what will be his legacy, the heritage for his son, grandchildren, and friends to remember in the years ahead?

Chester has always been seen as an imposing figure with a powerful magnetism, drawing people to him and commanding respect. Not a towering giant, his power has always come from within, from the hard times in the river's waterfront bars, soldiering in Nam, and climbing to power with the Gunslingers and Banditos. His power to rule started from his early years with the bikers to and grew in his time at Parchman. Over time, he became a man to be reckoned with.

The core of Chester's moral fiber was loyalty, trust. It was learned from the early days as novice biker, when a code of silence was drilled into him by Bear, Loser, and the other bikers. Trust equaled silence. Acceptance, approval, was the return for trust. Even when facing long-term imprisonment, life with the emptiness of a prison existence, he would not give his former friends up. They could have provided information about where he lived at the time of the Edwards murder, but he would not involve them, jeopardize them. He remained silent, loyal when none stepped forward.

Trust had been carved into his soul.

For his last fifteen years, his reliance was no longer on fast hands and powerful fists. He never used them again. He distanced himself from scams and memberships that could have provided his family income. Once he realized the futility of trusting in schemes, he put his confidence in his God.

Second on the list of Chester's legacy is his physical and mental strength. His "will" brought him victory in many a battle. In the mud of Nam, he lost one friend and acquired an antagonist, drugs, that would control him much of his adult life. Only his "Higher Power" would enable him to overcome it.

Added to the lasting inventory is compassion, tenderness. His heart was touched when conversations turned to Grandma's house, Sara Ann, his best friend Al, or his wife Cindy. Tears came when he went there. For years, his empathy was hidden, wrapped in layers of anger and bitterness, hidden so deep no one realized it. Now he had learned that tenderness and compassion weren't signs of weakness. This lesson came from a man who died on a cross for him; compassion became his strength.

Since his conversion, his compassionate potency from God's gift has been communicated to and heard by thousands, mostly young people.

He also passes on dependency on prayer. No telling how many times he took my hands into his to speak to the Father for me before I traveled. We always embraced each other when he was strong and I was weak, and when I was tough and he was not. Perhaps this is the most important item of the legacy Chester would pass on.

Last on his legacy is family. A component of life experiences once had been stolen from him. Alcohol and arguments between his parents, and later his spouse, robbed him of the feeling of family, and divorce caused him to divide his allegiance. He once wanted to make his grandparents his first family, but it eluded him when someone drove up to take him back to live with dad or mom.

When Cindy's daughter gave birth as an unwed mother to Jessica, Chester saw the promise of additional family and strongly suggested the baby be kept and not put out for adoption.

These are the attributes our hero left. All are admirable traits, fundamentals learned the hard way. However, for all the kids he spoke to or wrote, and men he taught to read, life was a little easier as they took a part of Chester. Cindy, Jason, and the rest of the family, I'm sure will find parts of this book hard to read, more difficult to identify with. This is the way Chester remembered it. The good times and the bad ones fashioned the final version.

The best part of his legacy is who he was; his spirit lives on and will continue as long as his story is read or told. The men who live, free or not, who knew him will also pass his prison legend on. His life, his testimony, made many of them better, and it will work it for all who read and believe.

So, goodbye old friend, and ride easy; we'll see you another day.

CPSIA information can be obtained
at www.ICGtesting.com
Printed in the USA
BVHW071438130620
581350BV00001B/23

9 781625 160140